FRED E. CASE is a professor in the Graduate School of Management at UCLA and is the author of *The Investment Guide to Home & Land Purchase*.

Investing in Real Estate

Fred E. Case

PRENTICE-HALL, INC., Englewood Cliffs, New Jersey 07632

Library of Congress Cataloging in Publication Data
Case, Frederick E
    Investing in real estate.

    (A Spectrum Book)
    Includes index.
    1. Real estate investment.   I. Title.
HD1375.C358   332.6'324   78-3486
ISBN 0-13-503219-9
ISBN 0-13-503201-6 pbk.

© 1978 by Prentice-Hall, Inc., Englewood Cliffs, New Jersey 07632

A Spectrum Book

10   9   8   7   6   5   4

Printed in the United States of America

PRENTICE-HALL INTERNATIONAL, INC., *London*
PRENTICE-HALL OF AUSTRALIA PTY. LIMITED, *Sydney*
PRENTICE-HALL OF CANADA, LTD., *Toronto*
PRENTICE-HALL OF INDIA PRIVATE LIMITED, *New Delhi*
PRENTICE-HALL OF JAPAN, INC., *Tokyo*
PRENTICE-HALL OF SOUTHEAST ASIA PTE. LTD., *Singapore*
WHITEHALL BOOKS LIMITED, *Wellington, New Zealand*

Contents

Preface

So many people have asked me how to invest successfully in real estate that I developed a series of checklists to help them look at raw land, homes, apartment houses, second homes, recreational property—all types of real estate investments. Over the last ten years these checklists became a book, and here it is. Parts of these checklists have been published in newspapers and magazines in all parts of the country. Requests for them became so frequent that I could no longer reply to the demands with my own limited resources.

The book is built around very basic, tested principles that have been translated into checklists and illustrative examples that will help you start your own real estate investment program.

If you have been investing in real estate, you will find help in organizing your activities in a more efficient and productive manner. You will also find suggestions on how to use an ordinary hand calculator to make complex investment analyses that normally are produced only at great expense on larger computers.

An important element in real estate investing is knowing where to find current information. So in this book you will find suggestions for building a real estate investment information library equal to those offered by many expensive real estate investment guidance services.

However, the book is only a tool, a means to an end that will be effective only if you use it. There is some hard work involved, but the returns can be quite good, particularly if you are finding that inflation, taxes, and rising prices are making it difficult to build an estate that you can use to get children through college and provide retirement for yourself.

Glossary

SOME REAL ESTATE INVESTMENT WORDS
YOU MIGHT NEED TO UNDERSTAND

Please Note: These definitions have been simplified so you can understand the how, what, and why of real estate investing. Their meanings are related to the manner in which they are used in this book. They are not intended to be precisely correct in a legal sense. In most cases you can turn to the Index and find the pages on which these words are discussed.

ABSTRACT OF TITLE   A history of all who have owned the property and the extent to which there may be claims against the title or restrictions on its use.

ACCELERATION CLAUSE   A requirement in a home loan that the borrower pay any remaining loan balance upon demand by the lender if the borrower pays off the loan ahead of schedule.

ACKNOWLEDGEMENT   A statement before a legally authorized public official (usually a notary public) that the person signing the document is doing so without being forced to do so and is the person named in the document.

AD VALOREM   Used primarily in property tax assessments, this term indicates that the value was determined by comparing properties and their prices in the real estate markets. (Literally, *ad valorem* means "according to value.")

ADVANCE COMMITMENT   A lender agrees, before a loan agreement has been signed, to make a loan on terms agreed upon with the borrower.

ADVERSE POSSESSION   A complex legal process in which a person (or persons) publicly uses and occupies a property in spite of the ownership claims or objections of others. Actual conditions necessary for obtaining title under this process vary according to laws in each state.

AGENT   Anyone who, for a fee or commission, agrees to represent another person in completing a transaction. *See also* Real Estate Broker (Agent, Sales Person).

AIR RIGHTS   The holder of such rights is permitted to use the air space above a parcel of land up to a height determined by local laws or by applicable state or federal laws. For example, the owner of an apartment above ground level owns air rights for the space occupied by the apartment. *See also* Property (Real Property).

AMENITY (INCOME)   Anything pleasing to a particular person but difficult to value or to price. Usually the amenity has extra value to the person owning it. For example, "pride of ownership" is an amenity that causes some persons to pay more for a particular property than is warranted from a comparison with other sales.

ALL-INCLUSIVE (WRAP-AROUND) MORTAGE   A loan for which several properties are pledged as security through the use of one loan document. *See also* Mortgage (Trust Deed).

AMORTIZE (AMORTIZATION)   To provide for equal periodic payments of money borrowed, as in a home loan.

ANNUITY   A series of equal payments received or paid for a period of time—years or months usually.

ANNUITY METHOD   A method of estimating the present value of a series of annuity payments (same amount of payment each period during the life of the payment period) using a mathematical table or formula to discount all future values to a present lump-sum amount.

APPRAISER   A person who, for a fee, establishes or estimates, in dollars, the market value of a property, or who estimates the value for a particular type of property use, or who estimates a dollar value that will aid his client in making an investment decision.

ASSESSED VALUE (PROPERTY TAXES) (*also* ASSESSMENT)   Depending upon your state's law: (a) the amount in dollars which the property tax assessor (appraiser) believes your property would sell for; or (b) the amount in dollars established by the property tax assessor on which your property tax liability will be estimated (this dollar amount may be less than the actual market value or price).

ASSESSMENT SPECIAL   A charge levied by government for special services provided to a particular property, it is usually included in the general property tax rate and related to the assessed value.

ASSET   Anything owned by an investor on which a dollar value can be placed.

ASSIGNMENT In mortgage lending particularly, the term refers to the transferring to another person the rights and duties outlined in a legal document, such as a mortgage or trust deed.

ASSUME (ASSUMPTION) In mortgage lending particularly, one party agrees to accept the responsibilities and duties of another party, relieving that party of further obligations under the terms of the lending agreement, unless the person assuming the obligations fails to perform as the agreement calls for.

AVERAGE Obviously, the term means typical—what most persons are doing. Technically it can also mean: (a) *Mean average*—all numbers are added and the sum is divided by the number of items; (b) *Median average*—all numbers are arranged in order according to amounts, the amount of the item in the middle of the array is the median.

BALLOON PAYMENT The last payment on a loan, which is usually much larger than the other payments.

BAND OF INVESTMENT A method of establishing a capitalization rate by determining the percentage of the total rate which relates to each investment return element. For example:

Equity .20 of total investment × .30 earning rate	= .06
Loan as percent of investment .80 × loan rate .09	= .072
Capitalization rate, band of investment method	= .132 or 13.2%

"BIGGER FOOL" THEORY A condition in which market expectations encourage buyers to base their purchase prices on what other buyers have paid or are paying. The buyer makes no effort to inquire carefully into market conditions or sales terms, but simply pays more and hopes he will not end up being the "bigger fool."

BINDER (DOWN PAYMENT) A money payment to guarantee that the buyer will perform and the seller will accept as promised in the preliminary negotiations relating to buying or selling property.

BUILDING CODE(S) Regulations imposed by local governments relating to the kinds of materials and the ways in which they are to be used in the construction or changing of a property.

CAPITAL GAIN Any increase in the value (or price) of a property over the original purchase price. As used in federal income tax law, the increase must occur over a specified period of time to qualify for special tax treatment.

CAPITALIZATION Estimating the value today of money to be received in the future either as a single amount (lump sum) or in regular amounts (annuity).

   STRAIGHT LINE The value today (present value) of an income stream assuming that the earning or percentage rate of return is constant and equal amounts of the investment are returned each year and the periodic payments are equal in amount. Direct-capitalization rate is divided into net income to obtain the value today of an income or amount to be received in the future. Annuity-income is paid in equal periodic amounts but the rate of return is related to that portion of the investment not yet recovered.

CAPITALIZATION FACTOR   A number that is multiplied by the net annual income to determine the value of the income over a particular time period.

CAPITALIZATION RATE   An amount expressed as a percent which is used with net income in a mathematical formula to determine the value today of the income to be received over an investment period; or, the value today of a lump sum to be received at a given time in the future.

CARRYING CHARGES   Additional amounts collected periodically, usually at the same time as the loan payments, and used to pay taxes, property insurance premiums, and other costs relating to owning a property.

CASH FLOW   The amount of cash received from the income produced by a property after all expenses of owning the property have been paid. Means the same as "spendable income."

CHATTEL (PROPERTY)   Any property not classified as real property, usually items attached in such a way that they can be moved easily. Typically, "chattel" includes clothing, furniture, refrigerators, stoves, washing machines, and similar kinds of equipment.

CLOSING COSTS (*also* TRANSFER COSTS)   All amounts paid by buyer and seller to assure the legal completion of the transfer of property rights.

COMMERCIAL BANK   A government chartered business that provides a variety of financial services such as consumer loans, business loans, home loans, and savings collections (either in checking accounts or savings accounts). This is not a savings and loan association. *See also* Federal Home Loan Bank, Federal Housing Administration, Federal National Mortgage Association, Federal Saving and Loan Insurance Corporation, Mutual Savings Bank, Savings and Loan Association, Veterans' Administration.

COMPOUND (COMPOUND INTEREST)   To provide an interest (or earning) rate on a periodic basis and to periodically add the earnings to the fixed amount already invested. In other words, interest is paid not only on the original investment but also on any amounts added to that original amount through previous interest payments.

COMPOUND AMOUNT OF ONE   Interest is paid on a single-payment investment and on any other interest already earned and paid.

COMPOUND AMOUNT OF ONE PER PERIOD (ANNUITY)   Interest is paid on a series of regular investments as well as on all interest earned on these investments.

CONDEMNATION   The process by which a public agency takes title to a property after paying the owner the market value and proving that the taking will benefit the general public. This process involves use of the right of *eminent domain*.

CONDOMINIUM ("CONDOS")   A method of buying property that allows each buyer to own exclusively some portion of the property and to share ownership of some portion of the property with others. For example, the owner of an apartment in an apartment-house condominium may paint, decorate, or change the interior at will; and exercise the more limited right (or title) to use halls, lobbies, parking places, swimming pools, tennis courts, and other facilities in conjunction with other owners. The condominium owner receives a title that permits him to finance his apartment and to purchase or sell it as though he owned a detached single-family home.

CONSTRUCTION LOAN (INTERIM)   A short-term loan (up to thirty-six months usually) to be used to pay construction costs of a property.

CONSUMER PRICE INDEX (CPI)   The current cost of buying a package of goods and services that a typical family need for daily living. The package contents stay roughly the same through time so that changes in the prices of individual items can be added together to reflect changes in the cost of "living." During each period the total cost is expressed as a percentage of a base period which is set at 100. An index of 120 means that the cost of living for that period is 20 percent higher than the base period.

CONTRACT (AGREEMENT) OF SALE   A written instrument containing the terms on which buyers and sellers agree for the exchange of a property.

CONTRACTOR   Anyone who, for a fee, agrees to complete work according to specifications presented in a written, legal agreement (contract).

GENERAL CONTRACTOR   Accepts responsibility for completing all the work although not doing all of it.

SUBCONTRACTOR   Hired by the general contractor or builder to complete specialized work such as plumbing, electrical, plastering, masonry, or other work.

CONVENTIONAL LOAN (MORTAGE OR TRUST DEED)   An instrument providing for the loan of money with property as security and without any form of governmental guarantee or insurance for the repayment of the loan according to the contract terms. *See also* Federal Housing Administration, Veterans' Administration.

CONVERT (CONVERTIBILITY)   The capacity of a property to be changed to another use which increases the value or earning power of the property.

CONVEYANCE   The transfer of the property interest from one person to another, as may be evidenced by transfer of title deed or other legal instrument.

COOPERATIVE   A method of owning property in which the investor receives a certificate of ownership (stock certificate) permitting occupancy and the use of a particular property. The title to the property is held by the cooperative organization which may use the title as security for mortgage loans.

CORPORATION   A form of investment organization in which the property consists of all the assets of a corporation. Investors buy shares in the corporation instead of ownership rights in the property. In case of loss, creditors or others with claims against the corporation can receive judgments only against the assets of the corporation and not against the assets of the individual stockholders.

COVENANT (CONDITIONS AND RESTRICTION) (C C AND R)   A legally enforceable agreement among property owners to restrict their use rights. For example, they agree to build homes of only a certain size, or to put up no fences, or to set the homes back from front lot lines by a certain distance.

CREDIT REPORT A history of the amounts of money borrowed and repaid by a particular person or organization.

CYCLE Changes that occur regularly in real estate market construction and sales, but not necessarily evenly nor predictably. The pattern of events tend to repeat in approximately the same order, such as: (1) level, (2) sharp increase, (3) leveling, (4) decline, (5) stagnation, (6) return to step one.

DEDICATION A private property owner transfers to public use a portion of land after acceptance of the gift by public officials.

DEED (*also* TITLE DEED) A legal document including who owns the rights to a property. Forms of such instruments include:

GRANT The buyer receives from the seller legally binding assurances that (1) no one else has any interest in the property except those listed, (2) the property has not already been sold to someone else, and (3) any other rights the seller obtains will be transferred to the buyer. (In some states a grant is used in place of a warranty deed.)

QUITCLAIM The seller gives the buyer all the rights the seller owns but the seller makes no claim about what the rights may be.

WARRANTY The seller provides the buyer with legally binding assurances that (1) the seller has the legal ability to sell the property, (2) no one else has any interests in the property except for those indicated, (3) no one else can interfere in the buyer's use of the property or, if they do, the seller will help stop such interference. (In some states a warranty deed may be used in place of a grant deed.)

DEFAULT The failure, usually on mortgage loans, of the borrower to repay a loan according to the loan contract agreement.

DEFERRED MAINTENANCE Failure of a property owner to make repairs, improvements, modernization necessary to maintain property rent or value.

DEFICIENCY JUDGEMENT (MORTGAGE LOANS) When the borrower fails to make payments according to lending contract terms, the lender may take legal steps to acquire title to the property. After acquiring title the lender must sell the property at public auction, and if the sale does not provide enough money to pay what is owed the lender, the lender may try to acquire what is owed by seizing other assets of the borrower. A court judgement that enables the lender to make up the difference is called a deficiency judgement. (*See also* Foreclosure.)

DEPOSIT RECEIPT Sometimes included in a sales contract or agreement, a written statement in which the buyer agrees to purchase property with a down payment and on terms acceptable to the seller. If the seller accepts this offer of the buyer, a contract has been completed.

DEPRECIATION The loss in value in a property (usually indicated by a lower price or lower rents than comparable properties) because of one or more of the following types of reasons:

1. PHYSICAL   Wear and tear and use;
2. FUNCTIONAL   Higher costs in using the property due to the manner of construction, equipment, or layout, as compared to other properties of about the same size, style, and age;
3. ECONOMIC   Market changes that make the property less attractive as compared to other properties or because of lower market prices;
4. LOCATIONAL   The immediate neighborhood lowers the capacity of the property to produce rents or lowers the property price; and
5. CONTINGENT   Unanticipated, nonrecurring activities that lower the price of the property or its capacity to produce rents.

DEPRECIATION (FEDERAL INCOME TAX)   A charge against income, defined according to Internal Revenue Service regulations and income tax law, to provide for the replacement of a wasting asset.

DECLINING BALANCE   Depreciation is charged at a constant percentage of the amount of the asset not yet depreciated.

STRAIGHT-LINE   An equal percentage of the total value of the asset is deducted each year.

SUM-OF-YEARS-DIGITS   is best explained by way of illustration. If the total life of a property is three years, depreciation for each year is calculated as follows:

Add $1 + 2 + 3$ $= 6$ years
First-year depreciation $= {}^3/_6$ value
Second-year depreciation $= {}^2/_6$ value
Third-year depreciation $= {}^1/_6$ value

DETERIORATION   Practically the same as depreciation, but may also be limited to meaning physical depreciation.

DISCOUNT   Assuming assets to be received in the future will have values lower than in the present, a discount is an estimate of the value today of a single amount or a series of periodic amounts to be received at a known time in the future. The difference between the current and future values of the asset is expressed as a percentage, also known as the "discount rate."

DURABILITY   The capacity of a property to resist wear, tear, and the force of weather and natural elements.

EARNED INCOME OR ORDINARY INCOME   According to federal tax law, the income on which taxes must be paid after recognition of allowable deductions and other credits. Such income is usually taxed at the highest rates—higher than rates on equivalent capital gains.

EASEMENT   An agreement that allows one party to use the property of another.

ECONOMICS   A study of the most effective means of assigning means of production to various ways of earning the income. Also:

—a study of the most effective means of allocating scarce resources to those who need them.

—a study of who pays and who benefits in any activity.

ECONOMIC INCOME (MARKET INCOME)   Returns (usually money) received from a property after the operating expenses have been paid but before payment of loan expenses and income taxes.

ECONOMIC LIFE   The period, in years or months, during which a property is expected to earn a net income or to produce rental income.

ECONOMIC (MARKET) RENT   Rents paid for similar properties by renters acting with some understanding of what the rents should be and who are not forced to pay a particular amount or any amount at all.

ECONOMIC VALUE   The amount in dollars that a property would bring if the property were exposed to the market long enough to attract buyers who understood what the property could be used for, what others would pay for the property, and with both buyer and seller not required to complete the transaction.

EMINENT DOMAIN   The right given to a public agency to take title to privately owned property by paying the market price and proving that the taking is for public good. *See also* Condemnation.

ENVIRONMENTAL IMPACT REPORT (EIR) OR ENVIRONMENTAL IMPACT STATEMENT (EIS)   A report required by any governmental agency which indicates how the use of a property will affect elements of the environment such as air, water, sight, sound, human health, government costs, and services.

EQUIPMENT (MECHANICAL OR CONVENIENCE)   Stoves, refrigerators, water heaters, clothes dryers, clothes washers, air conditioners or other equipment included as integral parts of the property and for which a price or rent is charged.

EQUITY   The amount of money in a property that belongs to the investor, in excess of what is owed on the property.

ESCROW   A service for buyers and sellers in which a third party (usually licensed by the state) assures that all terms of the sales contract are met before the title deed is transferred.

ESTATE   The total package of rights owned by a property holder.

EXPENSES   Deductions from income for payments needed to maintain the rents, such as:

CONTINGENT   Unusual expenses that occur very irregularly (wind, floods, and the like);

FIXED   Expenses that do not change as the property use levels change (property taxes, insurance premiums);

OPERATING   Outlays whose amounts are determined by the level of property usage;

RESERVES   Annual amounts placed in an account so that ultimately their totals will permit buying services or products which will affect the rental income over several years.

FEASIBILITY ANALYSIS A written statement that indicates (1) alternative uses for a property, (2) ways in which a property might be used to achieve a particular investment objective.

FEDERAL HOME LOAN BANK (FHLB) A Federally chartered agency, with twelve regional offices, that provides additional funds to members (usually savings and loan associations) for making home loans, with members using home loans they have made as security for repayment of the money they borrow.

FEDERAL HOUSING ADMINISTRATION (FHA) A Federally chartered agency that insures lenders against losses if they make loans according to FHA requirements. The borrower pays the insurance premium but the lender receives any proceeds from the insurance in case of default. An "FHA" loan is therefore any loan insured by the FHA.

FEDERAL NATIONAL MORTGAGE ASSOCIATION (FNMA, OR FANNY MAY) A Federally chartered agency that buys and sells FHA and VA loans at prices prevailing in the money/mortgage markets. The sellers usually plan to use the funds to provide additional home loans. The FNMA will also sell mortgages when it believes the terms are "appropriate."

FEDERAL SAVINGS AND LOAN INSURANCE CORPORATION (FSLIC) A Federally created agency that insures depositors against loss if the savings and loan association cannot return the savings. The accounts are insured only to a designated amount.

FEE SIMPLE (FEE ABSOLUTE, FEE) A form of title giving a private person the highest possible number of rights available to individuals.

FORECLOSURE A right given to a lender to force a public sale of a privately held property on which a loan has been made but for which the lender is not paying according to the lending contract.

FREE AND CLEAR Privately owned property without any kind of obligation against it that would reduce either the value or the sale price of the property.

FRONT MONEY The initial cash needed to start a project before other financing is obtained for the entire project.

FUNCTIONAL The capacity of a property to provide the services for which it was built with maximum efficiency and convenience and at minimum costs.

FURNISHINGS Anything movable in a property and included in the sale price, furnishings may include draperies, rugs, furniture, refrigerators, dish washers, clothes washers and dryers, air conditioners. These items should be listed in the sales contract.

GROSS INCOME MULTIPLIER (GIM) Used in estimating the value of a property by relating gross income to sale price, the multiplier is a single number obtained by dividing gross income into the sale price for a large number of comparable properties. The average of these numbers becomes a gross income multiplier.

HIGHEST AND BEST USE The uses to which a property could be put to produce the highest possible current net income and price or value.

HOME LOAN   Money borrowed to buy a home, it may be a trust deed or mortgage.

HYPOTHECATE   An owner of assets pledges his ownership interests in the assets as security for a loan, but reserves the right to collect any interest or income from the assets.

IMPOUNDS   An amount paid by the buyer to a lender in connection with the loan payment to cover payments for property taxes and insurance premiums.

INCOME   Money received for uses of a property:

> GROSS   The total money received for the uses of a property;
>
> NET   All money received for the uses of the property minus the costs of earning the income.

INFLATION   Price increases because the money supply has increased without an equivalent increase in the production of goods and services.

INTEREST RATE   The periodic amount, usually expressed as a percentage, that a borrower pays for the use of money:

> CONTRACT   The amount agreed upon between the lender and the buyer;
>
> NOMINAL   Same as contract rate;
>
> YIELD   Actual interest earned, usually same as contract rate except under conditions when there are costs to be deducted from interest income.

INTERNAL RATE OF RETURN (**IRR**)   The net income received from an investment during the entire life of the investment expressed as an annual percentage of the amount the investor has in his equity.

INVEST (INVESTMENT)   The process of carefully evaluating a property and setting a price which over a reasonably long period of time will permit the property to yield an income that pays back the original investment and a profit to the investor.

> Some say that any real estate purchase/sale transaction that produces a profit is an investment and that anything else is a speculation.

INVESTMENT VALUE   An expression in dollars of the worth of a property to a particular investor in the light of his investment objectives.

INVESTOR FEVER   A feeling that almost every investor gets after signing purchase papers and then realizes how much money is being invested and how much financial risk is involved. May be cured by referring again to the analyses made prior to deciding to invest.

JOINT VENTURE   An agreement among two or more persons to undertake a particular real estate investment on terms to which all parties agree.

KICKER   An additional amount paid beyond the terms of an agreement in order to complete a transaction.

LAND   The surface of the earth, an area below the earth, and the air space above the earth plus anything attached to the earth in such a manner as to indicate the attachment is intended to be reasonably permanent. Such attachments may include buildings, swimming pools, landscaping, and many other items.

LAND CONTRACT   A written agreement (contract) between a buyer and seller relating to the purchase of land only or of improved land, with the seller retaining title until the periodic payments equal a given amount, after which a mortgage or trust deed is created. Usually this type of agreement permits the buyer to acquire the property without a down payment or with only a minimal one.

LAND FEVER (BUILDING FEVER, PROPERTY FEVER)   A condition that encourages an investor to buy primarily on the basis of "enthusiasm," of "fear" that a good bargain may be purchased by someone else, or of a "feeling" that "everyone else is getting in ahead of me." Under such conditions an impartial evaluation of the investment is ignored in the hopes that an unusual profit can be made.

LEASE   A written agreement signed by a tenant (lessee) and the landlord or property owner (lessor) outlining the terms on which the rents are to be paid and the property is to be used:

    FLAT   Rents are the same dollar amount each payment period;

    GRADUATED   Rents change according to some standard, such as the Consumer Price Index (CPI);

    PERCENTAGE   Amount of rent relates to the amount of income or sales of the lessee;

    NET   The lessee (tenant) pays all expenses relating to using the property (usually this means the tenant pays maintenance, property taxes, and property insurance premiums);

    NET, NET   The landlord pays no expenses for the use and maintenance of the property.

LEASEBACK   A property user signs a lease which the property owner can use to secure financing, perhaps for the construction of a special property for use by the tenant.

    Or, if a property owner is unable to secure financing, the property is sold with the seller signing a lease to use the property and reserving the right to buy back the property at the end of the lease. The buyer of the property can use the lease to finance the construction of the building.

LEASEHOLD   The bundle of property rights owned by the lessor through the creation of a lease.

LEGAL DESCRIPTION   A statement of the dimensions of a property and its location in terms the courts will recognize, usually by Lot, Block, Tract number.

    METES AND BOUNDS   Property is described by direction and distance which relate to readily identifiable physical features on the land.

    GOVERNMENT DESCRIPTION   Location of the property from U.S. government north-south lines (meridians) and east-west lines (baselines).

LESSEE   Tenant, the one paying the rent for the use of a property.

LESSOR   The landlord, the one who collects the rent.

LEVERAGE   The process of using a maximum of borrowed money to improve the rate of return on the investor's equity.

LIEN   The rights of a lender in a property pledged by a borrower as security for a debt.

LIFE ESTATE   The bundle of property rights which a person owns during the lifetime of that person.

LIQUIDATE   The sale of assets to obtain cash, sometimes implying selling at a loss because the sale is forced.

LIQUIDITY   The quality of an investment which allows it to be sold readily for cash without a cut in price.

LISTING (LISTING AGREEMENT)   A written contract in which the seller of a property indicates the price and terms he would accept from a buyer:

    EXCLUSIVE AGENCY   Limits the selling to one agency (usually a real estate broker) which collects a commission from the sale—even if anyone other than the owner sells the property;

    EXCLUSIVE RIGHT   The listing agency may collect a commission on a completed sales no matter who sells the property;

    NET   The seller is guaranteed a minimum amount from the sale of the property;

    OPEN   Anyone who sells the property receives the commission.

LOAN COMMITMENT   Lender agrees to provide a loan in the amounts and terms indicated in the letter.

    TAKEOUT LETTER   A commitment letter

LOAN FEE   An amount charged a borrower as part of the process of securing a loan and beyond the interest charged.

LOAN TO VALUE RATIO   The percentage of an appraised value which determines the total amount of the loan.

MARKET   A listing of prices and terms at which properties are offered for sale and on which sales are completed:

    BUYERS' MARKET   Sellers offer more properties than buyers are demanding, so buyers get bargains;

    SELLERS' MARKET   Buyers demand more properties than sellers have for sale, so sellers get better prices.

MARKET ANALYSIS (MARKET REPORT, FEASIBILITY STUDY)   A report on the potentials for selling a property or using the property for a particular purpose; or an estimate of the terms and conditions on which properties can be bought and sold.

MECHANIC'S LIEN   A claim against a property by someone who has furnished labor, materials, or both but who has not been paid for them.

MODERNIZE   To change older elements in a property for newer ones which will prevent a loss of rents or of price, or which will improve rents or prices or reduce expenses.

MORTGAGE (TRUST DEED)   A contract pledging property as security for repayment of a loan.

MORTGAGE   There are two parties involved: (1) lender or mortgagee, (2) borrower or mortgagor.

TRUST DEED   There are three parties involved: (1) lender or beneficiary, (2) borrower or trustor, and (3) trustee, who enforces the contract.

ALL-INCLUSIVE OR WRAP-AROUND   One contract pledges all the rights in a property as security for a loan payment, although there is more than one mortgage or trust deed on the property, and the borrower wishes to consolidate all the loan payments into a single payment.

CONSTANT PAYMENT   A level periodic (usually monthly) payment that does not change during the life of the loan.

FIRST MORTGAGE   The lender has the first chance to recover any money owed by the public sale of a property on which the mortgage has not been repaid according to schedule.

JUNIOR (SECOND OR THIRD, ETC.)   The lender can recover any money owed by public sale of a property only after the holder of the prior or first mortgage has been repaid.

OPEN-END   Borrower can secure additional amounts using the existing loan agreement.

PURCHASE MONEY   The buyer pays part of the purchase price by giving the seller a mortgage on the property.

VARIABLE AMOUNT   The monthly loan payments change in order for the lender to charge more interest as the costs of borrowed money change.

VARIABLE RATE   The monthly payment usually stays the same but the length of the repayment period is extended so the lender can charge more interest because borrowed money is costing more in the money markets (sometimes referred to as VRM).

MORTGAGE INSURANCE   Protects the holder of the policy, usually a home lender, against loss if the terms of the mortgage are not met by the borrower. Mortgage insurance is provided by the Federal Housing Administration (FHA) and by private mortgage insurance companies.

MORTGAGEE   The person or organization providing funds to a borrower using a mortgage.

MORTGAGOR   The borrower who uses a mortgage to secure funds.

MULTIPLE LISTING   A written contract between the seller of a property and the sales agent permitting the agent to notify other agents of the agreement and to share with them any commission they may earn from selling the property.

MUTUAL SAVINGS BANK   State chartered financial institution that collects savings and uses them for a variety of productive investments, of which mortgage loans are the most numerous. Limited to the northeastern U.S.A.

NEIGHBORHOOD   An area in which approximately the same prices are paid for similar kinds of properties; or an area in which properties are used for approximately the same purposes and have approximately the same physical, economic, and use characteristics.

NONRECOURSE   The lender, if not paid, may not charge the borrower with any additional fees but may take title to the property pledged as security for the loan.

NOTICE OF COMPLETION   A public notice by the owners of the property that all work has been finished and that any financial charges against the property must be collected. Particularly useful in connection with a mechanic's lien which can be collected only within a given time (according to local law) after the filing of a notice of completion or the lien cannot be collected thereafter.

NOTICE OF DEFAULT   When a borrower has not paid according to the terms of the loan agreement, the lender must file a public notice in the public records that the buyer has not paid and the lender intends to foreclose.

NOTARY   A licensed official who observes the signing of legal documents and certifies that the signing has been done properly by the legally responsible parties.

OBSOLETE (OBSOLESCENCE)   A property suffering loss because it is no longer useful for producing income.

OPERATING EXPENSES   *See* Expenses.

OPTION   A payment to a seller to guarantee that the buyer can buy the property at a later date at the terms and price indicated in the option agreement.

  BINDER   Same as an option.

OTHER INCOME   Income produced by a property from other than rents. Such income derives from parking fees, washer-dryer-laundromat charges, use of recreational facilities, and many other sources. It is usually assumed to have a shorter duration and to be less stable than rental income when given a value.

OVERALL RATE   The net earnings per one hundred dollars of total property value, but expressed as a percentage.

OVERIMPROVEMENT   A condition under which the owner of a property has invested so much in buildings and other improvements that the property cannot command sufficient rents to pay for the improvements. In other words, the property—compared to other properties somewhat like it—is not at its highest and best use.

PARCEL   The land and improvements contained in a single ownership under one legal property description.

PARTICIPATION LOAN   A loan in which more than one lender provides loan funds to the borrower.

PARTNERSHIP   A legal agreement between two or more persons to participate according to the terms of the loan agreement in the income, expenses, and profits from the property investment.

  GENERAL PARTNERSHIP   One person is responsible for all financial obligations and operations of the investment, while the others have more limited responsibilities and returns.

  LIMITED PARTNERSHIP   Those who are responsible in a limited way for the debts and limited in participation in profits.

PAYBACK   The terms on which a loan is to be repaid.

PERFORMANCE BOND   A written agreement by which the provider of the bond agrees to see that anyone providing goods and services does so according to the agreement between the property owner and the contractors. If the contractors do not perform, the provider of the bond will either require the performance or provide equally acceptable performance from some other contractor while charging the original contractor for all expenses for doing this.

PERCENT   The number of dollars per one hundred dollars. For example, if you earned $5 by investing $100, your return would be $5 per $100, or 5 percent (sometimes written as 5%). Percentages can also be expressed in decimal form; our example would be written as .05 (no percent sign).

PLANS AND SPECIFICATIONS   A written statement accompanied by drawings and other exhibits which indicate the kinds of materials and workmanship to be used in completing, remodeling, renovating, rehabilitating an existing building, in constructing a new building, or in any work changing the physical structure of a property.

PLOTTAGE   Conditions under which two properties used as one have more value than the total value of each used independently.

POINTS (USED IN CONNECTION WITH MORTGAGE LOANS)   A statement of the percentage charges for the use of money.

POINTS	= one percentage point	= .1%
BASIC POINTS	= one tenth of one percentage point	= .01%
BASIS POINTS	= one one-hundredth of one percentage point	= .001%

PORTFOLIO (INVESTMENT)   The total of all the types of investments an investor owns, usually expressed in terms of dollars and returns for each type of investment.

PRE-PAYMENT PENALTY (CLAUSE)   A lender requirement that a home loan paid off ahead of the contract schedule will have to include financial penalties for the amounts paid.

PRESENT VALUE   The current worth of an asset that will become available in the future. Usually connected with establishing the value of a future rental income stream or a property price to be paid in the future.

  PRESENT VALUE OF ONE   Value today of a single amount to be received in the future.

  PRESENT VALUE OF ONE PER PERIOD (ANNUITY)   Value today of a series of periodic payments to be received in the future.

PRIME RATE   The rate of interest a lender charges borrowers considered most likely to repay their loans as required in the lending contract.

  MORTGAGE PRIME RATE   Interest rates on the best quality properties being purchased by the best qualified buyers.

PRINCIPAL (MORTGAGE OR TRUST DEED)   The amount of money owed on a home loan.

PRINCIPAL (AS IN A PARTNERSHIP)   The person bearing primary responsibility for a loan.

PRINCIPLE   A guide to action based on proven experiences of others. A basic belief useful in deciding what to do when the facts are insufficient or in conflict with each other.

A guide to action derived from predictable occurrences.

PROFIT   The money remaining to an investor after he has paid all costs of the investment, a fee for the management of his investment, and a return to himself for the use of his money. Profit cannot be calculated ahead of time; it is a residual whose amount is known only after the entire investment transaction has been completed.

PROPERTY   Anything of value. (A bundle of rights.)

PERSONAL PROPERTY   Easily moved items, such as furniture, equipment, and the like.

REAL PROPERTY   The bundle of use rights in a property; or land, buildings, any improvements to the land. (*See also* Realty.)

PROPERTY LIFE   Period during which property rights may be used.

ECONOMIC LIFE   Period during which property uses will produce income.

PHYSICAL (USEFUL) LIFE   Period during which the physical improvements will produce income.

PYRAMIDING   The process of using a small original cash investment to buy a property which will later be exchanged for another property of more value without additional cash investment from the investor. The process may be repeated many times, without any additional cash investment from the investor.

RATE OF RETURN   Percentage earned on an investment.

RATIO ANALYSIS   Expressing one numerical amount as a percentage of another numerical amount:

NET INCOME/EQUITY RATIO   Expenses as a percentage of investor's equity.

NET INCOME/MARKET VALUE   Earning on total investment.

EXPENSE/INCOME   Expenses as percentage of income.

REAL ESTATE   The total of the legally recognized rights in a particular piece of land and buildings and other improvements to the land. The term can also mean the business of buying and selling real property, as well as property or real property itself.

REAL ESTATE BROKER (AGENT, SALES PERSON)   Anyone licensed to sell real estate for a commission or payment for services. Though an agent may be hired by either buyer or seller, he or she usually represents the seller.

AGENT   Either a broker or a sales person.

BROKER   Responsible to his client for completing transactions as agreed upon.

SALES PERSON   Works with broker's clients but is primarily responsible to the broker for any services provided to the client.

REAL ESTATE CYCLE   A time period in which the prices or values of real estate increase, stay level, decline, and reach another level from which the cycle can start again. Many believe this cycle lasts eighteen to twenty years.

REAL ESTATE INVESTMENT TRUST (REIT)   An organization created under Federal law permitting a group of persons to invest in property using a special form of corporation that also gives the investors some income tax breaks not possible in an ordinary corporation.

REAL ESTATE SETTLEMENTS PROCEDURE (RESPA)   A Federal law that indicates how the terms of a purchase and sale are to be reported and completed.

REALTOR®   A patented term designating persons who buy and sell real estate for a commission and who belong to a real estate board chartered by the National Association of Realtors (NAR). The term, when written, must be capitalized.

REALTIST   A term designating persons who buy and sell real estate for a commission and who belong to a real estate board chartered by the National Association of Real Estate Brokers.

REALTY   Another term for real estate or property.

RECAPTURE   According to Federal income tax law, the difference between the amount received from the sale of a property and the amount of depreciation charged in excess of what it would be under straight-line depreciation.

RECORDING   Leaving a copy of a legal document with a legally designated public official who must make a copy of the document and record the date and time at which the document was received. All persons are notified in this manner of the interests of the persons named in the document.

REHABILITATE (OR RENOVATE)   To change a condition of a property in order to charge more rents, to reduce the cost of operating the property, or to increase the value or price of the property.

RENTAL SCHEDULE   A list of rents to be paid under the terms of a lease or a list of rents actually collected.

RETURN OF INVESTMENT   The amount of the total investment recovered each year from income. Always included in developing a capitalization rate when establishing the value of an income stream produced by land and buildings.

RETURN ON INVESTMENT   The percentage of earnings on the entire investment or on the remaining investment, including consideration for the use of money, risk, and other factors the investor feels he should be paid for. Always included in the capitalization rate when estimating the current value of income from land and buildings or income from land only.

REVERSIONARY CLAUSE OR AGREEMENT   Terms under which the seller of a property may recover property rights transferred to a seller.

RISK   The potential for losing the amount invested in a property.

SAFETY   Protection against the loss of income or value in a property.

SAVINGS AND LOAN ASSOCIATION   A financial institution, chartered either by Federal or state government, specializing in home loans. It is not a bank, nor does it provide all the services of a commercial bank. The primary function of an association is to collect savings from the local community and to make them available locally for home loans.

SCIENCE (OR SCIENTIFIC)   Actions taken on the basis of available facts and applicable theories. Also, the most reasonable conclusions to be made in the light of the facts. Generally, the terms imply reason, logic.

SECONDARY MORTGAGE MARKET   An opportunity provided lenders to buy and sell mortgages they have created in order to secure more cash for making additional home loans.

SENSITIVITY MEASURES   Estimates of the impact of different rates and earning conditions on the investment value of a property.

SERVICE (SERVICING)   Relates to the collection of amounts due on a mortgage.

SERVICE SYSTEMS   In relation to properties, the means used to provide heat, light, water, air conditioning, and sewage disposal to a property.

SINKING FUND   Setting aside an amount periodically at interest so that the total set aside will equal a given amount at a particular time.

SITE (LAND)   A portion of land identified by boundaries on which buildings and other improvements may be placed.

SPECULATION   The use of a maximum amount of other persons' monies for a short-term purchase of property with the hope that a large price increase will occur. Involves high degrees of all kinds of risks. Some say that in real estate a speculation is any property investment that produces a loss at time of sale.

SPENDABLE INCOME   *See* Cash Flow.

SUBDIVISION   The dividing of a single parcel of land into several lots or parcels.

SUBLET   A tenant leases to another tenant.

SUBORINATION (SUBORDINATE)   A person with first rights in case of foreclosure gives up these rights in favor of others with later rights to foreclosure; or whenever anyone with superior rights in property gives up those rights to another with inferior rights.

SUBROGATE   Replacing one person's rights for another's rights.

SYNDICATE (SYNDICATION)   An agreement among two or more persons to undertake a single, one-time property investment.

TAKEOUT LOAN   An agreement by a lender to provide long-term financing for a project now under construction and already financed on a short-term basis.

TAX BASIS   According to Federal income tax law, the value of the property on which taxes are to be paid.

TAX-FREE EXCHANGE According to Federal income tax law, legal provisions that permit property owners to exchange property equities under specified conditions without paying taxes at the time of the exchange.

TAX AVOIDANCE According to Federal income tax law, using all possible provisions of the tax law to reduce taxes to be paid.

TAX EVASION Using illegal means to reduce or eliminate taxes to be paid.

TAX SHELTER An investment with characteristics that reduce taxes to be paid.

TENANT Lessee or anyone paying an owner to use a property.

TENURE The period during which an owner of property rights can exercise those rights.

TERM (USUALLY MORTGAGE TERM) The number of years during which a mortgage or home loan is to be repaid; or the number of years during which an investment or money owed is returned.

TERMITE REPORT A statement by a professional person that a property is free of any damage from the action of termites and other insects, or that the damage listed in the report has been observed and can or cannot be corrected.

TIME-SHARING OWNERSHIPS Several investors own a property and, by agreement, share in the use of the property according to an agreed-upon time schedule.

TITLE Also called "deed," or "title deed," evidence of the total rights owned by an investor in a property.

TITLE ENCUMBRANCE (OR CLOUD) A restriction on a property owner's rights.

TITLE INSURANCE A private company issues a policy that protects the property owner's rights against the claims of others, except for those mentioned in the policy. Any claims against the property not identified in the policy which may later cause a loss are a basis for reimbursement to the policyholder.

TITLE SEARCH The process of searching public records to determine all possible rights in a given property and the ones who own the rights.

TRANSFER COSTS (CLOSING COSTS) All amounts paid by the buyer and the seller to assure legal transfer of property rights, exclusive of any interest payments.

TRUST DEED *See* Mortgage.

TOWNHOUSE Residential properties constructed with common adjoining walls but with each living unit having one floor on the ground.

TRUST A form of organization in which the property is managed by a trustee or trustees for the benefit of the investors in the trust. (*See also* Real Estate Investment Trust).

UNENCUMBERED A condition in which no claims exist against the rights of the property owner.

VACANCY AND COLLECTION LOSSES A charge deducted from expected gross income of a property to allow for noncollection of rents because units are not rented or rent cannot be collected. Gross scheduled income minus vacancy and collection losses equals gross operating income (GOI).

VALUATION (APPRAISAL)   An estimate, expressed in dollars, of the value of the total rights in a property.

VALUE   The amount paid by an informed buyer to an informed seller, with both acting without compulsion and with both understanding the uses to which the property could be put and usual market terms for selling and buying such properties.

LOAN VALUE   The amount of value expressed in dollars that a lender uses to determine the amount of loan to be made.

CAPITAL VALUE   The price paid for a property plus any price increases or minus any price decreases; or the total amount invested in a property.

SALVAGE VALUE   The portion of value left in a property at the end of a given period or event, such as at the end of a lease.

VETERANS' ADMINISTRATION (VA)   A Federal agency guaranteeing home loans to veterans who are identified by the VA as qualified for such benefits. In case the veteran fails to pay according to the loan terms, the VA takes title to the property and reimburses the lender for any losses in making the loan. The veteran pays nothing for the guarantee. [*See also* Federal Housing Administration (FHA).]

VARIANCE   Permission granted by a local governmental agency for a property owner to use a property in a manner not permitted in the zoning applicable to the property. (*See* Zoning.)

YIELD   The actual net earnings produced by a property expressed either as a percentage of the total property value or of the amount of investor equity.

ZONING   Regulations imposed by local governments on the kinds of uses to which a property may be put.

The Warmup:
From Home
To Income-Producing
Property

1

You own your home but you see your neighbors selling their homes for "fabulous" profits; and you wonder if you should do the same. Besides, you have heard all the stories of fortunes made in real estate, and you wonder if you could do as well. You may not be able to make a fortune, but there are ways you can move from home ownership to real estate investing while keeping some of the advantages of both forms of real estate ownership.

INVESTMENT CHOICES FOR THE HOME OWNER

Among the choices you have if you own your home are:

1. selling your home and using the proceeds to buy a larger home—some of the funds for a down payment on a larger home and the rest in some other form of investment,
2. trading your home for a larger home, avoiding many of the costs of buying and selling while increasing your real estate investment "stake,"

3. borrowing money on the basis of the equity you have in the home as a result of your original down payment, inflationary price increases, and your payments on the mortgage principal, and

4. changing your home to a rental property and at the appropriate time exchanging it for a rental income-producing property.

In this chapter you will learn how to convert your equity interest in a home into an income-producing property. The process will help you reduce your loss potentials, provide both income and capital or value increases, and reduce your income tax liabilities. The process is not "magic" nor does it guarantee absolute success. The process is a proven one that uses "science" to maximize opportunities for "good luck" when the time is right for deciding what to do.

IS IT LUCK OR SCIENCE?

Your neighbor drops in to talk about selling his home, which he bought just one year ago. He says he paid $75,000 for the home and just sold it for $125,000. When you congratulate him on his good luck, he says—almost casually—"Luck? Not me. I've been buying and selling homes and making profits for the last ten years!" As he explains what he has done, it sounds as though he has had remarkably and consistently good luck, always buying homes at prices below what he sold them for only a little later. Was luck the only ingredient, or did your neighbor unknowingly stumble onto some basic principles? Has your neighbor been doing this consistently, or did he have a lot of losses when he first started?

When you press him for answers to these questions, you find that he actually started investing in homes and income real estate fifteen years ago. In the first five years he barely broke even on some properties and actually lost money on others. He began to have more "luck" only after he tried to figure out why he had lost money so frequently and to study some of the many books written on real estate investing.

What would your neighbor have learned from his experiences and from his studying? *First:* Modest to large fortunes have been made—and lost—in real estate investing. *Second:* There is a portion of luck involved in almost every real estate investment because even the professional investors are unable to anticipate with consistent accuracy all the twists and turns in business and real estate markets. Most real estate investments extend over at least one year, usually many more, in which business and economic trends go up and down. *Third:* Some of the more predictable occurrences can be anticipated and reduced to basic principles for real estate investing. The purpose of this book is, of course, to provide, in reasonably brief format, the basic principles you should know to use more "science" than "luck" in winning your way to successful real estate investing.

FIRST FUNDAMENTAL PRINCIPLE

One of the most fundamental principles is that, though real estate investing is usually long-run, you will be enticed constantly into investments that will usually present only short-term speculative profits. Such deals are speculations rather than investments because you have to (a) time both your purchase and sale at precisely the right points, and (b) invest only a little of your own money and anticipate losing as much as you invest—or more. (We discuss timing in later chapters.) Perhaps even now you are being tempted by opportunities to buy inexpensive, recreationally oriented property in a beautiful wilderness area . . . or a condominium that you can use on weekends and rent out at other times. Or maybe you are considering a share in a "can't-lose" syndication or partnership that will return your investment in the first year by the purchase of a racquet ball court, a new apartment house, a shopping center with triple-A (top-credit) leases, farm land with fruit, or nut or grain crops. Your "instinctive" assumption that real estate is a good investment may be reinforced by the glamor and surefire profit that the investments offer.

If you want to invest in some such currently fashionable investments, go ahead! First, however, look at some of the basic ideas this book offers to help you make more—or at least lose less.

Once your home has proven to be a good investment, you will be tempted, as most persons are, to invest in land. The total price of land is usually reasonable, the down payment very small, and the monthly payments easy to make. Although there is no hard evidence, there is good reason to believe that more money has been lost in land speculation than has been made by investors through other forms of investment. However, as was true with the fashionable investments, there are ways of starting with land as your initial investment and making it profitable, as you will discover in the chapters devoted to land as an investment; however, your best opportunities will be found in income-producing investments.

PYRAMIDING AND LEVERAGE, THE BASICS OF REAL ESTATE INVESTING

One of the more successful ways of making profits in any kind of real estate investment is to learn how to use other people's money. How can you do that successfully? Perhaps a simple example will help you understand. Suppose that your successful neighbor tells you of a property that the two of you could buy, hold briefly, and then sell at a good profit, but the price is $90,000. Each of you would have to raise $45,000 in cash—but should you? Perhaps you could liquidate some of your investments and, with the cash you have, provide the $45,000. If you then were able to sell the property at a later date for $140,000 ($50,000 more than you paid), your share of $25,000 would represent a return of 55.5 percent. On the other hand, suppose you invested only $4,500 of your own cash and borrowed the rest of the money at 10 percent? If you held the investment for only one year you would pay $4,500 in interest. If you sold for the same price, your profit would be $20,500 (your $25,000 share minus $4,500 interest). On the original $4,500 investment (your down payment), your return is 455 percent—yes, four hundred and fifty-five percent!

This is a simplified demonstration of how to use money that does not belong strictly to you. If you are not sure at this point how this example relates to pyramiding and leverage, don't worry! This chapter will explain these techniques so you become familiar with them; later chapters will show you how to use them for winning in the real estate game. Here are the two basic concepts that can make you a more professional investor and put science into your decisions.

Leverage

Borrow as much of the purchase price of a real estate investment as you can at "reasonable rates." Rates are "reasonable" if they can be paid for out of the earnings of the investment. Picture the interest you are paying out one end of the lever and the income you are receiving on the other end. If you can keep the interest "end" down and the income "end" up, you are successfully practicing leverage.

For instance, if you own your own home, you can borrow the amount representing the value of the home in excess of what you owe on the mortgage. For example, suppose you can buy a home with a 9 percent mortgage. Select a home that you expect will have a minimal annual price increase of 9 percent overall. "Overall" means that the price should increase enough to permit you to pay interest not only on the mortgage but on your equity or down payment as well.

Let's take a more specific example. If you have built up a substantial equity in your home and would like to use it without moving from your home, you could discuss with a lender the possibilities of securing a new or additional mortgage loan equal to all or most of the equity which you now have in the home. You can then use this borrowed money to purchase an income-producing property. To determine whether the rate that the income-producing property will produce is sufficient for your needs, calculate the needed earning rate as follows:

Total purchase price of the property is	100%
Your down payment, using borrowed money on which you pay 9%, equals 30% of the purchase price; therefore .09 × .30	= .027
You can borrow the rest of the price of the income-producing property at 9.5% which equals 70% of the purchase price; therefore .095 × .70	= .0665
Minimum required earning rate on purchase	.0935 or 9½% (approx.)

If you buy an income-producing property, it must return a net income of $9.35 for each $1,000 of purchase price. If a property earns a net income of $40 per $1,000 of purchase price after all mortgage payments, it earns:

80% mortgage with 9% rate or .80 × .09	= .072
an equity of $200 earns $40 or .20 (20% equity) × .40	= .080
Earning rate on purchase price	.152 or 15.2%

The earning rate in this example (15.2%, or .152 in decimal) is obviously higher than the minimum earning rate needed (9½%). The interest end is down, and the income end is up. This is good leverage.

Pyramiding

Be careful to select a property that professionals believe will produce enough income to pay all expenses related to owning the property and also return some profit to you. Then, once you start investing in real estate, never sell for cash but always try to trade your property investment for another property in which you see opportunities for higher profits than you are now making. As you build the income-producing capability of your property, you are actually building a "pyramid" of equity.

To summarize briefly:

1. *Leverage*—borrow and use other people's money to increase your own profit potentials, and
2. *Pyramiding*—never sell for cash, but always trade for more profitable property.

Here is how these two techniques are put into effect, step by step:

1. Find an income-producing property (an apartment house for the initial investment) in a neighborhood in which prices have been increasing for at least the last six months to a year. In this case assume that you find an apartment with the potential for price increases of 1 percent per month.
2. Select a somewhat "neglected" property in comparison to other properties, but one with a potential for quick, relatively inexpensive repairs and improvements whose amounts can be recovered easily through rent increases. Or look for property that does not need additional investment but whose rents can be raised because they are below market levels.
3. Include in your financial planning:
   a. a property that will require no additional cash investment beyond your down payment,
   b. rental income from the property that pays all the costs of owning and operating the property;
   c. an available maximum mortgage equal to that part of the purchase price not covered by the down payment; 20 years at 9 percent interest usually proves to be "reasonable."
   d. property outlays and financing planned to minimize or eliminate any taxable income; and,
   e. when it is time for a new investment, the capability of trading present property for that new property. (At no time will any property be sold for cash.)
4. Plan to make your profit or equity build up from price increases, payments on the mortgage principal, and the total net income from the property.

Will this strategy work? A college graduate who was going to receive a substantial salary on his first job decided he wanted to cut his income tax liabilities and build a financial estate. He found a small four-unit apartment. Living in one unit and renting the other three, he spent his spare time improving all of the units so that he could raise the rents gradually. Over a period of ten years he continued to buy and trade for apartment houses with up to eight units in each apartment house. Today he owns a number of these small apartment houses consisting of 300 units total, and he is only in his early thirties. He has almost no income tax to report either from the real estate investments or his other income, and his equity or ''net worth'' in the units is in the hundreds of thousands of dollars.

APPLYING LEVERAGE CONCEPTS

You must be a bit skeptical about your ability to perform as well as that college graduate, but don't worry—you can do it!

Now take a look at Exhibit 1-1. It may look a little complicated, but let's see how simple it really is. The figures are hypothetical; but the income, price, and expense entries are each proportionate to one another.

Exhibit 1-1   Pyramiding and Leverage

		Changes for Each $1,000 Invested at the End of Investment Year			
		1	2	3	4
Start of Year 1:					
Mortgage*	$ 800				
Down payment (equity)	+ 200				
Purchase price	$1,000				
Equity Changes:					
Market price increase		$120	$254	$404	$ 573
Additions to mortgage principal		+ 21	+ 22	+ 24	+ 25
Annual equity buildup		$141	$276	$428	$ 598
			+141	+417	+ 845
Total equity, end of year			$417	$845	$1,443
Add down payment (equity)					+ 200
Total equity					$1,643
Gross Income:		$167	$209	$234	$ 262
Minus: Operating expenses**		– 42	– 52	– 59	– 66
Operating income		125	157	175	196
Minus: Property taxes**		– 20	– 22	– 25	– 28
Economic income		105	135	150	178
Minus: Mortgage payments		– 86	– 86	– 86	– 86
Cash flow		19	49	64	92
Add: Mortgage principal payments		+ 21	+ 22	+ 24	+ 25
Net income		40	71	88	117
Minus: Tax-allowed depreciation***		– 26	– 26	– 26	– 26
Taxable income		$ 14	$ 45	62	$ 91

Financial position at end of year 4:
  Equity Position
    Asset owned—property value $1,573
    Owed on mortgage   – 908
    Investor's total equity $ 665
    Original equity ($200)
    Return on original equity, $465/$200   233%
Income Position
    Assume 40% of taxable income was paid each year
    Total income after taxes $ 127.20
    Total rate on equity, 127.20/200   64%
    Average annual earning rate on equity, 64/4   = 18%

---

*Mortgage Terms:
  20 years @ 9% interest = monthly payment per $1,000 owed = $7.20 total annual
  payment (12 × 7.20) = $86.40
  Operating expense = 25% of gross income
**2% of previous year's market value.
***Assume for each $1,000 of purchase price: land = $300; building = $700.
  Building is depreciated at 3% per year ($700 × .03)   =$21.00
  Furnishings in apartments depreciated at 5% per year
  and equal $100 of each $1,000 property value ($100 × .05)   =   5.00
        Total depreciation per year $26.00

To keep the numbers simple, all the entries are in units of $1,000. In Exhibit 1-1, the purchase price is $1,000: By keeping this base figure even and simple, all other figures in the exhibit can now be computed very easily as "per $1,000." If, for example, you are talking about an expense of $50 ("per $1,000"), then the total expense for a $50,000 investment would be $2,500 ($50 × 50 units of a thousand each).

Now let's take a closer look at the figures themselves.

1. *Select property with the greatest gross income multiplier.* In Exhibit 1-1 each $1,000 of market price produces $167 annually in gross rental income. In other words, you have purchased a property on a multiple of six: The "six" is the gross income multiplier. If the real estate agents say the property is currently producing $167 in annual rental income, multiply the income by six to estimate the appropriate purchase price (6 × $167 = $1,002, or approximately $1,000).

You anticipate that, based on what is already happening in the local real estate markets, the property price (value) will increase by 1 percent per month so that at the end of the first year of investment the price will be $1,120 for a $120 increase. By the end of the fourth year the price would be

$1,573, a $573 increase over the original purchase price. So far the investment seems to be a good one, but keep referring to Exhibit 1-1 as we see what happens to the investment.

2. *Keep the down payment as low as possible.* In this case the best you could do was a 20 percent down payment, and financing from a mortgage of 9 percent of $800 (per $1,000 of purchase price) for twenty years. The monthly payments will total $86 (actually $7.20 per month for each $800 borrowed × 12 months = $86.40 rounded to $86).

Mortgage lenders follow the practice of crediting the first part of your payment to interest and the remainder to reduce the amount of the loan (the principal) that you owe. In this example, at the end of the first year you pay $65 interest (9 percent × the unpaid principal each month) and $21 on the principal. Each year, as you reduce the amount of money you owe, the dollar amount of interest is reduced consequently, more of the payment is used to repay the loan, although the total payment remains at the original $86. This is a fixed payment loan, the usual type of mortgage loan.

3. *Prepare a reasonably accurate estimate of the costs of owning and operating the property by consulting with other owners and property managers.* The costs of owning and operating the property area are estimated to average 25 percent of the gross income, ranging from $42 in year one to $66 in year four. Property taxes are estimated to equal 2 percent of the current market price, but because tax assessments always fall behind current market value, the 2 percent is based on the previous year's market value.

What have these expenses done to your income? In the first year, operating expenses produce an operating income of $125 and an "economic" or market income of $105. You are left with a cash flow after mortgage payments (because you want the property to pay all costs) of $19. However, because of the Federal income tax laws, which we will discuss later, you cannot count the payments on mortgage principal in reporting your taxable income; so you add back the $21 paid in principal to produce a net income of $40.

4. *Include in your expenses a sufficient amount to permit you to maintain your property at the highest possible rental earning potentials.* You will find that professional investors assume that everything about a property, except the land, needs occasional or regular repair, maintenance, of refurbishing. In order to be sure that each element in the property contributes to maximum rental returns, a charge is created to help overcome any rental earning losses. This expense, usually thought of as

"depreciation," is countered through the creation of reserve accounts in which money is set aside periodically eventually to be spent to overcome, as much as possible, the effects of depreciation.

The Internal Revenue Service allows you to deduct an amount representing a reasonable estimate of the rate at which your property would be depreciating or losing value under normal market conditions. You soon learn to differentiate between the amounts you must spend to overcome depreciation and the amounts the Federal income tax law allows you to charge for depreciation. Frequently the income tax deductions are higher than the actual amounts you are spending for depreciation so that you can achieve some additional financial advantage. However complex this may seem to you at this point, you will find information on income tax laws later, after you have mastered these principles.

In this exhibit, the furnishings (draperies, rugs, stoves, refrigerators) on your property are worth $100. (Remember this $100 is for each $1,000 you actually invest in the purchase price.) You decide that these items will need replacement every twenty years. In effect, you are saying that they are losing value (or depreciating) at 5 percent every year (5 percent × 20 years = 100 percent value). Also, the building is losing value: With an expected life of 33 years, the building itself is losing a little more than 3 percent of its value every year (3 percent × 33 years = 99 percent value). Using these estimates the total depreciation on building furnishings comes to $26 (per $1,000) each year. Check the arithmetic in the footnote of Exhibit 1-1.

5. *Minimize Federal income taxes (and perhaps state income taxes) on all income produced in excess of the actual expenses or of the expenses allowed by law.* The taxable income for the property ranges from $14 in the first year to $91 in the second year. Remember, however, that if you did not own the property and had earned the $40 net income produced by the property from another source, you would have had to report $40, not $14, for tax purposes. Further, even if the costs of owning and operating the property had produced a loss, the amount of the loss could have been deducted from other earned income.

Successful real estate investing therefore means that you must combine an understanding of the basics of real estate investing with a knowledge of current income tax law. Fortunately, you will find the principles easy to follow. Also there are many kinds of experts whom you can afford to hire to help you build your real estate fortune. To aid your understanding of the basic principles, let's generalize on what we've learned from Exhibit 1-1.

Never Pay More Than "Fair" Market Price

Gross income and market price do have a relationship to each other, and they do reflect real potentials. The key to the *right* relationship is the gross income multiplier. In the exhibit, the property was purchased for a multiple of six times the gross income—the six is the gross income multiplier. If you look in real estate advertisements, you will find many income-producing properties described in terms of a gross income multiplier (GIM). This claim is explained further in later chapters.

The Property Pays Its Way

After subtracting operating expenses, property taxes, and mortgage payments, the property is expected to produce a cash flow—or at least no loss. In other words, this property can produce enough income to pay all the costs of owning and operating it and some extra "cash," a result most fervently hoped for by most real estate investors.

Use Federal Income Tax Law to Maximum Advantage

For income tax purposes, the mortgage principal cannot be treated as an expense, so it is added back each year to the cash flow. However, income tax law permits the investor to deduct an allowance for expected value losses in the value of the building and the equipment, allowances defined as depreciation. Remember: an important aspect of income tax law is that the depreciation allowed need not be reflected in actual cash outlays.

Use Market Changes and Property Management to Build Equity

Each year the financial position of the taxpayer changes due to reductions in mortgage principal, changes in expenses, and other reasons. In the example at the end of the first year, the investor has increased his equity (or financial interest in the property) by the amount he paid on the mortgage principal as well as by the increase in the market price. How much has he earned in addition? Remember that he had an actual tax-sheltered cash flow because of depreciation realized each year.

Combine Leverage and Tax Law to Maximize Earnings

If an investor sells his property at the end of the first year, he has to pay a capital gains tax—a tax on the difference between what he paid and what he sold the property for. In our example, the purchase price was $1,000, with a cash down payment of only $200. Selling for $1,120, would produce a gain of $120 on a $200 down payment, or a gain of 60 percent. Since you deducted depreciation and are selling so quickly after purchase, you must add to the $120 gain the $26 depreciation. You must therefore pay taxes on a gain of $146. Since this is a capital gain, not earned income, your tax rate would be approximately 25 to 35 percent of the gain. This rate is lower than the 40 percent on earned income, because of a lot of income tax rules and regulations not considered at this point. A capital gains rate of even 35 percent is probably less than what you might have to pay on earned income. If you are in a tax bracket higher than 35 percent, you have clearly gained a financial advantage by investing in real estate. More importantly, you improved your financial position by investing wisely, not by working more or harder.

Another way of understanding the basic concepts of leverage, pyramiding, and real estate investment principles is presented in Exhibit 1-2. The solid lines indicate the four years of investment; the dotted lines are projections of what might happen during later years if you continue to hold this property. The shaded portion in the upper diagram indicates the amount of equity or investment buildup occurs because of price increases. The shaded are in the lower diagram indicates the annual net income you earn. The original purchase price is indicated as a straight line in the upper diagram, the original down payment as a straight line in the lower diagram.

One final word: The property would probably not increase in both value (or price) and net income indefinitely since it is limited in size. The final principle to remember is that you trade your equity in this property for an equity in a larger property so that you can increase your financial potentials. In other words, in year four you now have a total equity in the property of $1,643. Since you can use this as a 20 percent down payment on a larger property, you find one with a purchase price of $8,215 ($1,643 × 5). However, instead of selling your property, you trade it for the larger property. There are real estate agents who will help you do this and investors who are looking for smaller properties to exchange for their larger properties. Since you are using a multiple of six to guide your selection, you now have a property with a gross income potential of $1,369 ($8,215 ÷ 6) as compared to the other property with a $262 gross income. You have now increased your financial potentials substantially.

Exhibit 1-2 Basic Concepts of Leverage and Pyramiding

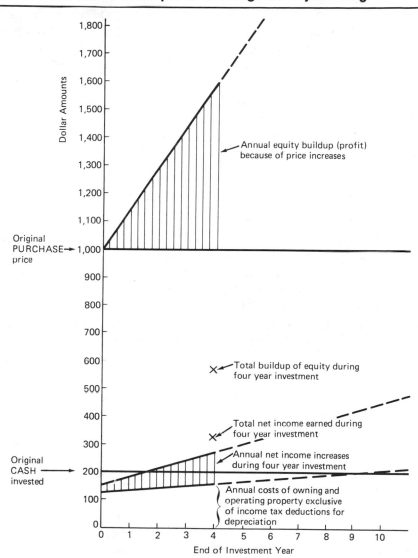

FROM HOME TO INVESTMENT PROPERTY

There are several ways to convert from a home owner to a professional investor. All methods require the constant advice of an experienced real estate broker and income tax advisor.

Let's assume, as one method, that you own a home but wish to convert it to an income-producing property. Here are the steps in brief.

First, you must offer your home as a rental unit. Though you may have to rent another unit somewhere else, the rent you receive from the home should offset the rent you pay elsewhere. After you have rented your home for a mininum period (at least six months), it is classified as an income-producing unit and can be traded for another income-producing unit.

Second, find an income-producing unit, usually a small apartment. Use the real estate broker to help you select such a unit and arrange for the exchange. Since you are not selling, you will have no cash receipts on which to pay a capital gains tax.

Third, since you will occupy one unit in the apartment house, be sure you find one that attracts you. Let the income tax advisor explain how to set up your tax records so that you can treat that part as an investment. The tax advisor will also help you treat costs and depreciation properly.

Suppose you do not wish to go through this process. Is there another way? Yes, you can sell your home and use the proceeds to buy an apartment house and declare a portion of the apartment as your home. If the share declared as a home is equal in value to the proceeds from the sale of your home, you have no tax to pay. If you realize a gain on your home sale and do not invest all the gain in an existing home in twelve months or in a new home (apartment unit) in eighteen months, you will have some small capital gain tax to pay. In any case, the capital gain tax is always less than what you would have paid if you had sold your home and used the proceeds to buy income-producing property that you did not plan to occupy.

Finally, if you do not want to move from your home but wish to invest, you might use some of your savings or borrow on the equity you have in your current home to purchase an income-producing property. However, you might try to find one that produces no reportable taxable income. Typically, such a property would have a high value potential but would need improvements and repairs. By using all the income to improve the property, you can increase its capital value until it is equal to that of the neighborhood, and at the same time increase your tax liability under capital gains provisions for a tax rate lower than that on earned income.

Let's summarize the principles very briefly before proceeding to the detail in later chapters:

1. Select an area of active real estate sales.
2. Determine the average market price.
3. Determine the average gross income.
4. Divide the market price by gross income to estimate the gross income multiplier.

5. Select a property neglected by its present owner either in terms of maintenance and repairs or in rents charged.

6. Buy the property, using a price based on the market multiple times the current gross income.

7. Develop the financial potential by planning a gross income and expense schedule that includes the costs of:
   a. operating the property,
   b. maintaining and improving the property so that rents can be raised as the market improves, and
   c. financing the property.

8. Use a tax advisor to help you deduct the proper amounts for tax-sheltered items (property taxes, depreciation, mortgage interest) so that you have no, or minimal, reportable income for tax purposes.

9. As you build your equity, look for a larger property to exchange for your property so that there is no tax liability created in the exchange.

10. Plan to watch market changes carefully so that you can keep building your equity and your financial future.

SECOND HOMES AND UNDEVELOPED LAND

Perhaps you feel that the purchase of an investment property is more than you want to undertake. Maybe you would be more interested in investing in a second home for leisure-time uses by your family, or in undeveloped land with the expectation of a dramatic increase in value without any improvement of the land. But be careful when you look to a second home or undeveloped land for investment purposes; they represent speculation much more than investment. In this book the emphasis is on income-producing properties, and neither a second home nor land fits that category. To give you some very simple ideas about such investments, two checklists and some suggestions for undertaking such investments are presented in the remainder of this chapter.

Second Homes

Families who purchase leisure homes usually plan to use them as they choose and to rent them out at other times. The rent is then supposed to be used to maintain the homes so that there is no taxable income earned from the property.

Changes in Federal tax laws in 1976, however, have made this alternative less attractive than in the past. The most important effect of these changes is that you must be willing to use your second home minimally during the year or not consider it as a major form of investment. The 1976 laws now limit your use of such a home to two weeks in every year or to 10 percent of the time it is rented, whichever is less.

To show you how to estimate how much the value of the home should increase each year to pay you for holding the property, a sample estimate sheet follows. In this table, there are two columns: the "Example" column and a blank column for you to use when necessary.

For each $1,000 of home investment:	*Example*	*Your Home*
Down payment: 20% of purchase price earning 10% equity		
.20 × 10 =	.02	_____
Mortgage: loan of 80% with interest rate of 9%		
.80 × .09 =	.072	_____
Property taxes: 2.5% on total price		
.025 × 1.00 =	.025	_____
Property insurance: .5% of property value		
.005 × 1.00 =	.0050	_____
Property maintenance, repairs: 3% annually ("depreciation")		
.03 × 1.0 =	.03	_____
Total costs	.152 or 15.2%	_____

The recreational home in the Example column has to increase in price by 15.2 percent each year to earn the rate desired on the equity and to cover the costs of holding and using the properties. Exhibit 1-3 is a checklist you can use to help select properties with such potentials.

Exhibit 1-3 Checklist for the Purchase of a Second or Leisure-Time Home

Instructions: Place a check for each "yes" answer. Rate the property as follows:
- 17-20 Good
- 15-16 Acceptable
- 14 or less Some possible problems

	Yes	No
1. Is the property located less than two hours' driving time from your home?	☐	☐

Exhibit 1-3 (cont.)

	Yes	No

2. Does the purchase price include the privilege of using any adjacent facilities such as:

_____ Recreational center
_____ Swimming pool
_____ Tennis courts
_____ Riding trails
_____ Golf course

If none are provided, check the answer "No"; otherwise a check on at least one item permits a "Yes" for the question. ☐ ☐

3. If there are fees for the use of facilities, are these fixed by the participating property owners? ☐ ☐

4. Is the road to your property an all-year road? ☐ ☐

5. Is water and electricity supplied to the property from safe, dependable sources? ☐ ☐

6. Is the sewage disposal system inspected and operated in a safe and dependable manner? ☐ ☐

7. Are there enforceable restrictions that will prevent neighbors from building their homes too close to yours? ☐ ☐

8. Are there enforceable restrictions to prevent neighbors from having animals or activities that will interfere with your quiet enjoyment of the home? ☐ ☐

9. Are you furnished with a statement, approved by an appropriate governmental agency, that describes fully the kind of property you are buying and any possible problems you may face during ownership? ☐ ☐

10. Have you visited the property? ☐ ☐

11. Have you talked to others who have bought property in the same area about their problems and pleasures? ☐ ☐

12. Is there a property owners' association to which you can belong (or must belong) that sets rules and general charges for the area? ☐ ☐

13. Are the property owners allowed to review costs for public facilities and services provided the property owners (i.e., road, water systems, trails, lighting, sewers, etc.)? ☐ ☐

14. Will lenders provide mortgage money to assist you in purchasing the property? ☐ ☐

15. Are there real estate agents who can help you in buying and selling property in which you are interested? ☐ ☐

16. Do you own the land on which the home is located? (You may only have a long-term lease.) ☐ ☐

17. Are there restrictions on what kind of home you can build and maintain? ☐ ☐

18. Are most of the homes in the area owned by persons who will use them regularly? ☐ ☐

19. Is the area free from any adverse influences such as smog, airplane flights, heavy traffic, and similar annoyances? ☐ ☐

20. Will all your family be enthusiastic about using this home for recreation in place of going to other places for vacations and long weekends? ☐ ☐

Undeveloped Land

For the present, assume that you are interested in buying undeveloped land and holding it until it can be developed by someone else who will pay you a substantial price. Later you will learn how to time your purchase to give yourself maximum opportunity for a "quick" profit. Quickness can be important, because from a financial viewpoint land ownership involves holding costs. Here are the calculations to determine how much your land value must increase each year to offset these costs and make a profit for you:

For each $1,000 of home investment:	*Example*	*Your Home*
Down payment: 20% @ your desired return of 15%		
.20 × .15 =	.03	_____
Loan: 80% at 10% interest rate		
.80 × .10 =	.08	_____
Property taxes: 2.5% of land value		
.025 × 1.00 =	.025	_____
Special taxes and assessments (usually		
for roads, road maintenance, etc.): 3% annually		
.030 × 1.00 =	.030	_____
Total costs	.165 or 16.5%	_____

Total costs indicate that your land must increase in value by 16.5% each year to earn the desired rate on your equity and pay the costs of carrying or holding this land until you can sell it. Obviously, 16.5 percent is a high rate of increase; you therefore want to search for land in areas where such increases have occurred or in areas where such rates are most likely to occur. To keep track of what you find out about various parcels of land that interest you, use the checklist in Exhibit 1-4.

Exhibit 1-4 Checklist for Buying Undeveloped Land for Investment Purposes

Instructions: Place a check for each "yes" answer. Rate the property as follows:
- 16-20 Good
- 15-19 Acceptable marginally
- 14 or Possible problems
- less

	Yes	*No*
1. Have you visited the land?	☐	☐
2. Do you have a report from the appropriate government agency (either a state agency or the Department of Housing and Urban Develop-		

Exhibit 1-4 (cont.)

	Yes	No
ment, a Federal agency) that identifies the possible problems in using the property?	☐	☐
3. Do you have a complete list of all the restrictions that you must agree to in developing or using the land?	☐	☐
4. Has a responsible person, such as a land surveyor, identified the actual dimensions of the land you are buying in an on-site visit with you?	☐	☐
5. Is there nearby land on which improvements are being made through homes and business property construction?	☐	☐
6. Can you secure either title insurance or an abstract and opinion, which protects you against possible title deficiencies?	☐	☐
7. Can you secure a loan to purchase the land and to build on it from a state or nationally chartered bank, mutual savings bank, or savings and loan association?	☐	☐
8. Are there employment potentials nearby so that families will be attracted to the area?	☐	☐
9. Can you reach the property over a publicly maintained and improved road?	☐	☐
10. Is safe water available to the site in sufficient quantity and at reasonable prices?	☐	☐
11. Is electricity and/or gas available to the site in sufficient quantities and at reasonable prices?	☐	☐
12. Is a safe, dependable sewage disposal system available for the site?	☐	☐
13. Are there privately enforced restrictions that will require you to build on the property according to certain building and architectural standards?	☐	☐
14. Are there public zoning and land-use planning laws that are enforced?	☐	☐
15. Are there environmental controls which will require you to furnish an environmental impact analysis?	☐	☐
16. Can you answer "yes" to at least three of the following relating to the location of the home with respect to driving time: _____ Shopping 5-15 minutes _____ Schools 15-30 minutes _____ Jobs 30-45 minutes _____ Recreation, parks 10-45 minutes		
17. Can you place a home or building on the property with a minimum of grading?	☐	☐
18. Will the view and privacy of the land be protected against future and current developments?	☐	☐
19. Can you grow any types of crops (fruit, grain, vegetables) on the land until you are ready to develop it?	☐	☐
20. Is there any type of building or improvement on the land that might be rented to produce income until the land is developed for other purposes?	☐	☐

NEXT STEPS

At this point you may feel the process is too complicated to master—that it really can't happen to you anyway. Not so: The entire purpose of this book is to take the mystery out of real estate investing. You can do your own investing, or know how and where to find others who can do it for you. Of course, there are risks in real estate investing. But you will learn what they are, how much risk to take, and how to shape your investments to meet the risks.

However, take the time to read the next chapter carefully because it contains the basic rules you must understand before you move into any type of real estate investment. Once you understand the rather simple rules offered, you are ready to follow the other steps which will help you become a professional real estate investor.

HOW TO DO IT

To help you to understand and remember the basics of real estate investing, meet Fred and Lola Samson. From time to time you will see them meet and solve problems of real estate investing in this book. When you first meet them, they are home owners, facing the problems of inflation, income shortages, rising property taxes, higher income taxes—all the problems typical home owners face. They are planning to become owners of income-producing properties, and they hope to enter their retirement years with assured additional income from solid real estate investments.

Fred and Lola are in their late thirties and have owned their home for ten years. Fred is employed in a local manufacturing firm as a production engineer and earns $22,000 a year. Lola works part-time as a secretary earning $12,000 a year. They have two children, one in senior high school and the other planning to enter the local community college.

The Samsons built the home they live in for a total land and building cost of $38,000. Recently, their home was re-appraised for tax purposes at a market value of $82,000. They are paying 7.5 percent interest on a mortgage of $30,000 with a 20-year term for a monthly loan payment of $241.68. The unpaid balance on the loan is $20,360.27.

Both Fred and Lola like to work around the house. Fred is reasonably competent at simple repairs and improvements, and Lola has a knack for decorating. Friends compliment them frequently on the "perfect look" of their house.

Facing increased income and property taxes, as well as anticipating their retirement and college educations for their children, they are looking for ways to improve their financial position. While driving home from work, Fred notices an older section of town in which many homes are being torn down to be replaced by apartment houses with ten to twenty units. Leaving work early one day, Fred visits local real estate brokerage offices and inquires about house prices and apartment house construction.

Fred learns that population growth and the attraction of the area are creating an increasing demand for rental units. Families, attracted to the area in search of rentals, frequently drive through the area in which Fred and Lola now live. A modest shopping center, good schools, local bus transportation, churches, and parks make the whole area most attractive. The real estate agents assure Fred that there are buyers for his home and that apartment units are available for his investment. Fred visits other real estate agents and receives the same information.

That night Fred and Lola take stock of where they are and where they want to go. Their combined annual income is $34,000 but is not likely to increase except for occasional cost of living increases. Their home costs $6,885 annually to own (loan payments $2,900; property taxes $2,050; property insurance $500; operating, maintenance, repairs, landscaping $1,435), or 20 percent of their annual income. Prospects are that rising prices might increase the percentage to 25 or 30 percent. Their original down payment of $8,000, combined with the price increases in the home, gives them an equity of $56,000.

The first thought of the Samsons is to sell their home and buy a new one. They could use $25,000 of their equity to buy a new home at a price of $100,000, pay off the unpaid balance of $20,000 of the loan and invest the rest of the proceeds, $11,000, in a savings account at 7 percent. However, the loan on the new home would be at 8.5 percent for 25 years and require a monthly payment of $603.92 monthly or $7,247.05 per year. The total costs of owning and operating the home, including the mortgage payment would probably equal $12,000 to $15,000 (12 to 18 percent of the current market value of the home). On the other hand, with the way local home prices are increasing, the home would probably increase in value at the rate of $100 to $120 per month, indicating a possible return on the price of 10 to 12 percent each year.

On the other hand, the Samsons like their home even though continued ownership might deprive them of profits from selling. They visit the local savings and loan association that holds their present loan and ask if they might be able to borrow money on their home to buy an apartment house. The lender says the loan could be made, but they would have to negotiate a new loan on current market terms and include the amount they still owed. They decide they might want a new loan of $45,000, which would give them $25,000 cash to invest elsewhere. However, the new loan would be for 25 years at 8.5 percent, with monthly payments of $362.35 and annual payments of $4,348.23.

A final alternative the Samsons consider is to move out of their home into an apartment, rent their home for at least six to eight months, and then trade for an apartment house. With a $56,000 equity they could trade for a very large apartment house.

Before deciding, the Samsons plan to investigate the apartment market. In trying to decide which real estate agent to use, they find one who is a member of a local real estate board that also includes a multiple listing service (MLS). This agent, with the professional designation of Realtor, has an inventory of all available apartment houses offered for sale in the area because of his membership in the multiple listing service.

First, the Samsons ask him how much apartment house they could buy for each dollar of cash paid down, and he tells them they can use a multiple of four or five. In other words, their $25,000 (proceeds from a loan) would buy $100,000 to $125,000; and the $56,000 would buy from $224,000 to $280,000 worth of apartment investment. Knowing that this was a venture into something very new to them, the Samsons decide they would look only at smaller units they could manage by themselves.

The first apartment the Realtor shows consists of eight units with a price of $125,000; the apartment has just been completed and is fully rented at $225 per unit. A slightly older ten-unit apartment also has a price of $125,000; it is of poorer quality and fully rented at a price of $175 per unit. The last apartment consists of eight units, is older, has one unit vacant with the remainder renting at $150 per unit—but the price is only $96,000. Further inquiry into the third apartment reveals that it is owned by an older man who because of illness has neglected the building.

The Samsons look at many other apartments in order to get a feel for the right price and the right rental rates. Finally, they decide that the first three units they saw represent the best choices in the local market. On their own they visit apartments listed for rental and discover the rents at $175 to $200 are very hard to find; further, most one-bedroom units rent at the lower end of the $175-to-$200 range, and two-bedroom units typically start at $200 and go to $325 for deluxe units.

They decide to investigate the older eight-unit apartment house first. Since it is smaller, it carries a smaller price; and they could use their talents to improve the units and get higher rents. Visiting the tenants, they find that some are there for short periods of time until they can find better units, while others are long-termers because of the low rents. All the tenants mention the shabby condition of the units and the difficulties they have getting repairs and replacements.

After a careful study of the entire building, the Samsons estimate they would have to make about $9,000 in repairs and replacements. They make this estimate after listing all the things to be done, totalling up the costs of materials for the jobs they felt they could do, and using bids from subcontractors for the more complicated work. They go to the Realtor with the list and suggest that the price on the apartment should be lowered. The Realtor indicates that perhaps the price could be lowered if the Samsons negotiated a loan to pay off the entire price at once with all cash.

When the Samsons visit the lender he informs them that their appraiser has placed a value on the apartment of $85,000 (because of its neglected condition) and that they could have a loan of only 75 percent of that or $64,000. Unfortunately, with only a $25,000 loan, the Samsons would have a cash total of only $89,000. They return to the Realtor and make an offer of only $90,000 (6 percent less). The seller indicates he would accept $92,000. At this point the Samsons realize that they would need not only $92,000 for the apartment but an additional $9,000 for the repairs. With a loan on the apartment house of $64,000, they would need a loan of $37,000 on their home. They return to the lender and explain the situation. The lender agrees to the $37,000 on their home which, with the $20,000 they still owe on their present mortgage, means a loan of $57,000. However, the lender indicates that the higher risks on this loan means that the loan could only be for 20 years and the interest rate would be 8.75 percent, requiring monthly payments of $503.72 and annual payments of $6,044.58.

The Samsons again take stock of what their financial position would be if they purchased the apartment unit:

Assuming they made no changes at first, current rents at $150 × 12 months × 7 units = $12,600 annually

Costs of owning:

Taxes	$ 1,800
Janitor, maintenance, repairs	5,670*
Mortgage payments	6,044
	$13,514, or a loss of $914

---

*They check with other property owners in the area and are told that the expenses would account for about 45 percent of their gross collected rents.

On the positive side, the Samsons show their calculations to an income tax advisor, and he points out that the building and furnishings have an estimated current value of $70,000 and that they could charge depreciation on this at the rate of 3 percent per year of $2,100. However, they would not be able to count their mortgage principal payments expenses for tax purposes so that their reconstructed statement would be:

Property taxes	$1,800
Maintenance, operations, etc.	5,670
Mortgage interest	4,944
Depreciation	2,100
Total expenses for tax purposes	14,514
Collected income	12,600
Loss for tax purposes	$1,914

The tax loss of $1,914 could be charged against other earned income so that the Samson's overall tax liability would be reduced. However, since depreciation is not an actual expense, their actual expenses, exclusive of payments on mortgage principal, would be $12,414. They would actually make $186 per year ($12,600-$12,414), and so they are assured the property will "pay its way."

The Samsons decide to buy the apartment. During the first year they fix up the apartments, installing new stoves, refrigerators, carpets, and drapes. The unrented apartment is listed and rented for $185 during the first month of ownership. At the end of the year, the Samsons may raise rents for the other tenants as their apartments are refurbished. At the end of the second year, they hope to raise all rents for an average rental of $225 and to rent all units. With a potential gross income of $21,600 and with apartments in the area selling at a multiple of eight times gross income, their apartment house will have a minimum market value of $172,000—simply by improving the units so that they are competitive in the marketplace. In addition, growth and inflation will probably increase this value by 10 to 15 percent.

The Samsons feel confident about their investment because they have made a very careful survey of market changes. They talked to Realtors, apartment investors, and tenants; and they know about the real potentials of the apartment house. Even if they have miscalculated, they can still afford to pay the new mortgage. (However, not all the payments can be credited to the apartment schedule for tax purposes since they are still paying $20,000 on their home.) They do face one or two years of demanding repair work and attention to the management of the tenants and the apartment unit. In later installments we will see how they fare.

First Rules
Of The Game

2

Winning in sports requires that you understand the fundamentals, that you know the rules within which you apply the fundamentals, and that you have a plan for winning. The same is true in successful real estate investing—fundamentals have been developed from the experiences of successful and unsuccessful investors. However, knowing the fundamentals is not enough; you must also have a systematic plan for using them within the rules limiting your activities.

Real estate investing fundamentals are derived from a variety of economic principles and business practices. Fortunately, they are neither complex nor difficult to apply. For example, once you have selected an investment property, you must understand how to operate it for maximum income returns and when to sell it to maximize value gains. The process can be likened to a sport in which you must decide to run, pass, or stall. Each of these three fundamental actions is easy to understand and execute, and the rules of the game will tell you how to execute. But *you* will have to decide when to use them and in what combinations.

A BASIC SYSTEMS APPROACH

One of the most important rules in real estate investing is always to know what to accomplish and to proceed to your objectives through a series of ordered steps (Exhibit 2-1). In fact, such a series of steps has been used to determine the order of presentation in this book. This systems approach is important because it requires a total approach in which, after looking at all your investments, you decide where real estate investments fit in and how they should be managed—all in the light of your objectives and the performance of your other investments.)

In the first chapter you owned a home but were ready to look to other forms of real estate investment. The first investment in income-producing

Exhibit 2-1   A Systems Approach to Real Estate Investing

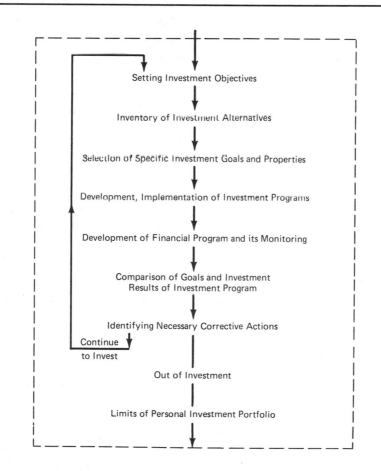

Setting Investment Objectives

Inventory of Investment Alternatives

Selection of Specific Investment Goals and Properties

Development, Implementation of Investment Programs

Development of Financial Program and its Monitoring

Comparison of Goals and Investment
Results of Investment Program

Identifying Necessary Corrective Actions

Continue
to Invest

Out of Investment

Limits of Personal Investment Portfolio

property is typically an apartment house, but there are other kinds—raw land, commercial and industrial properties, recreational developments—that might be equally attractive to you if you understand their particular opportunities and limitations. In this chapter you will be introduced to a systematic real estate investment approach that can be used for all types of real estate investment. Fundamentals and rules are offered, equally useful for any type of real estate investment you choose. Whatever your choice, the approach is the same for each.

Know Your Financial Limitations and Objectives

You must set limits on your personal investment portfolio to be sure that whatever you attempt can be accomplished with your assets and financial potentials. If you cannot do this, then (as indicated in Exhibit 2-1 by the arrow that crosses the dotted line at the top), you may have to seek the help of others in achieving your own personal portfolio goals. In any case, you must first decide what your investment objectives are: Do you want a capital gain? Do you want liquidity? Do you want a rapid income increase? Whatever the goals, you *must* state them explicitly and in order of priority.

Following are explanations of the more common investment goals:

1. Capital gains?   You buy a property for $50,000, hold it for five years, and then sell it for $60,000. Your gain of $10,000 is a capital gain, an increase in value.

2. Liquidity?   You buy a property in a very good location with very good leases for $50,000. A year after you buy the property you have a financial emergency that requires you to sell immediately. You are able to sell for the amount you paid, $50,000, very easily and without waiting. The property has liquidity—it sold easily, quickly, and without loss to you. To achieve liquidity in an investment you will have to bid with others for the property and take a somewhat lower rate of return and expectation of capital gain.

3. Rapid income increase?   You find property that can be rented as office space in a community in which several new businesses and industries are located. Your research tells you that there will be a need for a lot of office space within the next two or three years. You buy the property, modernize the offices, and contact the firms locating in your city. During the year of modernization and search for tenants, you receive little income. As your tenants increase in number and more businesses locate in the city, your income increases rapidly.

You enjoy the rapid increase in income because you anticipated business trends correctly, you picked an appropriate property, and you selected tenants who would meet your income requirements. After enjoying a rapid income increase for a time you will find that the income levels. You must then decide whether you want to repeat the process—that is the problem in seeking rapid income increases. They do not continue over long periods of time, but they do improve the value of a property so that it can be sold at a higher price.

4. Safety?   With the assistance of a property manager and an appraiser, you look for a property in a busy location, with tenants of solid business and credit reputations, who will sign long-term leases. For example, such property could be a well-located shopping center, office building, or industrial complex. In return for the safety you sacrifice rates of return and opportunities for large returns of cash annually.

5.Cash flow?   For cash flow, you want a property with minimum expenses and plenty of opportunities to take advantage of Federal income tax laws to reduce your taxable income. Cash flows are difficult to achieve in many properties because the competition to buy the properties is usually very keen; in light of higher purchase prices, your profit opportunities are fewer, but you do recover your original investment quicker. Older buildings in good locations offer many cash flow and long-range investment opportunities because they may be sold at a later date, removed, and replaced by a new investment opportunity.

6. Federal income tax shelter?   If you are seeking to use Federal income tax law to produce nontaxable income, you must start your investment process by consulting an income tax expert; then use a professional property manager to help you achieve a maximum income tax shelter. This type of investment is a complex process and is explained in a later chapter.

Inventory Your Opportunities

Once you have decided to invest, you must then take time to look at all the different ways real estate can help you obtain the objectives you have in mind. You should, for example, examine raw land, apartment houses, commercial property, and industrial property. Contact a real estate broker and others who have these properties for sale and ask them the questions that relate to your objectives. This approach is also discussed on later pages.

Be Specific and Analyze Carefully

Once you have selected your specific investment goals, you can then winnow out the properties you've looked at, leaving only those you feel relate directly to your goals. You must then go through a process of income, expense, and economic analyses (also discussed later). Frequently, goals must be modified so they will fit more carefully with each other. It is obviously foolish to purchase raw land and have an earned income investment objective. Clearly, the land cannot produce income unless you put an improvement or crop on it. This is a most ridiculous example, but it exemplifies the way some persons approach real estate investing. Investment goals can be achieved only through the property you select, and you must be very careful in what you select.

Implement Your Program

With the property selected and an evaluation of its potentials determined, you then must implement an investment management program. This requires careful attention to methods of financing, setting gross incomes, determining expenses, monitoring cash flows, considering income tax, financing costs, reacting to market changes, and a variety of other things also included in this text.

Monitor Results

A most important element in the systematic approach to real estate investing is to look from time to time at the goals you've set and compare them to the results you are achieving. At this point you may have to change the goals, accept the results as given, or look again at your entire investment program to see what must be done. The distinguishing feature of the "system" approach is that you identify the corrective actions after you've compared goals and results. You then return to the beginning of the process and either change your investment objectives or, if this cannot be done, change the properties you have. In fact, you may have to sell the investment because you are unable to achieve your investment goals. Or maybe you find your goals and your results matching nicely and you can now move on to other forms of real estate investment properties.

Remember Fundamentals

To repeat, the fundamentals of a systematic approach to investing are:

1. setting goals,
2. planning the way to reach these goals,
3. developing a program of investment to achieve these goals,
4. reviewing the process constantly to be sure that goals and programs are matched by equivalent results, and
5. identifying the necessary corrective action—either a change of investment actions or getting out of the investment entirely.

A basic assumption in this book is that you begin your real estate investing process by treating the purchase of a family home as a real estate investment. Careful attention to the investment as well as to the living qualities of a home provides a good foundation on which a substantial, if not large, family estate can be built. However, if you want to increase your real estate investment activity, you must have: (1) a working knowledge of the fundamentals and (2) an equity in your home or other financial assets to move upward in the real estate investment process.

SETTING GOALS AND KNOWING WHAT YOU WANT

Typically, you can achieve four goals through real estate investing:

1. risk reduction,
2. earnings,
3. capital gains, and
4. liquidity.

Unfortunately, they cannot all be achieved with equal success. You must decide in what order you will try to achieve them. For example, you may decide on a property that will increase in value (capital gains); but in order to achieve this goal, you may have to hold the property for some time, thus increasing your risk of losing it because real estate markets change so apidly. Perhaps you are undecided as to what you wish to accomplish; in that case you can look at various attractive property investments and evaluate each in terms of these goals. Use Exhibit 2-2 to help you decide what you want to do.

Exhibit 2-2 Rating Investment Goals

	Importance to You
1. *Risk Reduction* The rule is that the higher the risk, the greater the loss potentials. Risks to consider include changes in national or local business climate and real estate market prices, the neighborhood, the property, the site.	
2. *Earnings* Net income after all expenses of maintaining and financing the property. This may or may not be taxable. Real estate does provide maximum opportunities to acquire tax-sheltered income.	
3. *Capital Gains* Increase in the price or value of the property over the original cash or equity invested. Usually this takes time, so that income is delayed but income taxes are lower.	
4. *Liquidity* The ability to sell quickly without loss of equity or lowering of price below market levels.	

LIMITATIONS ON WHAT YOU CAN AND CANNOT DO

All four investment goals are influenced by:

1. the building,
2. the site,
3. the location of a given property, and
4. the real estate and business markets within which property is located.

Although precise analysis of the impact of each influence is not possible, the degree of influence can be expressed roughly as a range. Study, for a minute or two, Exhibit 2-3 before continuing . . .

Now note that in this chart each influence assigned is arranged in percentage form. In simple terms, the value of any property is influenced

**Exhibit 2-3   A Basis for Selecting a Real Estate Investment
(Read across, not down)**

Value Influence	Degree of Influence	Investment Goal Potentials*				Your Decision** (% assigned)
		Risk	Earning	Gains	Liquidity	
Building	20%–30%	2	1	4	3	
Site	25%–35%	4	2	1	3	
Immediate location (neighborhood)	30%–40%	2	3	1	4	
Business and real estate markets	10%–15%	3	2	4	1	

*1 is highest; 4 is lowest.
**Total assigned must equal 100%.

first by its immediate location or neighborhood; hence, "Immediate location (neighborhood)" is assigned an influence range of 30 to 40 percent, the highest on the chart. The site or lot, the building, and finally the market trends each represent a lower and lower range of influence, and ranges are therefore assigned in proportion to their effects.

In the "Investment Goal Potentials" columns, each goal is assigned a number from one to four. These numbers represent the degree of effect each influence has on each goal. For example, if a building is the foremost factor in the value of a property as a whole, then that property will likely yield good earnings first of all and minimize risk as a secondary benefit; but it will not be a very liquid possession nor will it reap high capital gains.

Finally, there is a blank column for your entries regarding a specific property. By filling in these boxes, you can use this chart several different ways.

Perhaps most obviously, the chart in Exhibit 2-3 enables you to relate a property to your particular investment goal very easily. Suppose, while being shown a property, you mark down on your chart that the building is the most influential factor in the value of the property; suppose further that you feel it represents approximately 40 percent of the value. After that, you feel that the location, the site, and markets influence the property value to successively lower degrees: You assign them percentages of 25, 20, and 15 percent, respectively. (Note that your ranges *must* total up to 100 percent.)

If you have sized up the value of the property accurately, then here is what the chart can tell you. If your investment goal is earning income, then this property should rank high in your consideration. Why? Because the chart ranks buildings as the number one influence on earnings. On the other hand, if you are looking for long-term capital gains, you might discount the worth of this property more than others you have seen. Again, the chart indicates that buildings are a relatively poor influence on capital gain investment goals.

Though the findings of the chart are by no means conclusive, they can serve as a ready guide for on-the-spot checklists. Your evaluation of all the property you see is at least systematized, guided by consistent principles.

The chart can also be used in another way, by letting your investment goals help you decide how much weight to put on each of the value influences. If your goal potential is capital gains, then start your search for a property in an excellent neighborhood with a well placed and developed site. On the other hand, if your goal is liquidity, then time your investment to take advantage of favorable real estate and business market conditions.

Suppose that you want to invest in an apartment house with the best potential for capital value increases. Find local neighborhoods in which quality apartments have been increasing in value. Within such areas look for a well maintained apartment house located on a site that maximizes the income potential by having the most units allowed by zoning laws. If your second objective is to reduce risk, select a newer property in the middle of the apartment district. In such an area you may have to pay a relatively high price for the property, thus reducing your net income potentials. Finally, you will not have to worry about liquidity and can give it small attention because of your careful analysis of the other factors. Under such conditions you might have decided to assign the following weights to the two apartments in which you are most interested:

| | Apartment Choice and Assigned Weights | |
	A	B
Building	30%	10%
Site	30	35
Immediate location	30	45
Market trends	10	10
Total	100%	100%

Your analysis indicates that you believe market changes will have only a minimal influence on the value of either apartment, so you can concentrate on the other three influences. Apartment A is equally balance in terms of building, site, and location. If you purchased Apartment A, you have decided that the building, site, and location are equally good, and that there is nothing more you would need to achieve your investment goals. On the other hand, Apartment B's immediate location is very favorable, carrying the greatest influence on total value; the lot is next, and the building is least important. Perhaps Apartment B would be the better investment because you could improve the building to maximize the potential for the site and the location, both of which are "number one" influences on gain.

Another way to use the chart is simply to select properties in which you are interested and use the chart to distinguish their potentials. For example, Apartment C you might rate as having an excellent building on a poor site in a marginal location in markets that are moving up rapidly. Your assigned percentages for Apartment C might be: building 30 percent, site 25 percent, location 30 percent, market trends 15 percent. Your assigned percentages for comparable Apartment D might be: building 30 percent, site 35 percent, location 20 percent, market trends 15 percent. In both cases your analysis indicates that the opportunities for capital gains and earnings are likely to be influenced adversely because of high risks, but that improving market trends would provide ample opportunities to liquidate at any time you choose.

TIMING

Timing may be important in sports, but it is absolutely critical in the real estate investment game. Prices change constantly in real estate markets and with them the potential land uses. Land uses and prices tend to go through cycles with difficult-to-predict durations (usually eighteen to twenty years), but cycles change in a reasonably predictable order of uses (See Exhibit 2-4).

In order to maximize your investment potentials, you have to time your investments so that you buy as values are starting to increase and sell before they decline. The rapidity of value increase and the changes in land uses are strongly influenced by business and real estate market changes. Take a look at the notations along the curve in Exhibit 2-4. Begin by looking for areas in which sharp population increases are occurring, because sharp population increases are usually the first clue to improving real estate investment potentials. If the population increases are built on solid growth potentials, then the next indication of better real estate markets is the installation of public electricity, gas, and water, to be followed not very long thereafter by the construction of sewers and sewage disposal facilities. In terms of land uses, there will be changes from agricultural to residential land subdividing.

To use Exhibit 2-4, look at the items, in lower case letters, on the outside of the land value change line for the clues as to where a particular area is in terms of the real estate cycle. On the inside of the curve, in capital letters, are the kinds of land use changes you will observe at a given time in the real estate cycle. Consider these indicators only as approximate statements, since each real estate market has unique characteristics that cause it to differ somewhat from general cycle changes.

You will find that your best investment potentials occur during the stability-growth-takeoff periods of the real estate cycle. You should begin to sell your investments when the property locations reach the leveling-stagnation stages. You should not invest in areas in the stagnation-decline stages. On the other hand, if you are a great risk-taker you may want to find areas in the slowing and change periods of the cycle and invest in them if local business and real estate market changes show strong signs of upward movement.

In average time terms, the ascending part of the cycle can be as little as twelve and as many as seventy-two months from stability to leveling. Cycle decline can take twelve to ninety-six months from stagnation to change. However, do not depend upon measures of time to determine the stage of the cycle; use the indicators on the chart.

BASIC RULES OF INCOME PROPERTY INVESTING

When you invest in an income-producing property, you should understand some basic rules for analysing property. Some of the most important rules are presented in this section.

Building and Site (Chapter 3)

The value of a real estate investment depends directly on its ability to produce either income periodically or a lump-sum price at the end of the investment. Most important, the land and the building must work together to maximize income potentials: They can be neither separated nor analysed separately from each other in order to determine the value of the investment. The joint nature of the services of the land and building influence the capacity of the property to produce income.

Exhibit 2-4 Characteristics of the Stages in the Land Use Life Cycles of Urban Areas

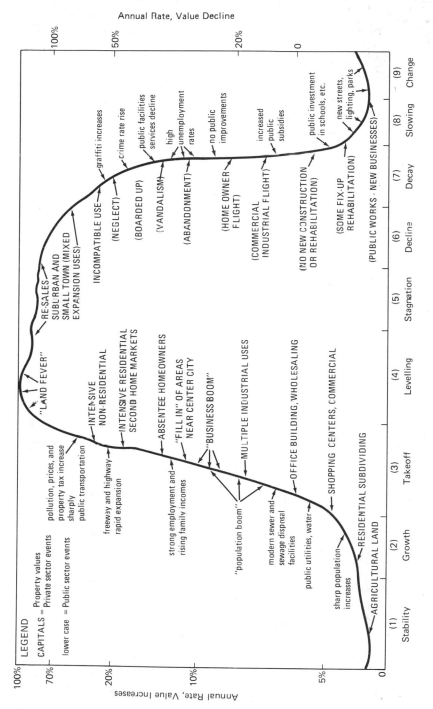

Annual Rate, Value Decline

100%   50%   20%   0

LEGEND
CAPITALS = Property values
CAPITALS = Private sector events
lower case = Public sector events

"LAND FEVER"

RE-SALES

SUBURBAN AND
SMALL TOWN (MIXED
EXPANSION USES)

INCOMPATIBLE USE

(NEGLECT)

(BOARDED UP)

(VANDALISM)

high
unemployment
rates

(ABANDONMENT)

no public
improvements

(HOME OWNER
FLIGHT)

(COMMERCIAL
INDUSTRIAL FLIGHT)

increased
public
subsidies

(NO NEW CONSTRUCTION
OR REHABILITATION)

public investment
in schools, etc.

(SOME FIX-UP
REHABILITATION)

new streets,
lighting, parks

(PUBLIC WORKS - NEW BUSINESSES)

graffiti increases

crime rate rise

public facilities
services decline

INTENSIVE
NON-RESIDENTIAL

INTENSIVE RESIDENTIAL
SECOND HOME MARKETS

ABSENTEE HOMEOWNERS

"FILL IN" OF AREAS
NEAR CENTER CITY

"BUSINESS BOOM"

MULTIPLE INDUSTRIAL USES

OFFICE BUILDING, WHOLESALING

SHOPPING CENTERS, COMMERCIAL

RESIDENTIAL SUBDIVIDING

AGRICULTURAL LAND

pollution, prices, and
property tax increase
sharply
public transportation

freeway and highway
rapid expansion

strong employment and
rising family incomes

"population boom"

modern sewer and
sewage disposal
facilities

public utilities, water

sharp population
increases

(1)   (2)   (3)   (4)   (5)   (6)   (7)   (8)   (9)
Stability Growth   Takeoff Levelling Stagnation Decline   Decay   Slowing   Change

100%   70%   20%   10%   5%   0

Annual Rate, Value Increases

57

Example. Would you like to own the Empire State Building? It is an important office building in the heart of New York City with good tenants. Would you want to own that building if it were located in the middle of the Appalachian mountains? Of course you wouldn't: The building was designed to permit the uses to the location required—a location in the center of financial and business activities which had to be housed in such office buildings as the Empire State.

Service Flows (Chapter 4)

Real estate offers a persistent flow of services with a terminal life, and unless those services are utilized at the time they are available they can never again be recovered. In other words, even if you do not use real estate, its value changes. If you do not obtain rent from the property on a continuing basis, the property is still deteriorating. Since the quality of improvements directly influences the capacity of the site and the location to warrant maximum rents, the full services you receive from the property depend on the improvements you put into the property. As any given point in time, you will never again have as good an opportunity to obtain as much net rental; you must utilize the services as they become available.

Example. You purchase an apartment house offering deluxe services and commanding the highest rents in the market. You face a financial bind and decide to neglect the apartments so you can use the cash to solve your financial difficulties. The tenants soon notice the decay in services and either ask for lower rents or move. You cash flow is diminished, and so is your income from the property. The value of the property is lower because the income is lower. If you now decide to return the cash and upgrade the property to previous levels, you have lost the income during the period of neglect. Since you were charging maximum rents in the first place you cannot now increase the rents to make up for the loss of income you have just experienced. And, remember, the property has only a given number of years to earn the highest rentals; if you do not earn during that period you have lost your opportunity to do so.

Continuing Expenditures (Chapter 4)

Due to the nature of the services flow, real property requires continuing expenditures to maintain income. Renters are always interested in using the most modern and most efficient types of properties. If your real estate investment is not maintained, renters will not be attracted and your property will decay. Failure to maintain an appropriate expenditure schedule will definitely affect the income-producing capacity of the property either immediately or in the future.

Example: You purchase a property in a rental apartment area. You can charge $500 per month per apartment, but you must provide air conditioning, a swimming pool, draperies, refrigerator, and stove. These features cost you $350 per month, leaving you $150 for your profit and other expenses. However, you decide to keep the furnishings longer than your investment plan called for—fifteen years instead of ten. Consequently, when tenants notice that other apartments have newer furnishings that operate more efficiently, they ask for lower rents or move. New tenants prefer the other, better equipped apartments.

Obviously, your expenditures are geared to the rents you plan to charge, whether you own an apartment house, a store, an industrial property, or any kind of property. If you cut your expenditures or neglect improvements, the property and your rents both suffer.

Long-Term Life (Chapter 5)

Real estate property is a remarkably durable form of investment. As a result, it's extremely costly to change the basic character of any property you buy. It is better to use the property as it is with minor modifications or to build a new property to your specifications, rather than to convert an old property substantially. Sometimes, of course, renovation or modernization of old properties is profitable, but these occasions are rather limited in comparison to the opportunities that exist in using a property as you find it.

Example: In 1890 a wealthy investor decided to build a ten-story deluxe office building with an open court, special iron work on the balconies and stairs, and a hydraulic elevator system. The building was located in the best part of downtown. By the early 1940s the local neighborhood was becoming shabby, so the building was rented for whatever uses would pay the rent. The building became shabbier and rents declined, but the costs of removing the building and the limited rental opportunities for new properties meant the building had to be kept by the investors. No one would buy the property. In the late 1960s a group of investors were looking for a rather small office building downtown for their activities—architecture, land use planning, investment consulting—with

sufficient extra space to generate some cash flow. They cleaned, reno-
vated, and returned the building to an appearance much like the original.
The building became an historical monument and a much sought-after
place for an office. Today this building gives every indication of being able
to last for a hundred years. Not all old buildings are as fortunate.

Special Characteristics (Chapter 6)

Real estate investors face a particular problem: No two real estate
parcels are precisely alike. Buildings may be precisely alike, but obviously
no two can occupy the same site, and sites differ. There is no effective way
of comparing precisely the quantity and quality of services offered by
different parcels of land. Valuation techniques will produce reasonably
reliable estimates, but deciding which of two properties is better or which
of two properties is' worth more in price still involves a large element of
judgement.

Example: You have an opportunity to buy one of two medical
office buildings, one across the street from the other. The buildings are of
the same size and quality construction. Both are well planned and desirable
office buildings, suitable as medical offices, pharmacies, optical supplies,
and the like. Which should you buy? The question is particularly thorny
when you find that one has an asking price 50 percent higher than the other?
You would have to establish the property's value by comparing
incomes—gross and net—and then see how the property suits your investment objectives. You find the rate of return on investment is the same for
either building; yet the total investment is 50 percent higher for the one
building. You also find that the more expensive building is a beautiful,
extremely well maintained building that caters to only "prestige" tenants.
Whoever owns the building has a lot of prestige in the community,
particularly since the building is visited regularly as a "showplace"
medical building. The other building has no prestige but a good reputation
as a medical office building, and it gets the spillover from the other
building. Both are medical buildings, yet each is unique.
Which do you buy? At this point you have to decide what you want:
Prestige (an amenity)? Assured income? A large or small total investment?
These wants are all subjective—it is your choice.

Lack of Standardization (Chapter 5)

Parcels cannot be graded, and properties are not standardized. Nor
can one parcel be substituted easily for another in any kind of comparison

process. For this reason, no investor should buy a real property until he has first looked at it personally. Inexperienced investors, particularly, should seek the assistance of qualified persons such as appraisers, property managers, lawyers, architects, and engineers. The role of these experts will be discussed in later chapters.

Example: You are offered two apartments for investment. The professional appraisal for each makes one sound almost identical to the other in size, rental schedules, levels of maintenance, tenant mix, and other important items. When you visit the properties, you find one in an older but well maintained neighborhood with tenants who are mostly retired. The other property is in a newly developing neighborhood, and the tenants are mostly younger people, newly married, usually with no children. One property has a distinctive appearance that reflects both the architecture, the painting of the exterior, and the use of landscaping. The other apartment is bare, modern architecture with a brightly painted exterior, and minimum landscaping. Clearly both are the same, yet different. Again your subjective feelings will probably have to help you decide which is the better investment for you.

At such times, when the decisions become difficult to make, the experts can help you make the right moves. Here is a listing of what they can do:

Architect—prepares plans and layouts for buildings; prepares plans and specifications to obtain bids on the costs of repairs, modernization, rehabilitation, new construction.

Contractor—according to the type of work you want done, a general contractor either does miscellaneous work or supervises the work of the other contractors (usually called subcontractors) to do electrical, plumbing, carpentry, cement, or other kinds of work.

Engineer—evaluates the structural qualities of a property and the equipment in it. Can estimate how well the property is suited for an intended use and what changes might have to be made in the building and equipment.

Appraiser—estimates the value of the property in comparison to other properties like it and in light of your investment objectives. May suggest ways of changing the property to improve its investment potentials or to meet the objectives you have set.

Lawyer—reviews contracts to determine whether they are legal and protect all your interests. Advises on how to deal with governmental agencies who are imposing requirements on your property. Will assist you in preparing proper lease contracts, or any kind of legal document relating to your buying and using a property.

Property manager—recommends appropriate rental schedules, arranges leases with tenants, supervises the operation of the property; may also advise on repairs, rehabilitation, modernization, and even timing of the sale in the light of your investment objectives.

Real estate broker—provides information on properties available for sale, terms of sale, general market conditions; will also assist in finding properties of the kind in which you wish to invest.

In every state brokers must be licensed and are called real estate agents, real estate brokers, or real estate salespersons. Anyone who regularly assists buyers and sellers for a fee must be licensed. Licensees who join a real estate board, agree to a code of ethics, and pay dues either to a real estate board, to a multiple listing board, or to both are usually known as "Realtors" or "Realtists."

Flexibility   All properties, but particularly commercial and industrial properties, should have flexible interior arrangements that can be changed to reflect changing market needs. Flexibility in the use of all the improvements on the property is most important if the property is to be held for any time in what are always dynamic and changing markets.

Example: For investment purposes office, commercial, and industrial properties are planned with maximum amounts of open space. Most interior walls are movable so that tenants can arrange the space to fit their needs. No tenant is locked into the space created for some other space user.

Property Management (Chapter 4)

An important element in realizing investment objectives is the development of appropriate property management and adequate financial management policies. In fact, you would be well-advised as an investor always to ask a property manager whether the income and expenses you are anticipating are realistic in the light of his experience with similar kinds of properties.

Example: A property manager charges according to the income he can produce. A professional manager can obtain carpenters, jaintors, electricians, and plumbers at proper prices; he can also supervise all repairs, maintenance, and rehabilitation to assure that it is done as requested, on time, and within a particular budget. Professional managers also take all calls from tenants, whenever they occur—and they usually occur at midnight or on holidays—collect rents, and arrange advantageous lease terms.

Adjacent Uses (Chapter 3)

A property is always affected by the uses to which adjacent properties are put. For this reason you must determine whether the uses of adjoining properties are compatible with those you intend for yours. The obviousness of this statement frequently is overlooked by investors who get so wrapped up in the special characteristics of a property they like that they realize only at a later date that adjoining uses hamper their capacity to maximize their investment potentials.

Example: You buy an apartment and plan to rent it to older tenants. When you inspect the property you find it adjacent to an all-night drive-in restaurant and across the street from a large all-night service station. Can you expect to attract older tenants who would prefer more quiet and less adjacent activity?

Governmental Controls (Chapter 3)

Governmental agencies are increasing their influence on the use of property. For example, environmental impact is emerging as a major consideration as regards the extent to which a government—local, county, state, or Federal—will allow a particular property to be used in a particular way. If there is any possibility that your uses will adversely affect the quality of air, the sight or sound or appearance of the local area, or the clearness of the water, you should seek the help of experts to help you determine whether you are likely to be running into additional controls on your uses.

Example: Building codes, planning and zoning requirements, environmental impact reports, and other factors have to be looked at. You'll find your checklist on these matters for analysis of the home is equally valuable for analysis of the environment of any kind of property.

Style (Chapter 3)

Style changes may cost you additional investment at some later date for modernizing, particularly if the building or property you are buying is not up to user preferences.

YOUR CHANCE TO PLAY THE GAME

To test your understanding of the ideas in this chapter, read the following case studies involving two families who plan to invest in real estate. In each case indicate what weights you would assign to the site-building-location-market and what priorities you would recommend in terms of risk reduction-earnings-capital gains-liquidity.

The Potential Investors

The Balsons are in their early thirties. Both are college graduates and both have promising careers. At present their combined income equals $50,000. They have an insurance plan, are buying a home, and find that regularly in the last two years they have had $5,000 to $10,000 in extra income. They put some in the stock market, with only fair returns on their investment. Most of the money they have placed in a savings account to earn maximum interest. Both have worked hard; they have remodeled an older home so that their equity in the home has risen from their down payment of $5,000 to more than $15,000.

The Chayles are in their late forties. Both are high school graduates, but the husband, Robert, had additional technical training in electronics. As a result he has worked for the same electronics firm for the last twenty years, helping them develop new electronic products from rough designs and plans. His work has earned him from time to time an extra bonus which he has always put in a savings account; he now has over $20,000 earning a maximum interest. His income is $28,000 and his wife has started to work lately, averaging about $1,000 per month. Their children have all finished college, have left home, but return for visits. Robert can look forward to a satisfactory but minimal pension if he chooses to retire in about ten years; he will have to retire in fifteen.

Possible Recommendations

The Balsons clearly should look for a property that will produce capital gains. Otherwise they can take somewhat larger risks, as long as the risk is limited to what they have invested. They need not worry about income; in fact, they would be better off not having additional income since it would put them in a higher bracket. They will want some liquidity in case their careers require their moving. In terms of weights, they would probably give minimum weight to market trends (10 percent) because they can wait until trends favor them. Next emphasis would be on a neighborhood that shows promise of growth and in which there are some older income units at lower prices (40 percent). They would have to plan to do some improvement work for themselves. Next, the site (35 percent) should be located in a zoning area that will allow larger income units to be placed on the property at a later date. Finally, the building (15 percent) need be in only good enough shape to be rentable, even if at minimum rents. The rents need not be enough to pay all property investment costs because the Balsons could use losses as an offset against their earned income, particularly since they seem to have considerable extra income in recent months.

The Chayles should seek to minimize their risk and to maximize both earnings and capital gains. Since they are established in the area and will probably not think of moving until retirement, they can give minimum weight to liquidity. Even if they have to sell, they could most likely wait for a favorable offer. They would want to let the market determine when to invest and would want to be sure that business conditions are favorable; so they would assign 15 percent. Since they want income and capital gain, they would weight the building and the site equally (25 percent each). They would look for an area which was midway up on the growth cycle. In that area they would probably want to buy an older, smaller, somewhat neglected apartment until that they could fix up and manage. They would want a neighborhood in which some new units were being built and which has been enjoying some population increases.

You may not agree with these recommendations. Your agreement, however, is not as important as using all the guides and considering each carefully in conjunction with the others.

USING REAL ESTATE INVESTING RULES

Any real estate investor must be aware of the following general principles:

First, success in real estate investing is directly related to your capacity to borrow properly. Since borrowing is essential to investment, you have to pay careful attention not only to the cost of borrowing but to the terms of borrowing, so that you have some flexibility in the repayment of the loan if the property is not producing the kind of income it should.

Next, the income from real estate must not only not only provide the investor with some interest or profit on the investment. But also, because the improvements to land are always losing some value, provision must be made for overcoming these losses of value. This provision is known by some as depreciation and by others as a recovery of capital. In any case some portion of the income has used to create a reserve account to either restore the property as a result of certain depreciation losses or provide a fund for the purchase of property.

Remember that in real estate there are no bargains. As the rate of return gets higher, the depreciation rate gets faster and the potential for loss gets greater. A basic principle in real estate investing is *you get exactly what you pay for*. If you buy a bargain in real estate, you are probably assuming a lot more risks than you anticipate. Even though you may have a higher earning potential, you also have a greater loss potential.

Real estate investment has the greatest potential in an inflationary period. Real estate prices and rents tend to keep pace with inflation; so if you have invested wisely, you can almost be assured not only of protecting your purchasing power but of enhancing your potential for additional capital gains.

Finally, it's important to remember that real estate requires continuing attention. If you're not able to devote a considerable portion of your own time to managing your real estate investment, then you should include in your investment calculations sufficient payment to have a professional manage it for you. The professional not only manages the property in terms of setting rents and controlling expenditures, but he also understands your total portfolio requirements and advises you on how to fit the real estate investment most closely with your overall portfolio needs.

In the next chapter you will learn how to recognize and analyse the most critical factors affecting your investment results.

Critical Elements
In Your Investment
Game Plan

3

You now understand the basic rules and, using them as a guide, have become interested in a small apartment house. First you inquire from your local banker and savings and loan officers about the reputation of the real estate broker offering the property for sale: you find he is a member of the local real estate board and has been selling properties in the local area for the last fifteen years. They assure you that he is reliable.

You visit the broker and he furnishes the following information about the apartment:

---

10 apartments, one bedroom each, current rents $185 per apartment per month.
Total gross income (allowing for vacancies):

Annual Expenses:		$15,000
Property taxes	$2,000	
Insurance	500	
Maintenance	300	
Mortgage payments	8,941	
Total expenses		$11,741
Net income		$ 3,259

The purchase price is listed at $135,000. The seller will arrange financing and is willing to accept a second mortgage if the first mortgage does not provide enough funds. The down payment asked for is $26,000.

From your viewpoint a return of $3,259 on an investment of $26,000 (13 percent) seems very attractive, particularly since you believe that you could ;'fix up'' the apartments and raise the rents. Your investigation of the area indicates that the apartment has been neglected and rents are at the lower range. Further, most of the tenants have been in the apartments for years so that the present owner has been willing to accept stability in tenant occupancy as a trade-off for somewhat lower rents.

Should you invest? The return looks good. The real estate broker assures you that the figures are accurate and typical of the properties he has listed for sale. He also assures you that he can help you secure a sufficiently large mortgage loan, so that you will not need to make a down payment of more than fifteen to twenty percent.

But wait. You have to think of what you might expect in the long run. To help you decide, the next two sections discuss critical information points and critical analytical points you should consider.

CRITICAL INFORMATION POINTS

You can estimate investment value with reasonable accuracy, and at the same time learn where data points are critical to meeting investment objectives, if the following data considerations are analyzed carefully:

Gross Income

Because property owners frequently allow rent concessions to secure and keep desirable tenants, a record of actual collected rents, preferably for a period of five years, is the only basis on which gross income can be estimated accurately. Scheduled rents are used as an indication of maximum possible income potential.

Vacancy and Collection Losses

Vacancy and collection losses are the means by which scheduled rents are adjusted to reflect collected rents. Losses from scheduled rents are caused by rental concessions, actual vacancies, loss of rent when one tenant leaves and another does not move in immediately. Frequently, an investor will set scheduled rents at the upper end of the market rent potential, expecting to have to make some adjustments through the vacancy and collection loss factor.

Expenses

Include in your calculations those expenses necessary to maintain the anticipated income collected. For newer properties expenses may equal as little as 20 or 30 percent of gross income, but for older properties as much as 75 or 80 percent. You determine the level of your expenses by the amounts necessary to achieve and maintain the level of gross income you have planned. Remember these are not forecasts but your explicit financial policies for making the property produce the returns you want—always recognizing that the market really determines the limits within which you can achieve your goals.

Operating Expenses. All types of expenses, incurred annually, that are influenced by the level of occupancy of the property—utilities, janitor, trash collection—are treated as operating expenses.

Fixed Expenses. Usually fixed expenses include property insurance premiums, property taxes, and license fees allocated on an annual basis. Their amounts are "fixed" in the sense that they are not related to the level of property use or occupancy.

Reserves. Some expenses necessary to maintain anticipated income are incurred in one year but are expected to be allocated over more than one year. Such items might be major repairs, such as roofs, or major maintenance, such as exterior and interior painting.

Contingent Expenses. These are unanticipated expenses, such as repair of storm damages. They may apply to only one year or to a number of years.

Financing Expenses. The first investment value estimate of a property is calculated without including any financing expenses. Since financing expenses can be negotiated, they tend to vary from investor to investor and are considered on whatever basis the investor may desire.

Income Tax Expenses. Income tax expenses are also related to the income status of each investor; therefore, they also vary from one investor to another and are treated in the analytical program on whatever basis the investor may desire.

Net Income

Net income is the amount capitalized to determine investment value. Usually it is the amount left after all but financing and income tax expenses have been deducted from gross income.

CRITICAL ANALYTICAL POINTS

An investor has to make a number of decisions before he can analyze real estate investment data. These areas of decision-making can be approached two ways: either you can make the decisions and let them determine how much you pay for a property; or you can, assuming the price is firm, adjust your decisions to accommodate the investment amount.

Length of Investment

The physical life of a property determines the maximum earning (or economic) life of a potential investment. The investor, after determining how long the property can earn the estimated net income, may or may not decide to stay invested during the entire economic life.

Earning Rate of Return

An investor's interest rate is related either to the investor's equity or his total property price. Using return on equity typically produces a higher earning rate.

Clearly you need to know a great deal more about the apartment house in which you are interested if you wish to become a serious professional real estate investor. At this point, therefore, you should prepare an analysis sheet as follows:

Note that you have not included mortgage expenses because you want to determine if the apartment can pay its way on an operating basis. If there is sufficient income to pay mortgage expenses, fine. Let the amount left after all operating expenses are paid determine how much in mortgage payments you want to assume.

In a similar manner you should determine whether the apartment is a good ''economic'' investment before you estimate its income tax poten-

	Annual Total
Number of apartments × annual scheduled rents	_____
Minus: Average income losses because of vacancies, uncollected rents, losing tenants	_____
Actual collected rents	_____
Expenses:	
Operating expenses (expenses whose amounts change as the number of tenants change)	_____
Fixed expenses:	
(property taxes, insurance, license fees)	_____
Reserves:	
(Amounts set aside each year to take care of painting and repairs and modernization)	_____
Total expenses	_____
Net earned income	_____

tials. If the apartment is not a good economic investment, income tax shelters have little meaning.

The next chapter demonstrates how to estimate these amounts precisely. Even before making estimates, however, you have to make some investment decisions. Although you make these decisions now, you may want to change them after you find how they affect your ability to invest in a particular property.

Recovery of Investment

Since real estate, particularly buildings and improvements, tends to lose value for a number of reasons, an investor wants to recover his investment price periodically, usually annually. Any investment amount not recovered in this manner must be recovered at the time the investment is sold.

Capitalization Rate

This rate, expressed as a percentage, includes provision for an earning rate of return and a recovery of investment rate.

Capitalization Method

Of the many ways of estimating the present value of the anticipated net income—a process known as "capitalization"—the most common method is to divide the net income by a capitalization rate. This is a very conservative method and, of the various capitalization methods, usually produces the most conservative or lowest investment value. The other most common method, the annuity method, multiplies the net income by a factor that reflects the anticipated earning rate and the recovery of investment rate. The factor can be developed from an algebraic formula or from tables prepared with the use of the formula.

Do not become worried about how to treat recovery of investment, capitalization rate, and capitalization methods. At this point all you need do is decide these things:

1. What is the approximate range of years during which you plan to keep this property as an investment?
2. What percent rate do you want to earn on the equity you plan to invest?

Typically real estate investors plan to invest eight to fifteen years in a particular property, the shorter period when stressing income and the longer period when looking for capital gains. The percentage they plan to earn on equity is always larger than what they could earn through either a long-term savings account or what is being earned by lenders on prime first loans. The percentage can range from lows of 8.0 to 9.5 percent to a high of 20 percent or more.

GAINING POINTS TO WIN

Gaining points in the real estate investment game begins with careful consideration of locational and financial considerations. For almost any kind of real estate investment property, the first step in locational analysis is defining the location, setting its boundaries. Boundaries are set by considering the area in which there is a similarity of land uses. Most investment value is achieved when similar or compatible land uses are grouped. For example, the most desirable apartment areas are those in which a variety of apartments are not only for rent but are also close to public transportation, shopping, and other amenities necessary for comfortable family living. After all, about one-half of all American families do rent and do want the same kind of neighborhood advantages found in detached single-family home areas.

Once the boundaries of a neighborhood have been set, the values of all properties inside those boundaries should be affected by the same forces and should respond in about the same manner. The basic forces most likely to affect values tend to be physical and geographic, political and legal, economic and market-oriented, and environmental. Although people also have an impact on value, presumably a given property and area attract those who find the area most desirable and so produce a population mix that maintains and enhances the quality of living in the area.

You will find that Exhibit 3-1 has some specific suggestions on analyzing an area in which you are thinking of investing. This analysis is slanted towards residential apartment areas; later, analyses are provided for other areas. There are forty questions, grouped by category, to which you provide "yes" or "no" answers. For each answer category you will find how to evaluate your number of *yes*s. If the area you are looking at does not rate at least "acceptable" in every category you might do well to look at another area or be prepared for higher investment risks.

Exhibit 3-1 Checking the Neighborhood for an Investment Property

Street Address _____

Description: Type of use _____

　　　　　　 Size: No. of rental units _____Rents _____
　　　　　　 or
　　　　　　 Square footage _____Rents _____

	Yes	No
1. Boundaries		
1.1 Is the area zoned for the use of the property?	☐	☐
1.2 Are there building codes which determine the quality and kind of construction?	☐	☐
1.3 Is the area protected from other kinds of uses by distinctive physical features, such as hills, rivers, water, major streets, or traffic arteries?	☐	☐
Good—3 *yes*s; Acceptable—2 *yes*s.		
2. Physical and geographic characteristics		
2.1 Buildings and improvements		
2.11 Are most of the existing area structures of about the same age and the others younger?	☐	☐
2.12 Are the area structures about the same size in terms of area and height?	☐	☐
2.13 Is the external appearance of the structures reasonably appealing and consistent?	☐	☐
2.14 Do the structures give evidence of being maintained and modernized?	☐	☐
Good—3 or more *yes*s; Acceptable—2 *yes*s.		

Exhibit 3-1 (cont.)

	Yes	*No*

2.2 Geographic

    2.21 Is the climate (temperature, weather) reasonably and consistently favorable to the property uses? ☐ ☐

    2.22 Do adjacent uses avoid detrimental impacts on land uses in the area? ☐ ☐

    2.23 Is the topography and soil suitable to the intended and existing uses? ☐ ☐

2.3 Hazards and nuisances

    2.31 Is the area free from dangers of high-speed traffic? ☐ ☐

    2.32 Is there airport traffic noise or other problems that can be avoided? ☐ ☐

    2.33 Is there freedom from noises, odors or other nuisances from industrial or commercial uses? ☐ ☐

    2.34 Is there good access to railroads, airports, and other public transportation? ☐ ☐

    2.35 Is the area free from dangers of heavy floods, rains, drainage from higher areas? ☐ ☐

    Good—4 or more *yes*s; Acceptable—3 *yes*s.

Comments: (Place here any additional items that you feel should be noted.)

2.4 Transportation: Is it adequate, dependable, relatively inexpensive, frequent with respect to:

    2.41 Jobs ☐ ☐

    2.42 Shopping ☐ ☐

    2.43 Recreation ☐ ☐

    2.44 Schools ☐ ☐

    2.45 Major central business district (banks, stores, service stations) ☐ ☐

    2.46 Major regional shopping center ☐ ☐

    2.47 Medical services ☐ ☐

    Good—4 or more *yes*s; Acceptable—3 *yes*s.

Comments:

3. *Political and Legal Characteristics*

    3.1 Is zoning enforced? ☐ ☐

    3.2 Are building codes enforced? ☐ ☐

    3.3 Has the local land use plan been revised in the last five years? ☐ ☐

    3.4 Are there private covenants or agreements to enforce building standards, property uses, and the quality of the area? ☐ ☐

    3.5 Is there adequate police and fire protection? ☐ ☐

    3.6 Are the property taxes reasonable compared to other areas? ☐ ☐

    What is average assessed values _____?

    What is the average tax bill per \$1,000 of market value _____?

Exhibit 3-1 (cont.)

3.7 Is the area free of special assessments for special services?   ☐   ☐
Are there assessments?
What are they? _____
What do they cost per $1,000 of market value? _____
3.8 Is the area free of special local taxes?
(Gross income or sales taxes)
Good—6 or more *yes*s; Acceptable—5 *yes*s.
Comments:

4. *Economic and Market Trends*
4.1 Is the area located so that it will benefit from future city
growth?   ☐   ☐
4.2 Are property values about the same?   ☐   ☐
4.3 Is the mixture of land uses compatible?   ☐   ☐
4.4 Is there evidence of land use changes leading to more intensive
land uses and higher values?   ☐   ☐
4.5 Are rentals in the area reasonable and competitive with each
other?   ☐   ☐
4.6 Are the utility rates reasonable compared to other similar areas?   ☐   ☐
What would be the typical monthly bill for:
Electricity _____
Water _____
Gas _____
Sewage disposal _____
Trash collection _____
Good—4 or more *yes*s; Acceptable—3 *yes*s.
Comments:

5. *Environmental Considerations*
5.1 Are the levels of pollution sufficiently low so as not to affect
human health?   ☐   ☐
Have there been smog alerts in the area? _____
Have the number of alerts been about average for the pollution
area? _____
5.2 Is the area free from excessive noise pollution?   ☐   ☐
5.3 Are the sewage disposal facilities and the water quality adequate
for the intended property use?   ☐   ☐
5.4 Is the area reasonably free from noise, ugly views?   ☐   ☐
Good—4 *yes*; Acceptable—3 *yes*s.
Comments:

Checking the Site

After you have found the area acceptable, check the lot on which the property is located. Though you may want to ask a surveyor, an engineer, or a contractor to help you, the list provided in Exhibit 3-2 can be used without such assistance. All you must do is be a careful observer and keep in mind what the typical user of the site might want.

Pay particular attention to the dimensions of the lot since you may want to add more rentable area at a future time, and you do not want to pay the costs of owning land you cannot use. Perhaps you may want a surveyor to mark the lot dimensions with metal stakes. Even though you do get the exact size of the lot, you should check with local governmental offices to determine how much of the total lot can be used.

Exhibit 3-2   Judging the Quality of a Site

The site, or the lot, provides the setting within which the building is arranged. There are many things about a site that can make it unattractive to the potential user. On the other hand, a good site is well worth a maximum price because it will help you earn maximum income from renting.

1. *Legal description and street address.* You will need the legal description of the lot for a number of purposes; therefore be sure you get it and be sure it is correct. The usual description will read: "Lot No. 27, Block 758 of Tract No. 384562." Or the tract may also have a name, such as "Sunset Acres." If there is a dispute as to what property you own, you will be required to furnish a legal description. If the property mentioned in the legal description is not the same as the one at the street address, the property you own will be the one at the legal address. The title insurance company or the real estate broker can usually check this for you.
2. *Dimensions and shape,* including a plot plan showing all improvements on the lot.
3. *Soil and subsoil*—does property show settling, are there unusual hazards (particularly for hillside properties)? Soil engineer reports?
4. *Drainage*—is there danger of flooding or excessive erosion?
5. *Topography*—how much of the site is usable? Any topographical hazards because of adjacent properties?
6. *Immediately adjacent uses*—is there a reasonable degree of privacy and freedom from annoyance from adjacent uses?
7. *Site utilization*—private- and public-use restrictions? Yard space as related to the location of walks, driveways, landscaping, and other improvements.
8. *Utilities*—availability to the lot of public works, sewage disposal, gas, electricity, phone lines, rates and quality of these services.
9. *Assessed value*—of the lot and improvements, total tax bill and tax rate, assessed value of lot compared to its market value.
10. *Access* from the lot to public streets and public ways.

If you decide to add more space, be sure that the soil and subsoil will bear the added weight and that you can secure the additional utilities needed. You may even have to analyze the environmental impact of any additional use and have the impact reviewed by a local office. A call to city hall should help you get the answers to such questions.

Are the Improvements Suitable?

By now you can appreciate that the neighborhood, site, and building must be compatible and work to reinforce each other if you are to realize your investment potentials. Though the qualities of all investment properties need analysis, each specific use—apartments, offices, shops, industrial properties—has special requirements. You cannot become an expert in doing specific building analysis, but there are some general characteristics you can ask about.

To help you check these important general characteristics, the following table is provided. The major characteristics are listed on the left side and comments relating to apartment houses on the right:

General Characteristic	Comments
1. Durability	1. Evidences of ability to resist use and weather. Quality of the workmanship and materials.
2. Structural soundness	2. Any evidences of failure in foundations, walls, roofs, floors, ceilings—cracks or appearance of major repairs.
3. Building space	3. Room sizes and uses. Potentials for changing and remodeling. Traffic patterns of building users. Natural light and ventilation. Convenience of electrical and appliance outlets.
4. Service systems (heat, light, water, air conditioning)	4. Capacities, convenience in using, efficiency, costs, age, condition.
5. Mechanical and convenience equipment (stoves, refrigerators, water heaters, freezers, washer-dryers)	5. Age, make, capacity, condition
6. Architecture and appearance	6. Compatibility with adjacent architecture, appeal, ability to withstand fads, evidences of maintenance and change to keep pace with market competition.

General Characteristic	*Comments*
7. Conformance to area standards	7. Maintenance, size, style, general appearance compared to its competitors in the area.
8. Floor plans	8. Room locations and size compared to user needs. Adequate closets, electrical outlets, equipment, windows, doorways. Adaptability to new uses.
9. Functional qualities	9. Are the apartments worth the rents that have to be charged? Can they be used easily, without danger and conveniently? Is there ample storage?

If you inquire locally, you may find inspection services that evaluate a property and furnish you with a list of possible repairs or other costs you might encounter. If such services are not available, you might contact local builders or contractors and ask them to evaluate the building in comparison to what they know to be the most desirable kinds of buildings for the uses you have in mind. A small expenditure for expert help at this point will pay rich dividends later.

GETTING FINANCIAL HELP

Before you agree on the final price for an investment property, keep some financial strategies in mind. By attending to these you will be able to negotiate a more favorable price and terms that fit your financial plan. These financial strategies relate to:

1. asking the seller a number of questions, and
2. dealing expertly with the lender.

1. Asking the Seller

The down payment you make in purchasing property is not the only cash you will need. There are also various closing costs to consider. In most cases determining the amounts of these closing costs and who pays them is left to the bargaining capacities of the buyer and seller. To assist you in your bargaining a check list of questions to ask the seller is found in Exhibit 3-3. (Also see Exhibit 3-4 for obtaining further financial information.)

Exhibit 3-3 Questions You Should Ask the Seller When You Are Considering Any Business or Commercial Property Investment.

1. On which date can the property become yours?
2. What is the total purchase price of the property?
3. How much cash down payment is required?
4. When does the down payment have to be made?
5. How much money must be secured from a first loan?
6. From whom might the loan be secured?
7. What will be the probable interest rate, years of loan, and monthly payment?
8. Will there be additional payments with the loan for insurance and taxes? How much for insurance _____ taxes _____?
9. Will there be any additional sums to be paid before the sale is completed?
10. What mechanical equipment and furnishings are included in the purchase price?

Equipment	*Furnishings*
_____	_____
_____	_____
_____	_____

11. What additional equipment and furnishings must be purchased and at what additional costs?

Equipment	*Furnishings*
_____	_____
_____	_____
_____	_____

12. What will buyer and seller pay of the following costs:

	Buyer	*Seller*
Real estate brokerage commission		
Loan fees (costs of securing the loan)		
Legal advice in preparing papers to transfer the property		
Title insurance or proof of title		
Preparation of title deed, recording		
Survey of property lines		
Property appraisal fees		
Taxes and assessments now due or paid		
Loan prepayment penalties (for existing loan)		
Insurance premium due or paid		
Termite and dry rot inspection		
Closing costs		
Other: _____		

13. Will the seller furnish information on the following for at least the past five years?
Utilities expenses
Property taxes
Operating costs (maintenance, repairs)
Modernization, rehabilitation, conversion expenditures
Rents collected
Copies of leases

Exhibit 3-3 (cont.)

14. Who will pay for the following and will these items be completed before the new owner takes possession?
Repairs
Decorating
Painting
Remodellings
Modernization
Replacements
Other: _____

12. If a professional property manager has been used, what are the terms of employment and his responsibilities? Or, if there is a resident manager, discuss with him the tenants and the problems of managing the property.
13. Are credit check reports available on the tenants?
14. What has been the history of rent delinquencies?

Exhibit 3-4   Tenant Questionnaire

Whenever you decide to invest in a property for the rental income it produces, you should survey the tenants, asking the questions listed below. If you do not receive a "yes" answer to each, discuss the question with the seller to determine whether you should investigate further before buying.

1. Do the rents the tenants say they are paying equal the ones called for in the leases?
2. Do the rental schedules furnished to you agree with the statements of the tenants about any special rental concessions they may have received for long-term leases or for other reasons?
3. Do the tenants agree that no changes have been made in the terms of the written leases and any amendments to them?
4. Have most of the tenants been occupants for at least one year?
5. Do the tenants indicate sufficient satisfaction with the present leases and rental terms to be willing to renew their leases?
6. Do the tenants' statements about security or other deposits and what will be done with them agree with the statements made by the seller on these items?
7. Have the tenants been satisfied with the services of the property manager?
8. Is a professional property management service used?
9. Have the tenants been furnished with copies of the property use rules and do they feel the rules are enforced in an appropriate manner?
10. Particularly for office and retail and industrial properties:

    10.1 Is the tenant one with a solid credit and business reputation?

    10.2 Has the tenant(s) been in business for at least five years?

    10.3 Has the tenant(s) rented this property for at least one year?

    10.4 Does the tenant(s) find that the property will meet any expansion needs for future business operations?

    10.5 Would the tenant renew the lease on the current terms? Or would the tenant agree to the rental increases (if you have this in mind)? _____

2. Dealing with the Lender

When you are ready to purchase an investment property, you will probably not have enough cash to pay for more than 25 percent of the purchase price and, if you are like most investors, you will prefer to pay not more than 10 percent down. Normally, you can secure the additional funds by borrowing from a commercial bank, a savings bank, a savings and loan association, or an insurance company, each of which has a different financing plan to offer you. They usually agree to lend the money if you agree to pay back the original amount you borrow in monthly installments, plus interest on what you have not repaid, and if you pledge the house as security for repayment of the loan. The pledging of the property as security is accomplished by means of a mortgage or deed of trust: This document protects the lender inasmuch as if you fail to make your payments according to the loan terms, the lender can have your house sold publicly and apply the proceeds to the amounts owed him. In this section we shall discuss the kinds of terms (dollar amount of the loan, the interest rate, the period of repayment, and other requirements) the lenders usually offer to prospective buyers.

Savings and Loan Associations.   These are financial institutions, chartered by either state or Federal agencies, for the purpose of collecting savings in local communities and then making these funds available locally for the purchase, primarily of single-family homes, although they do provide a limited amount of financing for other types of property purchases. The principal difference between a Federally chartered and a state chartered association is that state chartered associations can sometimes make loans on more different types of properties than Federally chartered associations; they may also be able to be slightly more liberal in their lending terms.

The typical savings and loan association, because it specializes in home and apartment loans, can make relatively large loans for relatively long terms. That is, it can make a loan representing a relatively high percentage of the total purchase price—often up to 80 percent of what you pay for the home—and can give you up to twenty, or in exceptional cases, up to thirty years to repay the loan. This type of loan is known as a conventional loan since its repayment is neither guaranteed nor insured by any governmental agency and it can be made by any type of lending institution. The amount of the purchase price which can be financed and the terms on which the money is to be repaid are determined by the charter provisions of the association; provisions are the same for all Federally chartered associations but differ for the state chartered associations. As long as the associations do not exceed the loan-to-value ratios and the terms set forth in their charters, they may introduce any modifications they feel are proper. This means that different lending terms are offered by different savings and loan associations in the same local community.

Savings and loan associations not only make loans for the purchase of homes, but will also make loans for home repairs and improvements. They do not make loans for the purchase of personal property, such as an automobile, furniture, or a trip.

Commercial Banks. These banks, also chartered by either Federal or state agencies for the purpose of collecting local savings, make loans primarily to businessmen, although an important part of their total business usually includes home loans. The difference between the Federally chartered and state chartered associations is about the same as that for savings and loan associations. For example, many state chartered banks can make loans with only land as security, whereas the Federally chartered banks cannot.

Compared with savings and loan associations, commercial banks' commercial mortgage loans are usually for a smaller percentage of the purchase price, usually between 60 and 70 percent, and for shorter periods of time, usually fifteen years. In addition, commercial banks are often more selective in making home loans because they prefer to lend money for nonresidential properties or for business purposes. You will probably secure the best bank terms if you seek a home loan from the bank with which you have been making deposits or doing other business.

Savings Banks. Found in the New England and East Coast states, savings banks are more like savings and loan associations than like commercial banks. They also specialize in home loans with terms very similar to those of savings and loan associations, although they make more of other types of loans than the associations.

Insurance Companies. This type of lender makes loans through agents, but all loans must be approved by the company. Because of the manner in which they receive their funds, the insurance companies tend to prefer large loans on business properties or good quality single-family homes. Their loan-to-value ratios are often quite high, averaging between 60 and 80 percent of purchase price, and the length of the loans between twenty and thirty years. Their interest rates also tend to be at the low end of the prevailing scale of market rates. They are typically selective in the properties they finance, preferring larger, newer properties in well-established neighborhoods.

Insurance companies have developed various types of mortgage insurance plans, which they sometimes prefer the borrower to take out but may not make an absolute requirement for obtaining the loan. These insurance policies usually have a term equal to the term of the loan and provide proceeds for paying off the loan if the principal wage earner dies or is incapacitated. Some of the policies also have a cash value that can be used (1) to pay off the loan before its date of maturity, (2) as an endowment at the end of the loan period, or (3) for monthly payments to the insured or his beneficiaries.

Selecting a Lender. Securing money for a home mortgage is somewhat akin to shopping for an automobile. Of variety of financing models, some are standard and some can be assembled to meet a special need. For this reason the prospective borrower should spend some time getting acquainted with the various lenders in his area and determining what kinds of loans they prefer to make and the terms they usually expect. Exhibit 3-5 is a checklist indicating some of the questions to consider before making a final decision on the type of lender to do business with.

Exhibit 3-5   Some Questions to Ask Lenders

Although all home mortgage lenders may seem the same, they differ in many different ways. One way is in the fees charged in connection with the process of making a loan. Once you have found a property to buy, you will find it helpful—and financially sound—to visit more than one lender and get answers to the questions listed below:

Policy on Loan-Making:
1. What would determine the amount and terms of the loan if the property is approved?
2. How long will it take to secure the loan?
3. What is the maximum loan-to-value ratio permitted? What is the average size of a typical loan?
4. What is the maximum interest rate, or is the rate regulated? What is the average rate on a typical loan?
5. What is the maximum term, in years?
6. Does the lender make construction loans? If so, on what terms?
7. Does the lender make FHA loans? VA loans? Are they making them now?
8. In which areas does the lender prefer to make loans?
9. Which costs, of those listed below, would be charged for the loan and what would be their amounts?

Exhibit 3-5 (cont.)

Item	Dollar Amount
Escrow fee	
Notary fee	
Loan office fee	
Appraisal fee	
Credit report	
Title policy	
Termite report	
Recording fee—trust deed	
Recording fee—grant deed	
Drawing trust deed and note	
Miscellaneous legal fees	
Fire insurance premium	
Prepayment penalty	
Loan points	
Others:	

Policy on Property:
10. What does the lender expect of the house in terms of architecture, age, size, condition, and location?
11. How is the value defined? (The value serves as the basis for establishing the amount of the loan.)

Policy on Borrower:
12. What are the limits on the number and amounts of mortgage loans that can be made to one person?
13. Will the lender give a first mortgage (or trust deed) if the buyer also has to use a second mortgage to pay for the house?
14. What type of borrower does the lender prefer in terms of:
    a. Size of loan requested
    b. Borrower's income
    c. Borrower's occupation

Exhibit 3-5 (cont.)

15. What relation does the lender establish between the borrower's income and the amount the lender will approve?

Name of lending institution _____

Location _____

How to Use the Mortgage Payment Table

Exhibit 3-6 shows the monthly payment to be made each month for each $1,000 borrowed at a given rate of interest for a given period of years.

Example A. I borrow $10,000 to buy a home, and I agree to pay 6 percent interest for twenty years. By cross-referencing the column headed "6%" and the row labeled "20 years," I obtain the figure $7.17 which I multiply by 10 ($10,000 ÷ $1,000). The answer, $71.70, is the amount I must pay monthly to repay the 6 percent loan in twenty years.

If I multiply the $71.70 by 12, the answer of $860.40 is the amount I will pay on the loan annually.

If I multiply $860.40 by 20, the answer of $17,208 is the total amount of money I will repay to the lender for lending me $10,000 for twenty years at 6% interest. The $7,208 over the $10,000 I borrowed represents the cost to me of using the lender's money.

Example B. Suppose I borrow $1,000 for twenty years at 6.5 percent interest? The table does not have 6.5 percent interest figures.

The figure for 7% for 20 years is	$7.76
The figure for 6% for 20 years is	7.17
The difference between the two figures is	.59

If I multiply .59 × .5 the answer is .295 (or half the difference). If I add .295 to $7.17 (the smaller amount), the answer of $7.47 (rounded to the nearest cent) is the amount I pay monthly at 6.5% interest for twenty years.

Example C. Suppose I borrow $12,225 at 6.6 percent for twenty years?

The figure for 7% for 20 years is	$7.76
The figure for 6% for 20 years is	7.17
The difference between the two figures is	.59

Exhibit 3-6 Monthly Payment per $1,000 of Loan Needed to Amortize the Loan*

Number of Years	*Interest Rate* 1%	2%	3%	4%	5%	6%	7%	8%	9%	10%
1	83.79	84.24	84.69	85.15	85.61	86.01		86.99	87.45	87.92
2	42.10	42.54	42.99	43.43	43.88	44.33	44.78	45.23	45.68	46.14
3	28.21	28.64	29.09	29.53	29.98	30.43	30.88	31.34	31.80	32.27
4	21.26	21.70	22.14	22.58	23.03	23.49	23.95	24.41	24.89	25.36
5	17.09	17.53	17.97	18.42	18.88	19.34	19.81	20.28	20.76	21.25
6	14.32	14.75	15.20	15.65	16.11	16.58	17.05	17.53	18.03	18.53
7	12.34	12.77	13.22	13.67	14.14	14.61	15.10	15.59	16.09	16.60
8	10.84	11.28	11.73	12.19	12.66	13.15	13.64	14.14	14.65	15.17
9	9.69	10.13	10.58	11.05	11.52	12.01	12.51	13.02	13.54	14.08
10	8.76	9.20	9.66	10.13	10.61	11.11	11.62	12.13	12.67	13.22
11	8.00	8.45	8.91	9.38	9.87	10.37	10.89	11.42	11.96	12.52
12	7.37	7.82	8.28	8.76	9.25	9.76	10.29	10.82	11.38	11.95
13	6.84	7.28	7.75	8.24	8.74	9.25	9.79	10.33	10.90	11.48
14	6.38	6.83	7.30	7.79	8.29	8.82	9.36	9.91	10.49	11.08
15	5.98	6.44	6.91	7.40	7.91	8.44	8.99	9.56	10.14	10.75
16	5.64	6.01	6.57	7.06	7.58	8.12	8.63	9.25	9.85	10.46
17	5.33	5.79	6.27	6.77	7.29	7.84	8.40	8.98	9.59	10.21
18	5.06	5.52	6.00	6.51	7.04	7.59	8.16	8.75	9.36	10.00
19	4.82	5.28	5.76	6.27	6.81	7.37	7.95	8.55	9.17	9.81
20	4.60	5.01	5.55	6.06	6.60	7.17	7.76	8.36	9.00	9.65
21	4.40	4.86	5.36	5.88	6.42	6.99	7.59	8.20	8.85	9.51
22	4.22	4.69	5.18	5.71	6.26	6.84	7.44	8.06	8.71	9.38
23	4.01	4.52	5.03	5.55	6.11	6.69	7.30	7.93	8.59	9.27
24	3.91	4.37	4.88	5.41	5.97	6.56	7.18	7.82	8.49	9.17
25	3.77	4.24	4.75	5.28	5.85	6.45	7.07	7.72	8.39	9.09
26	3.64	4.11	4.62	5.17	5.74	6.34	6.97	7.63	8.31	9.01
27	3.52	4.00	4.51	5.06	5.64	6.24	6.88	7.54	8.23	8.94
28	3.41	3.89	4.41	4.96	5.54	6.16	6.80	7.47	8.16	8.88
29	3.31	3.79	4.31	4.86	5.45	6.08	6.73	7.40	8.10	8.82
30	3.22	3.70	4.22	4.78	5.37	6.00	6.66	7.34	8.05	8.78

*This table is based on the assumption that the final payment would differ from preceding payments because it would be used to make up deficiencies caused by rounding to nearest cent.

If I multiply .59 × .6 the answer is .354. If I add .354 to the lower of the two figures above ($7.17 + .354), the answer is $7.524, the amount I pay monthly for each $1,000. If I multiply $7.524 × 12.225 ($12,225 ÷ $1,000) the answer of $91.98 is the monthly mortgage payment I must make.

COMPROMISES FOR REAL ESTATE INVESTORS

You will soon discover that no single property can fit all the investment goals and rules you have developed. Even if you tried to build a property to your specifications, you would find some things "not quite right." Your goal is to anticipate these problems and have some basic strategies for dealing with them. To help you, some suggestions are listed; these should help you devise other approaches to meet your special needs.

1. *Location is usually more important than the buildings on the lot.* You can always make repairs and improvements to a building, but you cannot do anything to change the qualities of a location.
2. *An older property is preferable to a new property* if you want to be reasonably certain about income and cost potentials and are seeking the most rentable space for each investment dollar.
3. *Good workmanship* is preferable to *good materials* if you have to make a choice. Workmanship can overcome the defects of poor materials, but you would pay constantly for poor workmanship. Hopefully you can avoid this kind of choice, because poor workmanship and poor materials mean extra costs and continuing problems.
4. *Low down payments are preferable* because they increase the earning rates on your equity. However, be sure you have a financial reserve in case the property does not produce enough net income at times to pay for the financing.
5. *Plain properties without distinctive architectural or other characteristics* are the most durable investments. Luxuries or extras may make the property look better, but they do not improve the income potentials.
6. *In a given market, smaller units* will usually be more salable, easier to manage, and easier to keep rented in changing markets. Any apartment property with more than twenty units will require professional management.
7. *Size of the property and units within the property* should fit the average for the market. Smaller or larger units often present problems that result in lower prices and higher costs.
8. *Use experts when in doubt.* The costs of using appraisers, builders, lenders, and lawyers are considerably less than those associated with making mistakes. If your investment cannot produce enough income to let you pay for such expert help, then it may be the wrong investment.
9. *Convertibility*—the property should lend itself to changes as the market changes so that you can always maximize rent potentials.
10. *Flexibility*—the space in the property should be easily changed to meet different user needs at minimal costs of time and money.

11. *Energy saving potential is more important than style of appearance*—given increasing shortages of natural gas and rising prices of fuel, energy saving has become paramount for successful real estate investing.

12. *Specifying repairs to be made before buying* is a safer, less costly financial strategy. Estimate them ahead of time, thereby being able to negotiate for a lower price.

Planning Your Game Strategies

4

Estimating the value of your home is a very subjective process which relates to how you plan to use the home, the pleasures you expect to receive from owning the home, the potential for earning money through an increase in the value of the home—and many other factors. Typically you reach your final decision as to what to pay by comparing what others have paid for similar homes. On the other hand, the estimation of the value of an income-producing property can be quite complex: It begins with an estimate of the value to you of the potential net earnings, and it then includes information about what others have paid for such properties and what it might cost you to build a similar kind of new property. And because there are many types of income-producing properties—apartment houses, stores, office buildings, industrial parks, golf courses, and many others—the analytical process has to be varied slightly for each one. Fortunately, the basic strategies in analyzing income-producing properties are the same no matter how the properties may be used.

The analytical strategies for income-producing properties require that you obtain accurate and complete answers to these questions:

1. *How much gross income is produced from the various earning potentials in the property?* In an apartment house, for example, income can be produced from rents, parking, vending machines, laundry room equipment, and many other items.
2. *What expenditures will be incurred in producing the gross income?* All properties have three classes of expenses:
    a. *operating*—they fluctuate with the levels of use of the property;
    b. *fixed*—they remain fixed in amount no matter how the property is used; such as property taxes, insurance, license fees; and
    c. *reserves*—amounts spent in one year which should be allocated as expenditures for several years, such as installing new roofs or the painting of the exterior and interior of the building.
3. *How will financing and income taxes affect the value of the investment?* This is a highly personal consideration which relates to your personal finances.
4. *What will be the net income after paying expenses, financing, and income taxes?*
5. *How long will the net income continue and how much do you want to earn on your investment?* Depending on your investment goals, you may want to earn a given dollar amount, try for capital gains or a value increase, or seek a given rate of return based on the amount of money you have invested in the property, the amount you pay for the property, or other criteria.
6. *What is the amount you are willing to (or should) invest now to achieve the investment goals you have selected?* The process of placing a present value on your anticipated future stream of income is known as capitalization. This is a simple process involving easily understood analytical methods. In simplest terms, the process is:

	Gross income
MINUS	*Operating, fixed, reserve expenditures*
EQUALS	Net income
MINUS	*Financing costs*
EQUALS	Cash flow
MINUS	*Allowed deductions from income tax*
EQUALS	Cash flow and tax-sheltered income

APPLYING YOUR GAME PLAN

You can use a "standard" game plan for analysing all real estate investment income properties if you use the six basic questions. To help you understand how to use the questions in all situations, the standard format for analyzing an apartment house investment is presented in Exhibit 4-1, and the application of that analysis to an actual apartment investment is presented in Exhibit 4-2a and 4-2b. Formats for other types of properties are presented in later chapters, but the basic format is the same. In the remainder of this chapter you will find ideas for making your own analysis, using a professional to advise you on a potential investment.

When applying Exhibit 4-1 to an apartment investment, remember that the records furnished to you by the present owner may be incomplete or inaccurate. You should ask for records over the last five years, if possible, together with a statement from an accountant as to the accuracy of the records. If a professional property manager has been used, ask for a certified copy of those records. Even then check all statements with the experiences of investors who have owned or who currently own such apartments. You will find many investors willing to share their experiences with you. If you cannot find them, then pay a professional property manager to help you in such analyses.

The following comments about the process of analysis should also help.

Exhibit 4-1   A Standard Plan for Analyzing Income Investment Properties (using an apartment house as an example)

(all amounts are annual)

1. *Rental Income Schedules and Estimates*

Number of rental units	x	Rents (Room count, sq. ft. range)	Monthly	x 12	Amounts reported	Market levels
Furnished:						
_____	x	(_____, ____)	_____	x 12 _____		_____
_____	x	(_____, ____)	_____	x 12 _____		_____
_____	x	(_____, ____)	_____	x 12 _____		_____
_____	x	(_____, ____)	_____	x 12 _____		_____
Unfurnished:						
_____	x	(_____, ____)	_____	x 12 _____		_____
_____	x	(_____, ____)	_____	x 12 _____		_____
_____	x	(_____, ____)	_____	x 12 _____		_____
_____	x	(_____, ____)	_____	x 12 _____		_____
_____	x	(_____, ____)	_____	x 12 _____		_____
Total Rental Income Estimates				_____		_____

Exhibit 4-1 (cont.)

2. *Plus Other Income (Concessions, Vending Machines, Laundry Room, Parking, Furniture)*
Type:

_____   _____   _____

_____   _____   _____

_____   _____   _____

Gross Income Estimates   _____   _____

3. *Minus Vacancy and Collection Loss Provisions*

   Percent (%)   x Gross income estimates   _____   _____

4. *Effective Gross Income Estimate*   =========   =========

	As reported	As adjusted

4. *Effective Gross Income Estimate* $ _____ $ _____
   Minus the following items

5. *Expenses Analysis*
   5.1 Operating expenses (the amounts of these vary with the amount of occupancy)

	As reported	As adjusted
Janitor (include free apartment rent)	$_____	$_____
Social security, unemployment	_____	_____
Gardener	_____	_____
Trash and garbage collection		
Supplies (cleaning, etc.)	_____	_____
Utilities (not paid by tenants)		
Gas	_____	_____
Water	_____	_____
Electricity	_____	_____
Maintenance:		
Building exterior	_____	_____
Building interior	_____	_____
Elevator	_____	_____
Pool	_____	_____
Other	_____	_____
Advertising	_____	_____
Fees (identify)	_____	_____
Licenses	_____	_____
Management:		
Resident (plus free rent)	_____	_____
Nonresident (% of #4)	_____	_____
Other (identify)	_____	_____
	_____	_____
Total operating expenses	$ _____	$ _____

Exhibit 4-1 (cont.)

5.2 Replacement reserves (total amounts prorated annually)

Furniture $_____ $_____
Stoves
Refrigerators
Air Conditioner
Draperies, rugs
Elevator
Painting
Roof
Other (identify)

      Total replacement and other reserves $ _____ $ _____

5.3 Fixed expenses (do not change with occupancy or use levels)

Property taxes $_____ $_____
Insurance premiums
Licenses, fees
Others (identify)

      Total fixed expenses $_____ $_____

      Total expenses (as percent of item #4 ____) $_____

6. *Estimated Investment Value of the Anticipated Net Income*

6.1 Net income estimate:

Gross adjusted income (item #4) $_____
Minus: Total expenses (item #5)   _____
Estimated net income $_____

7. *Capitalization Rate Development*

First mortgage rate _____% × loan amount as percent of price   _____% = _____%

Second mortgage rate _____% × loan amount as percent of price   _____% = _____%

Equity (your money) earning rate _____% × amount as percent of price   _____% = _____%

Average interest rate to be earned by the investment   Total   _____

Period of investments in years ____ divided by 100 =

Recapture rate +   _____
Capitalization rate   _____

8. *Investment Value Estimate*

8.1 Before recognizing mortgage or financing payments

Estimated net income (Item #6.1) $_____
Minus: Land value $____ × Average interest rate ____%   _____
(This is the amount of total income earned by location or land)
Net income attributed to buildings and improvements $_____
Estimated building value: Net income to buildings divided by
    capitalization rate $_____
Add: Estimated land value   +_____
    Estimated investment value of the total property $_____

Exhibit 4-1 (cont.)

8.2 After recognizing mortgage or financing payments
    Estimated net income (Item #6.1) $_____
    Minus: Annual mortgage payments (interest + principal)   _____
    Net income after financing $_____
    Estimated building value: Net income to building
       divided by capitalization rate $_____
    Add: Estimated land value   +_____
       Estimated investment value of the property   =_____
    Add: Amount of the mortgage principal repaid   +_____
       Investment value of the property with financing   =_____

8.3 After recognizing the impact of income taxes
       Estimated net income (Item #6.1) $_____
    Minus: Interest payments on mortgage $_____
       Depreciation allowed: Building   _____
                   Furnishings   _____
                   Other   _____
      Other (type) _____   _____
      _____   _____

      Total tax allowable deductions $_____
      Net income to be capitalized after tax allowances $_____

    Investment value recognizing income tax impact
    (Using rate of return as basis) Net income/your equity ____% Net
    income/price of property   ____%

9. *Other measures of investment value*
  9.1 Value prior to mortgage
      Land value (Item #8.1) $_____
      Plus: Building value (Item #8.1)   _____
      Estimated investment value $_____

  9.2 After recognizing financing
      Land value (Item #8.2) $_____
      Plus: Building value (Item #8.2)   _____
         Total amount of mortgage   _____
      Estimated investment value $_____

  9.3 Using a gross multiplier
      Gross adjusted income (Item #8.2) $_____
      X Typical market multiplier
      Estimated market investment value $_____

  9.4 Comparison of investment values using rates of return
      Economic return (Estimated net income,
      Item #6.1 divided by purchase price)   ____%
      Economic return (Estimated net income
      Items #6.1 divided by your down payment)   ____%
      Return after taxes:
      Based on your equity (Item #8.3)   ____%
      Based on net after taxes   ____%

10. *Estimated investment value using market information*
  10.1 After surveying the market and obtaining prices of comparable properties:
       Highest prices paid for comparables $_____
       Lowest prices paid   _____
       Most frequent price paid (Mode)   _____
       Price midway between High/Low   _____

Exhibit 4-1 (cont.)

Cost to reproduce a comparable property
Per square foot x
total square feet in building .... $_____
Market prices of comparable properties
Price per rented unit .... $_____
Price per square foot .... _____
Price per room .... _____

Appendix A

Developing a market value estimate and a gross multiplier

	Date on comparable properties				
Bases for Comparisons	#1	#2	#3	#4	#5
Blocks from your property					
Number of rental units					

For individual units:
Number of units: 1 bedroom(sq. ft.) _____
            2 bedroom(sq. ft.) _____
            3 bedroom(sq. ft.) _____
            4 bedroom(sq. ft.) _____
Rents per unit:
Number of units   × monthly rent   × 12
1 bedroom _____ × $ _____ × 12   _____
2 bedroom _____ × $ _____ × 12   _____
3 bedroom _____ × $ _____ × 12   _____
4 bedroom _____ × $ _____ × 12   _____
Other bedroom __ × $ _____ × 12   _____
Total annual scheduled rents   _____
Sales price   _____
Sales terms: Down payment   _____
           Mortgage rate and years   _____
           Mortgage amount   _____
           Furnished: Drapes, rugs, equipment   _____
           Furniture   _____
Gross Multiplier (Price divided by rents)
Comparison to your property: (Comments)   _____

General comments about investment values (What do tenants pay, for example)

Data Base:		
Purchase price—market price		$100,000
(land $20,000; buildings $80,000)		
Equity—down payment		25,000
First mortgage loan—amount		75,000
Interest rate		.085
Term		15 years (180 months)
Monthly payments		$738.54
Transfer Costs—Initially		
—End of period		
Income tax rate	50%	
Anticipated market changes—		
Annual average % increase		
Market price	5%	
Rents	4%	
Expenses	3%	
Property taxes		
Financial Goals		
Investment period	5 years	
Return on market price	8%	
Return on equity	15%	

Apartment purchased on January 1 of the first year of investment

Rental Schedule and Estimates

Always consider two kinds of rental schedules: (1) the rents as
scheduled, and (2) the rents actually collected. A lease may call for
monthly rental payments of $225, but the previous owner may have given
one month's free rent for a one-year lease. You should ask the tenants what
rents they have been paying. Find out how long the tenants have been
occupying the property and whether some have been given rental concessions. If not immediately, then eventually, you will want all rents to be
equal to the best possible market rents.

Other Income

You may or may not want to include this income in your overall
property investment analysis. This income is undependable, usually costly
to produce, and difficult to anticipate. If you do include it, be very
conservative in your estimates of the potential net income. Typically, this
income is earned from vending machines, parking, laundry equipment,
and furniture rentals.

Exhibit 4-2b Investment Analysis of Seven-Unit Unfurnished Apartment

Investment Year
(All data are for the end of the year)

	Years				
	1	*2*	*3*	*4*	*5*
Market value, end of year	$105,000	$110,250	$115,763	$121,551	$127,628
Investment analysis					
Gross scheduled rents	15,000	15,600	16,224	16,873	17,548
Minus: Vacancy, collection losses (.06 × scheduled rents)	900	936	973	1,012	1,053
Effective gross income	$ 14,100	$ 14,664	$ 15,251	$ 15,861	$ 16,495
Minus:					
Total expenses (fixed, operating)	4,230	4,357	4,488	4,622	4,761
Property taxes	2,625	2,756	2,894	3,039	3,191
Net Earned Income	7,295	7,551	7,869	8,200	8,543
Minus:					
Depreciation allowance (3% straight-line on building)	2,400	2,400	2,400	2,400	2,400
Mortgage interest payments	5,744	5,534	5,305	5,056	4,785
Taxable income	$ 899	$ 383	$ 164	$ 744	$ 1,358
Taxes due (50% bracket)	0	0	82	372	679
Add back					
Depreciation allowance	2,400	2,400	2,400	2,400	2,400
Minus					
Mortgage principal payments	3,118	3,328	3,557	3,806	4,077
Cash flow—gross	$ 4,619	$ 5,345	$ 5,957	$ 6,206	$ 6,477
Minus					
Income taxes paid	0	0	82	372	679
Cash flow spendable	$ 4,619	$ 5,345	$ 5,875	$ 5,834	$ 5,798
Financial Status					
Market value of property					
Minus:					
Balance due on mortgage	$ 72,413	$ 69,598	$ 66,533	$ 63,198	$ 59,568
Minus:					
Current equity	$ 32,587	$ 40,652	$ 49,230	$ 58,353	$ 68,060
Financial Gain	$ 7,587	$ 15,652	$ 24,230	$ 38,196	$ 34,568
Ratio analysis					
Net income/market value	6.90%	6.85%	6.80%	6.75%	6.69%
Net income/current equity	22.23%	18.57%	15.98%	14.05%	12.55%

Recheck using the gross income multiplier

Gross effective income $14,100 × market multiplier 7.5 = $105,750

Vacancy and Collection Losses

This is an error or "fudge" factor. Plan to keep your rents at the highest possible levels, but circumstances may keep you from earning all you have anticipated. For example, a tenant leaves and you spend one or two weeks cleaning the apartment before renting it again; then, because you want a very desirable tenant to stay, you may grant some minor rental concessions. You can estimate such amounts by talking to neighborhood investors or simply by using a percentage, such as 5 percent, initially and then adjusting it later as you gain experience in operating apartment properties.

In estimating expenditure amounts, follow the principle of charging an "average" annual amount you believe you can achieve using competent management practices.

In trying to decide what amounts to include for expenditures, follow the basic principle that you want to expend enough to be able to maintain the gross rents you have scheduled. You do not want to charge more because you would have to increase rents. You do not want to charge less because you cannot then maintain proper service levels—and you can thus lose tenants.

Expenses

Referring again to Exhibit 4-1, here are some suggestions on how to estimate amounts to include in expenses:

Janitor—Include a charge even if you plan to do the work. Sometimes a janitor is given a free apartment. Even so, include the value of the apartment as an expense.

Gardener—This is the same type of expense as the janitor expense and should be treated in the same way.

Social Security Payroll Taxes—When you hire others, there may be taxes even if they are "independent contractors." Be sure to consult with appropriate state and Federal agencies about this matter.

Utilities—These are utilities relating only to public areas. Tenants should be charged for their own utilities; preferably, each apartment should have separate meters.

Maintenance—These costs include both labor and materials. Usually you should expect to have others to do this work. Even if you do some of the work yourself, you should include a charge for your services.

Advertising—Include any form of advertising costs: classified advertising, letters, signs, etc.

Fees—Some local jurisdictions charge special fees or require licenses. You should investigate.

Management—Sometimes tenants are given reduced rents to serve as resident managers to collect rents, receive complaints, handle service or maintenance problems. These reductions should be included as costs. A good real estate investment should earn enough for you to have professional managers who will handle all problems connected with setting rents and paying expenses.

Reserves

Since you want to estimate average annual amounts necessary to achieve the level of incomes you have forecasted, you would not want to charge some large expenditures to a single year's income. For example, you paint the exterior of the building only about every five years, and you therefore amortize this expenditure over five years to obtain an average annual cost. Furnishings, such as stoves, refrigerators, other kinds of mechanical equipment have to be replaced about every ten years; so you would charge one-tenth of the costs every year. Draperies, rugs, furniture have lives as short as five years. Make an inventory of such possible expenditures and convert them to annual amounts.

Fixed Expenses

Although previous years' bills help you estimate what property taxes, insurance, and license costs have been in the past, be sure to check with government officials and insurance brokers to determine whether increases in these amounts may be anticipated. Given the inflationary pressures seemingly basic to our economy, you should almost always anticipate increases in these amounts.

After deducting all expenses, you have an estimated net income which represents the earnings of that property under average investor's conditions, since you have estimated these amounts by using average amounts typical for such properties. This net income can be called "market" or "economic" net income because it represents what a typical investor should be able to earn. It is the "target" you want to aim for as you use the property for your investment purposes.

You then can consider how much money you can borrow to finance the property's purchase, since you want the property to pay for itself if possible. Obtain various loan commitments to determine how each will add to the costs of owning the property. Remember, by using a maximum amount of loan money, you increase the potentials for higher rates of return on the money you invest.

CONVERTING PROPERTY INCOME TO AN INVESTMENT VALUE

When you invest in real estate you hope to make a "profit" by (1) receiving a net income from the property, that is, earning on your investment (net income is gross income minus the expenses of earning the income but not including any costs of financing), and (2) receiving an amount from the sale of the property that is greater than what you have invested (capital gain).

There will be two basic occasions when you will have to estimate your profit potentials: (1) when you have been invested for some time and you wish to estimate what your total investment might be, and (2) when you can buy the rights to receive income and a capital gain at some future date.

There are mathematical means of estimating the value of your investment in varieties of situations that fit into these classes:

1. A single amount invested in the past (perhaps land) on which you want to earn interest so you want to know what to ask for the property (compound amount of one, Exhibit B).
2. When you invest in a property now and hope that it will increase in value at a minimum rate of interest until you decide to sell at some future date (compound amount of one, Exhibit B).
3. When you have been spending money on an investment and you wish to recover all that you have spent plus interest on what you have spent and you wish to know what your total value invested may equal (compound amount of one per period, Exhibit C).
4. When you can buy the right to receive income from a property and you wish to know what to pay (present value of one per period, Exhibit E).
5. When you can buy the right to full ownership to a property but the right cannot be exercised until a given number of years in the future (present value of one, Exhibit D).
6. When you wish to estimate your annual mortgage payment when borrowing to invest (mortgage payment installment to amortize 1, Exhibit G).
7. When you wish to estimate how much to deposit periodically at a given rate

of interest for a number of years so that the total will equal a particular amount (sinking fund, exhibit F).

Key Decisions on Your Part

Before you can estimate the value of a past or potential real estate investment you must make two key decisions:

1. What interest rate do you wish to earn on your investment? (This is expressed as a percentage.)
2. How long you wish to hold your investment. (This is the earning period.)

The age of the property should always be considered in estimating the investment period. Clearly, you cannot earn income if the building is too old or no longer usable. You may not want to stay invested during the entire potential earning life of the property but only during the period when you can earn the net income you have been considering.

Typically, a real estate investor seeking maximum earning potential and capital gains will stay invested eight to fifteen years. If you are seeking long-term capital gains and less income, the period may be twenty to twenty-five years. For most purposes the investment period should be longer than twenty years. Always remember the life cycle of real estate markets and properties and let them influence you in deciding how long to stay invested.

Investors commonly decide what their rates of return should be by using a buildup method illustrated in Exhibit 4-1. In this method you:

1. Select the financing terms you wish and then multiply the mortgage rate by a percentage that represents the relationships between the loan amount and the purchase price:
   Purchase price $100,000
   Loan amount $80,000
   Loan/purchase price ratio..............80,000/100,000 = .80 or 80%
   Mortgage loan interest rate ......08 or 8%
   Impact of financing
   on earning rate................ .08 × .80 or .064 or 6.4% new rate
2. Determine your equity. In this case it is $20,000 or 20 percent of the purchase price if you borrow no other money. You decide that you wish to earn 25 percent on your equity; the impact of your equity decision on the capitalization rate equals:
   $$.20 \times .25 = .05 \text{ or } 5\%$$

3. The capitalization rate will be .064 + .05 = .114 or 11.4%.

Let's say that, after determining your capitalization rate, you find a property and estimate that the net market or economic rent would be $10,000 annually; let's assume further that you wish to stay invested for twenty years. You might calculate the investment value of the property in any of these ways:

1. $10,000 net income divided by 11.4 percent equals $87,719, the value to you now of receiving that income stream for an unspecified time. (Of course, when you finally sell the property you will receive an amount which must also be considered, but we will discuss that later.)

2. Your initial investment in the property is $20,000, for which you receive $10,000 net income. Your return on investment is 50 percent.

3. The net income is $10,000. You borrow $80,000 on which you must pay interest in the first year of $6,400 ($80,000 × .08 interest). Then: $10,000 − $6,400 = $3,600, or 18 percent on your original down payment after letting the property pay for the financing. (This does not include the principal payment.)

4. With a net income of $10,000, you borrow $80,000 at 8 percent interest to be repaid in 25 years so that your annual mortgage payment is $7,409. Your net income is $2,590 after the property income pays all the costs of the loan. The earning rate on your equity ($20,000) is 12.8 percent.

5. The net income is $10,000. The Federal income tax law allows you to deduct an annual depreciation amount based on the remaining life and current value of the building and the furnishings in the building. These deductions do not represent actual cash payments, but only deductions allowed by current Federal income tax law. The deductions are expressed as a percentage of value.

   Assume that the building you purchase has a value of $75,000 for tax purposes, and you are allowed a 2-percent deduction annually or $1,500. The furnishings are estimated to have a value of $8,000, and you are allowed an 8-percent deduction on their value or $640. (Federal income tax law is discussed in depth in Chapter 7.)

   For tax purposes, your net income is $10,000 minus the mortgage interest ($6,400), building depreciation ($1,500), furnishings depreciation ($640): $10,000 − $8,540 = $1,460 income on which taxes are due. If you did not have a real estate investment, you would have paid on $10,000 income; if you were in a 50-percent income tax bracket, you would pay $5,000 in taxes. As it is, you pay only $1,460 × .50, or $730. You have received a total of $8,540 in earned, tax-sheltered income.

At this point you can see that the value of a real estate investment can be estimated in many ways, depending on your personal goals and financial situation.

Measures of Investment Value

In Exhibit 4-1 (section 9) there are four methods suggested for estimating the value of this investment.

1. *Prior to mortgage:*

Land value (obtained from the market survey)	$25,000
Value of the income stream (building value)	+87,719
Value of the investment	$112,719

2. *After financing*:

Land value (obtained from the market survey)	$25,000
Income stream value minus the mortgage $2,590/11.4%	22,719
Principal payments on mortgage (loan amount)	+80,000
Value of the investment	$127,719

3. *Using a gross multiplier*: From a survey of comparable properties, you determine:

Average sale price	$110,000
Average gross collected income	÷ 16,000
Multiplier ($110,000 ÷ $16,000)	6.88
Estimated gross collected rents	$ 17,000
Estimated investment value	
($17,000 × 6.88)	$116,875 (or $117,000)

4. *Other value estimate comparisons using rates of return:*

a. Economic return	$ 10,000
Estimated purchase price	117,000
Investment value ($10,000	
÷ $117,000)	9.4%
b. Annual economic return	$ 10,000
Down payment	20,000
Investment value ($10,000	
÷ $20,000)	50%
c. Return after taxes (including	
tax-sheltered income)	$ 8,540
Equity	20,000
Investment value ($8,540	
÷ $20,000)	43%*

*Plus the value of other income you did not have to pay taxes on because of the tax shelter in the real estate.

On a practical basis you can expect to pay the market price, which your survey has shown to be $117,000. This means that you earn an overall rate of 14.53% (1.0000 divided by 6.88, the multiplier). You might now wish to recalculate some of your estimates using the procedures just outlined to sharpen your estimates. To help you review the process, refer again to Exhibits 4-2a and 4.2b.

In Exhibit 4-2 the assumption is that you stay invested for only five years and that continued inflation will increase the market value of the property and the costs of operating it. Checking the investment value using a gross multiplier indicated that the market value should be approximately $100,000 (gross rent $15,000 x a multiplier of 7).

There are several ways of estimating an appropriate earning rate. This rate, also called a capitalization rate when used to convert anticipated future lump sums or income streams to present value, can be developed by:

Other Ways to Develop Capitalization Rates

Band of Investment

Percent of purchase price represented by equity .20 × earning rate .08	.016
Percent of purchase price represented by first mortgage .70 × interest rate .09	.063
Percent of purchase price represented by second mortgage .10 × interest rate .12	.012
Total capitalization rate (9.1%)	.091

Market Method. The market rate is calculated by dividing the net income earnings from a given type of property by the sales price of the property.

Net income from property A (land only), $1,000; value of land, $10,000—
$1,000/$10,000 equals an interest or capitalization rate of .10

Net income from property B (land only), $2,200; value of land, $22,000—
$2,200/$22,000 equals capitalization rate of .10

Net income from property C (land only), $1,700; value of land, $17,000—
$1,700/$17,000 equals a capitalization rate of .10

Conclusion: The rate at which income from unimproved land should be capitalized is .10 or 10%.

Buildup Method. In this method you start with the earning rate from long-term minimum risk investments, such as long-term government bonds, and add additional percentages for various kinds of risks: The amounts reflecting the investor's opinion of the influence of these risks on the value of the investment. For example:

Earning rate of long-term government bonds.	.0875
Liquidity	.0115
Quality of income	.0152
Durability and quantity of the income	.0175
Capitalization rate	.1317 or 13.17%

The Overall Rate. This rate for a real estate investment is the average rate of interest and recovery for the building and the land. For example:

Capitalization rate of building is .15 in which building equals .60 of the investment.
Earning rate on the land is   .10 in which land equals   .40 of the investment.

Capitalization rate = $(.15 \times .60) + (.10 \times .40) = .13$, or 13%

Estimating Value Without Using Tables

The exhibits may scare you into believing that you could never make the kinds of calculations included in those tables. However, before you decide you cannot do this, take a few moments to review what some investors do. They use a method of estimating the value of a potential income stream from an investment by using a direct capitalization method. In other words, the only investment calculation they bother with is the one in which they estimate the value of an investment according to the net income stream that they estimate will be earned by the property during the period of desired investment. The method is called "direct capitalization." Examine the methodology that follows; you will find it quite simple.

Assume that you have an opportunity to invest in a property which is producing an annual net income of $1,000. You decide that the property will earn this amount for five years. You wish to estimate how much to pay now. These are the steps to follow:

1. Your desired earning rate . . . . .10%(.10)
2. Period of investment . . . . .5 years
3. Annual recovery rate* . . . .$^1/_5$ — .20
4. Net income $1,000
5. Value of the investment . . . .$1,000/.30 = $3,333.33

*In real estate you expect the income to pay you interest (earning on your investment) and to help you pay for the recovery of the original investment. This is an assumption many conservative investors make because they assume that some portion of their investments (usually the buildings) will either cease earning income after the investment period or will require heavy investments for modernization and rehabilitation at the end of the investment period.

To understand how this calculation works look at Exhibit A.

Exhibit A—Direct Capitalization Example

Interest rate (earning rate): 10% (.10) Investment period: 5 years
Recovery rate: ($^1/_5$ years) 20% (.20) Capitalization rate: 10%+20%=30%(.30)
Net income (annual): $1,000
Investment value: $1,000/30 = $3,333.33
Proof of calculation:

End of year	Net income	Earning	Recovery
1	$1,000	$ 333.33	$ 666.67
2	1,000	333.33	666.67
3	1,000	333.33	666.67
4	1,000	333.33	666.67
5	1,000	333.33	666.67
TOTALS	$5,000	$1,666.65	$3,333.35

Determining the Total Capitalization Rate

The relationships between value, net income stream, and return on and of investment are expressed in the formula:

$$V = \frac{I}{F}$$

where: V = value to be estimated.
I = net income to be capitalized,
F = capitalization factor.

In the *direct* capitalization method, the capitalization factor *(F)* is expressed by the result of dividing the number one by the sum of the interest earning rate and the annual recovery rate. It can also be expressed as a percentage rate that is multiplied by the net income. In all other capitalization methods, the figure for F is obtained from a table and multiplied by the net income stream.

Examples.   The following cases involve direct capitalization only, but they indicate how basic relationships between value, net income, and the capitalization factor can be determined by our formula:

1. You plan to invest in a property that will earn $1,000 annually; you also plan an investment period of twenty-five years, and expect a rate of return of 6

percent. The return of investment must be 4 percent $(1.0 \div 25 \text{ years} - .04)$. What is the value of the property (V)? Using the simple direct capitalization method:

$$V = \frac{I}{F}$$

$$V = \frac{\$1,000}{.10} \quad (.10 = .06 + .04)$$

$$V = \$10,000$$

The value of the property should not be more than $10,000.

2. A property has a value of $10,000 and an annual net income of $1,000. What is the capitalization rate and what is the capitalization factor? To find the rate:

$$R = \frac{I}{V}$$

$$R = \frac{\$1,000}{\$10,000}$$

$$R = .10 \quad (\text{or } 10\%)$$

To find the factor:

$$F = \frac{I}{V}$$

$$F = \frac{\$10,000}{\$1,000}$$

$$F = 10$$

3. A property has an annual value of $10,000, a capitalization rate of .10, and a capitalization factor of 10. What is the net income?

$$I = F \times V$$

$$I = .10 \times \$10,000$$

$$I = \$1,000$$

or,

$$I = \frac{V}{R}$$

$$I = \frac{\$10,000}{10}$$

$$I = \$1,000$$

Exhibits 4-3a and 4-3b provide examples of how to use a direct method of capitalization and a capitalization rate that includes both return of and return on capital to estimate the value of a property. (Exhibit 4-3b contains the answers to the problems in Exhibit 4-3a; to keep you "honest" until you have had a chance to work on the problems, the answers are placed at the end of this chapter.) This method is used widely because it is easy to understand and produces a very conservative estimate of the value of an investment property.

Example. You wish to buy a property earning $10,000 a year and you determine that the land has a value of $50,000. You also determine that a proper earning rate would be 8 percent and that the building will have a life of 25 years. Since you don't know the value of the building, you want to estimate the total property value—land *and* building. Your total capitalization rate would be calculated as follows:

Capitalization factor (1.0 ÷ 25 years)	.04 (4%)
Capitalization rate	.08 (8%)
Total capitalization rate	.12 (12%)

The value of the property is then calculated:

Income earned by land ($50,000 × .08)	$4,000
Income earned by building ($10,000 − $4,000)	6,000

Using your total capitalization rate, you then calculate the value of the building:

$$V = \frac{I}{F}$$

$$V = \frac{\$6,000}{.12}$$

$$V = \$50,000$$

All you have to do now is add the value of the building, calculated at $50,000, to the value of the property ($50,000) for a total property value of $100,000.

Now try working with some of the practice exercises in Exhibit 4-3 before going on to the following example.

Example. An investor wishes to earn 8 percent on his investments; he plans to stay invested for fifty years.

Exhibit 4-3a Straight-Line Capitalization Problems

Problems:
1. What would be the capitalization rate in each of the following instances, assuming 8% return on investment and the indicated number of years for recovery of investment?

_____ 10 years _____ 15 years _____ 33 years _____ 40 years

2. In each of the following, indicate the dollar amounts to be allocated to return of capital and return on capital in the first year assuming an overall rate as given and an economic life of 25 years:

| | | | amounts to |
Return on	Return of	Net income	Capitalization over-all rate
_____	_____	$ 1,000	12%
_____	_____	$10,000	16%
_____	_____	$15,000	10%

3. The basic formula for capitalizing is $V = I \div F$.

Where:
V = value to be estimated,
I = net income to be capitalized,
F = capitalization factor, determined by the capitalization rate and the length of the investment period.

Supply the missing item in each of the following problems:

V	=	I	÷	F
$10,000		$ 250		_____
_____		$1,000		20 years and 8% return on investment
$120,000		_____		50 years and 9% return on investment

4. By what percentage could the net income decline each year in the following examples and still permit a continued earning of the same rate on the remaining capital?

_____ 8% return on investment, economic life of 25 years

_____ 9% return on investment, economic life of 40 years

_____10% return on investment, economic life of 50 years

5. What would be the rate of return on the last year's equity in each of the following examples, assuming no decline in net income?

	Net income	Return on	Return of
_____	$ 1,000	6%	25 years
_____	$26,000	8%	40 years
_____	$10,200	9%	20 years

(Answers are in Exhibit 4-3a, at the end of this chapter.)

1. He can buy vacant, unimproved land used for parking purposes that returns an annual income of $1,500 net annually. What is the value of the land based on the earning stream and an 8 percent interest rate?
   Answer: $1,500/.08 equals $18,750

2. He can buy a property with an apartment house on it that produces a net annual income of $5,500. The land has an estimated value of $20,000. What is the value of the total property?
   Answer: Land value $20,000 × .08 equals $1,600 earnings by the land. Total net income of $5,500 minus $1,600 equals $3,900. Capitalization rate is interest rate .08 plus recovery rate of .02 (assuming a 50-year investment period). $3,900/(.08 plus .02) equals $39,000.

Many investment analysts feel that the direct method of capitalization, which we have discussed so far, is not the method to use in estimating real estate investment values. Instead they believe that income should be treated in the same manner as is income from other forms of investment through the use of discount tables. A discount table assumes that if you are planning to receive a stream or a lump sum of money benefits sometime in the future but wish to buy them now, their represented values should be less than their future value. If I wished to borrow $100 from you now and promised to repay it in one year, you would want me to return not only the the $100 but interest on that $100. If the current interest rate were 8 percent, you would expect to receive $108 one year from now. In other words, by investing $100 (a loan to me) now, you expect to receive more than $100—$108—when I repay the loan. The purpose of the discount tables is to help you calculate easily the present value of income streams or lump-sum monies to be received at a known time in the future.

The following illustrations should help you appreciate how valuable these tables can be in estimating real estate investment values. The formulas used in these calculations are included on page 118-119.

Example 1 I can purchase a property now for $100,000 and sell it in ten years at $250,000. Since I expect to earn 9.5 percent on any money I invest, should I undertake this investment?
The solution:

a. $100,000 × compound amount of one, or 2.47822 = $247,822. Yes, undertake the investment. Or

b. $250,000 × present value of a lump sum for 10 years .403514 = $100,878.50

Example 2. I can purchase a property that will produce an annual net income of $10,000 for the next fifteen years. If I wish to earn 11 percent on my investment, what should I pay now for the right to receive this income?

The solution: $10,000 × present value of one year for 15 years, or $7.19087 = $71,908.70.

Example 3. I purchased a property five years ago for $100,000. I wish to sell it today at a price that will pay me 7.5 percent annually for holding the investment. What price should I ask?

The solution: $100,000 × compound amount of one per year for five years or 1.435269 or $143,526.90.

Example 4. The property I purchased five years ago has required me to pay $2,000 annually in taxes. I wish to recover these payments and receive an 8.5 percent return on them. How much more should I add to the price?

The solution: ($2,000 × compound amount of one per year or 5.925373 = $11,850.15)

Solving these problems requires the use of basic capitalization tables or a calculator that permits using the equations on which the tables are based. In this chapter we will discuss the basic tables—how they are developed and how they are used effectively in almost any kind of real estate investment problem. Samples of the tables are also provided. You must understand how to use these tables.

Using Tables and Formulas to Estimate Investment Values

If you rely on the direct method of capitalization, you will be able to estimate only the simplest form of real estate investment, that which relates to the net income earned by a property. The other investment situations mentioned earlier can be estimated only if you learn a little some thing about the tables. These tables are based on the simpler kinds of arithmetic you might have learned in high school, or even in the lower grades. In some schools it is called business mathematics. The entire system is based on the simple assumption that if you have invested money you should earn interest on it (compounding). In other words, if you invested $1 a year ago and wish to earn 10% on your investment, you would expect to receive $1.10 today. This is similar to what happens when you make a deposit in a savings account. On the other hand if you paid $1 today for the right to receive an income of $1 one year from now, and you wish to earn 10% on your investment, you would pay only 90¢ (10% of one dollar is ten cents). This is called discounting. This is all very abstract, so some examples will help you understand the tables and how to use them, or even to prepare your own.

Compound Amount of One (Exhibit B)

This table helps you to estimate how much you have already invested or what your single sum investment may equal in the future. For example, suppose that you had purchased a lot for $1,000 five years ago. You wish to earn 10% on your investment during the investment or holding period. You have an opportunity to sell today but you must set the price.

To estimate your investment do the following: (See Exhibit B)

1. Original investment $1,000
2. Earning rate desired   10% (.10)
3. Investment period   5 years
4. Factor to determine value   1.6105
5. Price you should charge today $1,000 × 1.6105 = $1,610.50

Exhibit B   Compound Tables: Compound Amount of One

Interest rate (earning rate): 10% (.10) Investment period: 5 years
Net income (annual): $1,000 (one payment at end of first year)
Investment value: $1,000 × 1.6105 = $1,610.50
Proof of calculation:

End of year	Initial investment	Earning on	Accumulated value
1	$1,000	$100	$1,100
2		110	1,210
3		121	1,331
4		133.10	1,464.10
5		146.40	1,610.50

This table can also be used if you were thinking about paying $1,000 for a property today and planned to sell it in five years. If you wished to earn 10% per year, you would have to have an increase in property value to $1,610.50.

The Rule of 72

If you wished to earn 10% on an investment and were wondering how long you would have to hold the investment for the compounded rate of 10% to double the value of the investment, divide 10 into 72. This would indicate that the investment would double in 7.2 years. For any single amount invested, if you know the interest rate you wish to earn, you can estimate how many years it will take your investment to double. Simply divide 72 by the interest rate.

Compound Amount of One Per Period (Exhibit C)

Suppose that you had purchased the lot for $1,000 five years ago. Also suppose that for each of the five years you had to pay taxes on the property. For the sake of the example, assume that the taxes were $1,000 a year. How much more would you have to charge for the property in order to recover all the taxes you paid and also to pay yourself 10% on those amounts? This is how you would estimate your total:

1. Your desired earning rate   10% (.10)
2. Periods during which taxes were paid   5 years
3. Amounts paid annually in taxes $1,000
4. Total invested $1,000 × 6.1051 = $6,105.10

Exhibit C   Compound Tables: Compound Amount of One Per Year

Interest rate (earning rate): 10% (.10) Investment period: 5 years
Net income (annual): $1,000 (received at end of each year for 5 years)
Investment value: $1,000 × 6.1051 = $6,105.10

End of year	Annual payment (income)	Earning on	Accumulated value (end of year)
1	$1,000	$ 0	$1,000
2	1,000	100	2,100
3	1,000	210	2,310
4	1,000	331	3,641
5	1,000	464.10	6,105.10
TOTALS	$5,000 +	$1,105.10 =	$6,105.10

Present Value of One (Exhibit D)

In the next investment situation assume that you can buy a property now which someone else guarantees to buy for a fixed price at a later date. You wish to estimate how much to pay for the property now.

1. Your desired earning rate   10%(.10)
2. Your investment period   5 years
3. Amount to be received at end of five years $1,000
4. Present value of the investment $1,000 × .6209 = $620.90

Exhibit D   Discount Tables: Present Value of One (A single sum)

Interest rate (earning rate): 10%(.10) Investment period: 5 years
Net income (annual): $1,000 (received at start of first year)
Investment value: $1,000 × .6209 = $620.92

End of year	Earning On	Original investment $620.92	Accumulated investment
1	$62.09		$ 683.01
2	68.30		751.31
3	75.13		826.44
4	82.64		909.09
5	90.91		1,000.00
TOTALS	$379.07	+ $620.92 =	$ 999.99
			(or $1,000, error due to rounding)

Present Value of One Per Period (Exhibit E)

Suppose that in addition to the assurance of the repurchase of the property for $1,000 in five years you were also assured that you would receive an annual net income of $1,000. What should you pay now for the right to receive that income for five years?

1. Your desired earning rate   10%(.10)
2. Your investment period   5 years
3. Amount to be received annually (net income) $1,000
4. Present value of the income stream $1,000 × 3.7908 = $3,790.80

Exhibit E   Discount Tables: Present Value of One Per Period

Interest rate (earning rate): 10%(.10) Investment period: 5 years
Net income (annual): $1,000 (received at start of first year)
Investment value: $1,000 × 3.7908 = $3,790.80 (invested at start of year one)

End of year	Income received	Earning on	Recovery of	Unrecovered investment $3,790.80
1	$1,000	$ 379.08	$ 620.92	3,169.88
2	1,000	316.99	683.01	2,486.87
3	1,000	248.69	751.31	1,735.55
4	1,000	173.56	826.44	909.11
5	1,000	90.91	909.09	.02
				(due to rounding)
	$5,000 =	$1,209.23 +	$3,090.77	

Sinking Fund (Exhibit F)

Suppose that as you receive the $1,000 at the end of each of five years you wish to set some of it aside so that you will have $1,000 at the end of the five years. Also assume that you would want the deposited money to earn 10%. What amount should you deposit each year?

1. Your desired earning rate   10%
2. Your investment period   5 years
3. Amount you wish to have at the end of fifth year $1,000
4. Annual required investment $1,000 × .1638 = $163.80

Exhibit F   Discount Tables: Sinking Fund (Periodic investment to equal a desired amount)

Interest rate (earning rate): 10%(.10) Investment period: 5 years
Amount to be recovered through periodic investments: $1,000
Annual deposit required to equal the amount to be recovered: $1,000 × .1638 = $163.80

Year	Start of year total	Earning on acc. invest.	Deposit End of year	End of year total
1	0	0	$163.80	$163.80
2	$163.80	$16.38	163.80	343.98
3	343.98	34.40	163.80	542.18
4	542.18	54.22	163.80	760.20
5	760.20	76.02	163.80	1,000.02*

*2¢ extra because of rounding.

Estimating Mortgage Payment (Exhibit G)

One final table and then you will have an opportunity to see how to use all the tables in various types of income-producing real estate investments. Almost all real estate investments will have to be made with the use of some borrowed money, using a mortgage instrument. When you borrow the total amount, you repay each period (either monthly or annually in most cases) a fixed amount, part of which represents repayment of the amount you borrowed and part of which represents payment of interest to the lender for the money borrowed. Your periodic payment would be calculated as follows:

1. Mortgage interest   10%
2. Length of the loan   5 years
3. Amount borrowed $1,000
4. Periodic loan payment $1,000 × .26380* = $263.80

Exhibit G   Compound Tables: Mortgage Payments

Interest rate (earning rate): 10%(.10) Earning period: 5 years loan period)
Loan Amount: $1,000
Annual payment: $1,000 × .263.80 = $263.80

	Payment	To Interest	To principal	Loan unpaid
Start of year 1				$1,000
End of year 1	$263.80	$100	$163.80	836.20
2	263.80	83.62	180.18	656.02
3	263.80	65.60	198.20	457.82
4	263.80	45.78	218.02	239.80
5	263.80	23.98	239.82*	0
TOTALS	$1,319.00	= $318.98	$1,000.02	

*2¢ over because of rounding

Sample tables for estimating the values of income producing properties are provided in the Appendix. For the following examples only the amounts and tables presented so far will be used.

Example A: You purchased a lot 5 years ago for $1,000.
       You pay taxes each year of $1,000
       Your earning rate is 10%

*This is known as a mortgage constant. It is the average percentage of principal and interest which you are repaying each year. The percentage is calculated on the remaining unpaid principal.

Your total investment to date is:

$1,000 × 1.6105 (Exhibit B) = 1,610.50 (original
purchase price)
$1,000 × 6.1051 = 6,105.10 (taxes annually)
$7,715.60 (total investment)

Example B: You are very conservative and wish to calculate the value of
the investment where you will receive $1,000 each year and then
have the chance to sell the property for $1,000 at the end of five years.
Present value of $1,000 is
$1,000/(.10 + .20)
(exhibit A) = $3,333.33 (value of income)
Present value of $1,000
to be received in five years = 620.92 (Exhibit D)
Value of the investment $3,954.25

Using the Mortgage Constant for Investment Planning

In some real estate markets investors expect the property to pay the
entire costs of any financing. In fact, they plan the investment so that the
net operating income (which has been used in the chapter to estimate
property value) pays all the mortgage costs—principal and interest. They
reason that the mortgage payment on principal represents an increase in
equity that is being paid entirely from the investment. They also hope that
there will be an increase in the price (or value) when they sell.

In this form of investment analysis the procedure is:

1. Net operating income = $1,000
2. Property price = $8,950
3. Mortgage constant = 1,000 divided by 8,950 = .1117
4. Review the annual mortgage payment tables to find all constants equal to
.1117. You will find that the constant .1117 represents the following kinds
of loan terms:
8% loan between 16 and 17 years (constants range—.1096 to 1129)
8.5% 17 to 18 years (.1104–.1133)
9.0% 19 years (.1117)
9.5% 20-21 years (.1134–.1115)

Knowing this, the investor can bargain for different loans within the
limits indicated by this review.
On the other hand the investor might have been given a constant of

.1117 as the one the lender would allow. By dividing \$1,000 by .1117 the investor knows that he cannot afford to pay more than \$8,950 for the property.

Developing Your Own Investment Capitalization Tables

Although some tables are provided in the Appendix you will find that they are often not right for the investment calculation you are making. The formulas used to prepare the tables are quite simple and can be used easily if you have a hand calculator. In fact, you will find that many of the less expensive hand calculators already have programs in them that include all these tables. Some of the calculators are especially manufactured for real estate investment analysis; look for them.

If you have an inexpensive calculator that permits addition, subtraction, multiplication, division, and raising to a power, you have all that you need. In the next few paragraphs you will be guided in using these calculators to prepare any of the tables already mentioned.

Compound Tables (Compound amount of one and one per period)

Definitions: ERNR—earning rate, expressed as a percent
         INVP—period for holding the investment, investment period
         *—raise to a power. Multiplying a number by itself, for example—3^3 is three to the third power or $3 \times 3 \times 3 = 27$
         $4^4 = 4 \times 4 \times 4 \times 4 = 1024$

A. Compound Amount of One (CPO)

    CPO = $(1 + \text{ERNR})^{*\text{INVP}}$

    ERNR (earning rate) = 10% or .10 INVP (investment period = 5 years

    CPO = $(1 + .10)^5 = 1.10 \times 1.10 \times 1.10 \times 1.10 \times 1.10 = 1.610$

    Invested amount = \$1,000, rate = 10%, period = 5 years, value = \$1,000 $\times$ 1.610 = \$1,610.

B. Compound Amount of One Per Period (CPA) (one per period is also called annuity)

    CPA = $([(1 + \text{ERNR})^{*\text{INVP}}] - 1)$ divided by ERNR

  Example: ERNR = 10%, INVP = 5 years

        (a) $1 + .10 = 1.10$

        (b) $(1.10)^5 = 1.61$

(c) $1.61 - 1 = .61$
(d) $.61$ divided by $.10 = 6.1000$
Invested amount annually $= \$1,000$, ERNR $= 10\%$, INVP $= 5$ years
Investment value $= \$1,000 \times 6.1000 = \$6,100$

Present Value Tables (Present value of one or one per period)

A. Present value of one PVO
   PVO $= 1$ divided by $(1 + \text{ERNR})^{*\text{INVP}}$
   ERNR $= 10\% (.10)$ INVP $= 5$ years
   (a) $1 + .10 = 1.10$
   (b) $(1.10)^5 = 1.61$
   (c) 1 divided by $1.61 = .6211$
   Amount to be received in five years $= \$1,000$
   Present value of this amount is $\$1,000 \times .6211 = \$621.10$
B. Present value of one per year PVA
   PVA $= (1 + \text{ERNR})^{*\text{INVP}} - 1$ divided by $(1 + \text{ERNR})^{*\text{INVP}}$ multiplied by ERNR
       $(1 + .10)^5 - 1$ divided by $(1 + .10)^5$ multiplied by $.10$
   ERNR $= 10\% (.10)$ INVP $= 5$ years
   (a) $(1 + .10)^5 = 1.6105$
   (b) $1.6105 - 1 = .6105$
   (c) 1.6105 multiplied by $.10 = .1611$
   (d) $.6105$ divided by $.1611 = 3.7896$
   Annual income to be received $- \$1,000$ for five years
   Present value of the income $\$1,000 \times 3.7896 = \$3,789.60$

Mortgage Payment Table

The mortgage payment table can be developed by dividing one by the amount derived from the present value of one per year table.
For example:
Amount borrowed $\$1,000$. Length of loan 5 years. Interest rate 10%
PVA 5 years, 10% equals 3.7896
Mortgage payment $= 1$ divided by 3.7896 or $.263880$
Annual mortgage payment equals $\$1,000 \times .26388$ or $\$263.88$

Mortgage loans are usually arranged through the use of monthly payments. You can estimate the monthly payment by dividing the annual figure by 12. For example the annual mortgage payment was estimated at $\$263.88$. The monthly payment would be approximately $\$263.88$ divided by 12 or $21.99. However, if you wish to be more precise you may use the tables which show the monthly amounts. For example, 10% annually is .883% monthly and five years equal 60 monthly periods. Using the column instalment to amortize $160 months the monthly payment is $21.25 ($1000 × .021247) and $21.25 × 12 is $254.96 the annual payment. The difference between the two annual payments occurs because the monthly calculations are compounded on a monthly basis so that the effective interest rate is slightly higher than the nominal 10 per cent in the contract.

Sinking Fund Table

The sinking fund table can be developed by dividing one by the amount derived from the compound amount of one (the accumulation of one per period) per period.

For example: Amount to be recovered at end of five years $1,000, at 10% interest

CPA for 10% five years = 6.10510, one divided by 6.10510 = .163797

Amount to be deposited annually $1,000 × .163797 = $183.80

END RUNS IN THE INVESTMENT ANALYSIS GAME

Experienced real estate investors develop short-cut, "rule-of-thumb" means of making quick estimates of value. Later these estimates are refined and checked by using the more complex methods to be discussed. Great care must be used in selecting widely comparable properties—age, size, income, expenses, and so on.

Gross Multipliers

Value is estimated by searching the market place for similar type properties and finding the relationship between gross scheduled income and sales price.

Property	Sales Price	Gross Income	Price/Income Ratio
A	$ 300,000	$ 37,500	8.0
B	360,000	46,200	7.8
C	295,000	37,300	7.9

D	325,000	40,600	8.0
E	350,000	42,000	8.1
	$1,620,000 ÷	$203,600 =	7.96 or 8.0 GM

Gross income of property being studied $43,500

$$\times \quad 8$$

Estimated market value $348,000

Overall Rate

You develop the following market information:

Property	Sales Price	Adjusted Net Income*	Income/Price
A	$ 300,000	$ 21,000	.07
B	360,000	25,200	.07
C	295,000	20,100	.068
D	325,000	21,200	.065
E	340,000	24,500	.072
	$1,620,000	$112,000	.07

*Reflects typical actual cash outlays exclusive of financing.

Adjusted net income of property being studied $23,400

Overall average rate .07

Estimated investment value $23,400/.07 $348,000

Broker's Net

Only property taxes (2.5 percent), insurance, and minimum mainte-nance costs (2 percent) are subtracted from gross. Usually this shows the highest earning potential.

Property	Sales Price	Adjusted Net Income	Income/Price
A	$ 300,000	$ 35,500	12.0%
B	360,000	43,700	12.0%
C	295,000	35,200	11.9%
D	325,000	38,300	11.8%
E	340,000	39,700	11.7%
	$1,620,000	$192,400	11.9% or 12.0%

Property taxes   .025
Insurance   .010
Maintenance   .020
                      _____
                      .055 × Gross = expenses
Broker's net income of property being studied $41,100
Estimated value $41,100/.12 = $342,500
        or
Asking price of property = $345,000
Earning rate from comparable 12%
Required broker's net = ($345,000 × .12) = $41,400

Which Strategy Is Right?

Mathematically, all answers are correct. The one right for your purpose depends on your investment and market expectations. The important assumption underlying all assumptions is that you should use mortgage financing as a means of earning a higher rate of return on your equity. To accomplish this, you must secure financing at an interest rate equal to or less than your desired earning rate. Further, this method assumes that you want to earn the same rate on your equity as your equity increases. Finally, good investment strategy requires that you use net income and capital gains as the measures of your success. The property is only a means of achieving your investment goals, and when your monitoring of the property's investment performance indicates that it is no longer performing according to your expectations, you must look for another investment.

All the tools discussed in this chapter must be related to your basic investment goals, and the tools must be used to develop strategies that will help you reach your goals. Are you conservative? Do you want to minimize your risks? Use high capitalization rates, short periods of investment, and the direct methods of capitalization. Have you found a good property in an excellent location in which the cycle is just moving up? Use lower rates, seek capital gains, use leverage and the discount tables to estimate the value of your investment. Or simply use all possible methods of analyzing the investment potential, array your answers according to amounts, and keep your purchase and goals within the midrange of strategies.

Exhibit 4-3b   ANSWERS

ANSWERS:

1. 10 years = 1.0/10 or .10 + .08 (earning rate)   = .18 capitalization rate
    15 years = 1.0/15 or .07 + .08   = .17
    33 years = 1.0/33 or .033 + .08   = .133
    40 years = 1.0/40 or .025 + .08   = .125

2. Economic life of 25 years equals 1.0/25 or .04 annual recovery rate

Capitalization rate	*Proportion of net income for recovery*	*Dollar amounts of*	
		Return of	*Return on*
.12	.04/.12 = .33 × $1,000	$ 333	$667 ($1,000-333)
.16	.04/.16 = .25 × $10,000	$2500	$7500 ($10,000-2,500)
.10	.04/.10 = .40 × $15,000	$6000	$4000 ($10,000-6,000)

3. I $250/V $10,000 = .025 $\left(F \dfrac{I}{V} = F \right)$

    I $1,000/.13 (1/20 = .05 + .08) F = $7692 V $\left(\dfrac{I}{F} = V \right)$

    $120,000 V × .11(1/50 = .02 + .09) F = $13,200 I (VF = I)

4. .08 × .04(1/25) divided by .08 + .04 = .0267 or 2.67%
    .09 × .025(1/40) divided by .09 + .025 = .0196 or 1.96%
    .10 × .02(1/50) divided by .10 + .02 = .0167 or 1.67%

5. Net income $1,000 divided by .06 + .04 (1/25) = $10,000 value
    $10,000 × .04 = $400 equity returned each year, last year equity is $400
    Income is divided $600 to return on $400 return of. In last year $400 equity earns $600
    return of or $600/400 = 1.50 or 150% return on.
    .025(1/40) plus .08 = .125 capital rate. .025/.125 × $26,000 = $5,200 equity return
    $26,000-5,200 = $20,800/5200 = 4.000 or 400% return on.
    .05(1/20) plus .09 = .4 capital rate. .05/.14 × $10,200 = $3,642 annual equity return
    $10,200-3,642 = $6,357/3,642 = 1.7455 or 176% return on equity.

Checking Your
Game Plan
(Estimating Value)

You have completed your analysis of the expected gross and net income flows from the potential investment property, and you know how much that income stream is worth to you. But is this what you should pay for the property? If you offer less than what sellers will accept, you will never acquire the property. On the other hand, if you could buy vacant land and build a new property for less than what you might pay for an existing property, clearly you would want to build the new property (if you can wait during construction). Only under unusual circumstances would you want to pay for an existing property more than what it would cost to create a new one, or than what a seller would accept.

THE MARKET AND THE "BIGGER FOOL"

In this chapter we will discuss the "bigger fool" theory and the upper limits on purchase prices. In using the bigger fool theory, you let the prices that others are paying for properties guide you in estimating what you will pay; however, you are careful not to be caught in a foolish bidding game in which you let others determine what you will do. Equally important, you will use the opportunities and costs associated with building a new property to set an upper limit on what you will pay for any property.

Since the processes we will discuss are those of a professional appraiser, you might consider hiring an appraiser to do this type of analysis. If you have the time, you will find that you can do a reasonably competent appraisal yourself if you understand what questions to ask and how to use the answers to arrive at a value estimate.

MARKET PRICES

In letting the actions of others guide you in setting a price on your investment choice, you must remember

1. to select properties that closely resemble the one you are interested in.
2. to inquire into the circumstances under which the sales were completed (for example, the price set in a sale by one relative to another, or a sale by someone in financial difficulties, might be suspect),
3. to discover the terms of the sale.

Although many properties similar to yours may be available for comparison, you need use only the three most closely similar to your property with respect to items 1 through 7 in Exhibit 5-1. However, in order to complete the comparisons you must be certain that the comparable properties were actually sold and that you can secure information on down payment, loans, and loan terms. You cannot rely on the statements of sellers who hope to sell as to what they expect to receive for their properties.

Exhibit 5-1 What Should This Property Sell for As Compared to Other Similar Properties in the Neighborhood Which Have Been Sold Recently?

One of the most effective means of deciding how much you should pay for a property is to compare it with others sold recently in the neighborhood. The following checklist indicates the kinds of items most likely to affect the sale price. You can get information about these from persons who have recently purchased or from local real estate offices. There is no way to get an easy answer as to what you should pay even after you have collected all the information. You must decide for yourself what you think you would want to pay after you have seen what other persons have paid.

Exhibit 5-1 (cont.)

Comparison Factor	Home I Am Planning to Buy	A	B	C
Address	_____	_____	_____	_____
1. Lot size (dimensions) (sq. ft.)	_____	_____	_____	_____
2. Bldg. (sq. ft.)	_____	_____	_____	_____
3. Room count (by units) (total rooms) (bedrooms) (baths)	__/__/__	__/__/__	__/__/__	__/__/__
4. Age of property in years	_____	_____	_____	_____
5. Date of sale	_____	_____	_____	_____
6. Costs of repairs (to bring to desired level)	_____	_____	_____	_____
7. Type of architecture	_____	_____	_____	_____
8. Terms of sales Down payment	_____	_____	_____	_____

	1st	2nd	1st	2nd	1st	2nd	1st	2nd
Size of loans	_____	_____	_____	_____	_____	_____	_____	_____
Terms of loans	_____	_____	_____	_____	_____	_____	_____	_____
Interest rate	_____	_____	_____	_____	_____	_____	_____	_____

Comparison Factor	Home I Am Planning to Buy	A	B	C
9. Rental schedules (No. bedrooms/ monthly rentals)	__/__	__/__	__/__	__/__
10. Gross scheduled rents	_____	_____	_____	_____
Vacancy/collection loss rate	_____	_____	_____	_____
Total expenses	_____	_____	_____	_____
11. Conditions of sales	_____	_____	_____	_____
Parties	_____	_____	_____	_____
Cause of sale	_____	_____	_____	_____
Sale price as per cent of asking price	_____	_____	_____	_____
12. Other factors: _____	_____	_____	_____	_____

Sales of typical properties in the neighborhood:
Range: from $ _____ to $ _____
Average sales prices $ _____
(number of properties
considered was _____)

Exhibit 5-1 (cont.)

Estimated value of _____ ,
    as compared with
    Property A, its value is $_____ because _____

    Property B, its value is $_____ because _____

    Property C, its value is $_____ because _____

    Typical area properties $_____ because _____

    The final estimate is $_____ because _____

Where do you get information about completed sales? Usually real estate brokers are willing to provide the information, particularly if they believe that you will be a future buyer. When asking, however, do not accept merely oral statements; ask to see the actual records. And you can be even more certain about the information if you contact the buyer, the seller, and the lending institution that provided the financing. In some states title insurance companies can provide such information for a small price. Usually for about $5 to $10 per property you can ask them to provide a specified number of sales after you indicate the area in which the sales should be found and the general characteristics of the type of properties you want to analyze.

The kinds of information pertaining to terms and conditions are indicated in items 8 through 11 in Exhibit 5-1. In asking these questions you are making certain that there are no unusual circumstances associated with the comparable sale that might distort the price paid for the property.

NARROWING YOUR CHOICES

As a final check, get a feeling of the ranges of sales prices for properties similar to yours. You can obtain this information from real estate offices. In some states the tax assessor is required to maintain records of current sales and his estimates of the market values of all assessed properties based on an analysis of sales. You should inquire locally whether your local tax assessment records can be used for this purpose. You might also check with the appraisers working for local financial institutions, particularly if you are planning to borrow funds from one of them.

In fact, if you have narrowed your choice to one or two properties, you might ask a financial institution to make an appraisal for loan purposes. There is a charge for such appraisals, ranging from $25 to perhaps $200, depending upon the size of the property and the details wanted in the appraisal. You might even talk to institutional appraisers and see if they are available on a private basis to make an appraisal for you.

Let's say you have determined the appropriate price range for the property in which you are interested and what you believe to be a "typical" or "average" sales price for a property you wish to purchase. Now you must estimate the value of your property in comparison with each of the three properties you are using for comparison purposes. For example, you might say that in comparison with property A, your property should have a sale price of $175,000 (compared to a sale price of $145,000 for property A) because your property is slightly larger, newer, and maintained in better condition. So you have determined that your property should sell for $175,000 in comparison with property A, $182,000 in comparison with property B, and $172,000 in comparison with property C.

Which amount do you use? You could average $175,000 + $182,000 + $172,000 divided by 3 (the number of properties) = $176,000. You might also select $175,000 since it is between the highest and lowest estimates. Or you might start with $172,000 as your lowest bid and decide that you will not pay more than $182,000.

Or you might use the reliability of your information to weight your decision, thus·

Property	Reliability of Answer	Adjusted Price
A $175,000	100%	$175,000
B $182,000	97%	$176,300
C $172,000	50%	Not used

In any case you will have become an expert on property prices if you have done a careful job of evaluating completed sales in the market that interests you. In the process you may even find a property you believe is a "bargain" based on the kinds of net income capitalization analyses discussed in earlier chapters. Professional appraisers usually are content to establish a price estimate within 5 percent of the final sales price. If you paid $175,000 for the property after careful analysis, you might still have been able to purchase at a plus or minus $8,750 (5 percent of $175,000) of your estimate; however, if your analysis convinces you that $175,000 is the right price for you, do not worry about what might have been.

Many buyers are content to use the gross multiplier method discussed in the previous chapter in lieu of both the more complicated net income capitalization and the elaborate market comparison methods. If you do decide to use a gross multiplier method, be sure that: (a) your properties are very comparable in terms of location, site, and building; (b) the operating expenses are about the same; and (c) you have a maximum number of properties to use for comparison purposes.

Always keep in mind the bigger fool theory: if you pay what the other buyers are paying without determining what and why they paid those prices, then you are the "bigger fool." Don't become a member of the Bigger Fool Club by careless analysis or by relying on what other "fools" have paid.

ESTIMATING THE COST OF NEW STRUCTURE AND FEATURES

To avoid becoming a bigger fool, what procedures can you use to check your answer? One means is to estimate what new structures would cost to build and how the used property you are interested in would compare to it.

There are many problems associated with estimating the cost to build something new or the cost of something already built. However, you may decide that you have the money and the patience to build a new apartment house if you cannot find an existing one that is satisfactory.

When you are estimating the possible cost value of an existing apartment house, you will have to decide whether you want your estimates based on the costs of building an exact replica or one that provides the same functional services but that is more modern. An apartment house that is ten years old may have older, perhaps obsolete, heating or plumbing systems or outdated mechanical equipment such as stoves, refrigerators, air conditioning. Most appraisers resolve the issue by estimating what it might cost to build a replica ("cost to reproduce") and then deduct from that estimate the costs of curing some of the problems arising from age or obsolescence.

You can estimate costs by using a cost service that gives you the costs of building typical properties. To use the service you simply look through it to find examples of properties like the one in which you are interested. When you find an appropriate example, you will also find instructions on how to use the book.

You might also ask contractors to make estimates of what they would charge to build the apartment house. These estimates can vary quite widely sometimes so that you may have to decide which one is best or simply average the estimates. The best course is to select only contractors who are building apartment houses just like the one in which you are interested and have them furnish estimates based on what they had charged to construct, modified to reflect any costs changes which might have occurred since they built. You should expect to pay for such estimates unless you are seriously considering using the contractor to construct a new apartment.

Finally, you might pay a professional appraiser to make a cost estimate.

However, let us assume for the moment, that you will try to make an estimate yourself and want to know what steps should be followed:

A. Define a Bench Mark Apartment.   Costs are based on the quantity and quality of the apartment you wish to build. To do this, define the apartment in these terms:

1. *Size*
    a. total square feet for the main building and any garages and other support buildings,
    b. numbers of rooms, room sizes and room uses,
    c. height of building.
2. *Kinds of construction*—frame (all wood), frame plus veneer (external walls of stone or brick or stucco), basements or under-the-building garages, dry wall or stucco walls internally.
3. *Quality of construction*—the best, medium, or cheapest materials, equipment, hardware or furnishings.
4. *Architectural style*—clear and well defined or nondescript.
5. *Kinds of equipment*—(price, capacity, energy savings) for kitchen and baths, plus plumbing, heating, air conditioning.
6. *Other improvements*—garages, other buildings, landscaping, concrete or asphalt walks and drives, swimming pools.

B. Estimate the Costs New.   Refer to Exhibit 5-2, Item 1 for a list of the costs to consider in estimating the costs of building a new structure just like the one in which you are interested. Such costs can also be estimated from plans prepared by an architect.

Exhibit 5-2   Estimating the Costs of Building an Apartment House

1. Total Costs New

1.1 The main building

First floor	_____ sq.ft. × $_____	= $_____
Second floor	_____ sq.ft. × $_____	= _____
Stairs, porches	_____ sq.ft. × $_____	= _____
Basement	_____ sq.ft. × $_____	= _____
Underground garage	_____ sq.ft. × $_____	= _____
Total cost of main building		$_____

1.2 The garage

Car spaces	_____ sq.ft. × $_____	= $_____
Storage space	_____ sq.ft. × $_____	= _____
Total costs of garage and storage space		$_____

1.3 Landscaping and walks

Car-driveways	_____ sq. ft. × $_____	= $_____
Pedestrian walkways	_____ sq. ft. × $_____	= $_____
Landscaping (lawns, etc.)	_____ sq. ft. × $_____	= _____
Total costs of landscaping and walks		$_____

1.4 Other costs

Swimming pool $_____

Other (specify)   _____

Total other costs   _____

1.5 Summary, total sum of all costs $_____

Architectural, engineering costs   _____

Financing costs during construction   _____

Other holding costs   _____

Total of all costs, exclusive of land $ _____

2. Total Costs to Construct Property

Total of all costs (previous page) $_____

Minus:

Costs to repair or put property in working order (depreciation)

Replace wornout equipment $_____

Repair worn items in building   _____

To modernize or update   _____

Overcome the age of the building   _____

Total costs to overcome depreciation   _____

Cost of structures in their present condition $_____

Add:

Land costs   _____

Acquisition costs (title transfer costs)   _____

Total costs to reproduce or replace the property $_____

Exhibit 5-2 (cont.)

2. Total Costs to Construct Property (cont.)

Explanation of the Building Cost Factors Used

The cost per square foot was obtained after discussing the subject property with local real estate men and building contractors.

Real estate operators classified the construction of the subject property as typical of the neighborhood and used the following cost factors to estimate the cost to reproduce the property.

Building contractors' estimates averaged slightly higher than the realtors' estimates, but an investigation of the reasons for this showed that the contractors were anticipating rising costs and were protecting themselves by quoting slightly higher than market prices. Contractors agreed generally that the real estate operators' estimates were more representative of the market as of the date of the appraisal. The real estate operators' estimates were used for this appraisal.

3. Depreciation Schedule

Physical: Items to be cured: Total cost: Basis for cost:

Physical Incurable:

Physical—wear, tear, use, age
An actual estimate of wearing qualities of building
Requires consideration of condition of materials, effects of weather, resistance to use

Functional: Items to be cured: Total cost: Basis for cost:

Functional Incurable:
Incurable items and basis for costing:

Functional—style, efficiency, modern
Is building as efficient for use intended as other buildings?
Is the appearance such as to classify it as outdated?
Is equipment not as efficient or too costly, even if it is still in operating condition?
Must ignore any reference to actual physical condition.

Economic: Items to be cured: Total cost: Basis for cost:

Exhibit 5-2 (cont.)

3. Depreciation Schedule (cont.)

   Economic items which are incurable:

_____
_____
_____
_____

  Economic—location, market events
        Measure of those items which affect value but which cannot be remedied
        or controlled by property owner
        Changes in immediate environment
        Changes in the economic region
        Changes in business or real estate market conditions

Contingent: Items to be cured: Total cost: Basis for cost:

_____ _____ _____
_____ _____ _____
_____ _____ _____
_____ _____ _____

Contingent items which are incurable:

_____
_____
_____
_____

  Contingent
        Cannot be anticipated or predicted
        Involve effects of fires, storms, earthquakes, usually natural phenomena

___

There are five kinds of costs to consider:

1. main structure,
2. the garage and other support buildings,
3. landscaping and walks,
4. miscellaneous other costs to include swimming pools, recreation rooms, tennis or squash courts, and
5. holding and extra costs such as architectural and engineering fees, financing costs, title acquisition costs, payment to you for funds which you will use during construction and on which you will earn no interest or profit.

To these costs add the costs of the land and you have the total costs of the property in a new condition. But the property is not new.

THINGS THAT LOWER VALUE

   C. Deduct for Value Losses.   The lower value of an existing or older property, as compared to that of a newly completed building, is due to depreciation. Depreciation occurs because of the age of the building (wood, metal, glass do wear out or become less useful), wear and tear to which the building has been subjected, lack of modern equipment, outdated style, poor floor plans—a number of items. You can decide what kinds of depreciation exist in any building by comparing it with others that will compete with it for rentals.

Once you have found the items that cause a loss of value in the property (depreciation), subtract them from the cost new in order to develop an estimate of what you would pay for the existing building. Since you have observed some depreciation and will want to cure it, you subtract the costs of curing from the costs new.

Suppose you also decide there are some other deficiencies in the property that cannot be cured but which will lessen your ability to charge maximum rents. Use your best judgement in deciding how much they should affect the price of the property and subtract them from the costs you have estimated.

You now have an estimate of the value of the property that exists and the costs to build a new structure somewhat like the one you want. You can compare this with your previous estimates of the price of the property based on an income capitalization process or a market comparison procedure.

STRATEGIC CHOICES

At this point you can appreciate the hazards and problems of trying to estimate the costs of a new property. Even the best of experienced cost estimators differ in making such estimates. If you ask contractors to provide you with their estimates of costs to construct, you find even wider differences. In thinking about building a new apartment house, you should anticipate that the differences between what you have estimated and what the final structure might cost can vary from 20 to 50 percent. That's right! If you estimated the costs to build at $150,000 for the existing property we have been discussing, the final costs could equal $180,000 to $225,000. The final costs are always higher than what you have estimated because so many things can happen during construction: strikes, rising materials prices, additional items originally overlooked. The list can be quite long.

However, if you discuss costs with some experienced contractors, appraisers, and mortgage loan officers, using Exhibit 5-2 as a guide to the kinds of costs to consider, you will develop an understanding of the appropriate range within which your costs new will be found. After that, you have to use your best judgement as to what to do about these costs.

Typically, only experienced investors will undertake the construction of a new property. If you are going to build, proceed with caution, and use all the good advice you can obtain and afford.

IF YOU DECIDE TO BUILD . . .

If you decide to build, there are some important ideas to keep in mind. First, you will be working at least with an architect, a general contractor, and subcontractors. Selecting and working with them is crucial to your financial success.

Securing Bids

Before you can proceed with building, you have to develop a set of plans. There are ready-made, draftsman-prepared, and architect-prepared plans. Their costs vary, but usually the first two types can be purchased for a flat price; the architect, however, may charge a flat fee, a percentage based on the estimated costs to build, or a combination of fee and percentage. Experienced investors have learned that an architect can not only provide you with the best building for the site, but, in the process, find ways of reducing construction costs and operating expenses. You should explore each possibility.

If your investment is fairly large, you might consider asking a property manager to work with you in planning your investment. A property manager can suggest ways of arranging space, selecting materials, and planning ahead on ways to economize on maintenance and operational costs. Even if you do not use a property manager, take your plans to one; ask and pay for his advice on the efficiency with which the property can be operated.

The architect prepares blueprints (drawings of what the property will be like, including detailed plans of the various service elements) and specifications (a listing of the precise types of materials and equipment to be used), which together provide a basis for general contractors to submit bids for construction. The general contractors will then use the plans and specifications to call for bids from subcontractors.

Typically the general contractor excavates and constructs foundations, and does the carpentry and masonry work. Subcontractors install plumbing and heating equipment, electrical wiring, roofing, plastering, cement work, masonry work, and other specialized construction tasks. The contractor will hire "subs" (usually based on the lowest bid) and pay them, submitting bills to you with an additional amount for his services.

Selecting a Contractor

Since the contractor is crucial to the success of your project, there are some rules you can follow in selecting the most qualified. A low bid is not always the best basis for selecting a contractor. A contractor may bid low and expect to make up his profits through changes and extra work you will invariably ask during construction. He may also bid low because he plans to use poor materials and less qualified workmen.

How then should a contractor be selected if not on the basis of the lowest bid? First you should ask for evidence that the contractor has the experience to build what you want built. Ask to see some of the projects he has completed. Talk to some of his former clients.

The greatest problems in working with contractors arise from their financial instability. Too frequently they overcommit on work and run large materials and labor bills which force them into bankruptcy. You should ask for evidence of financial stability, perhaps a credit report. You can ask for credit references from bankers, materials suppliers, and his subcontractors.

There are trade associations to which contractors can belong. If a contractor does belong to one, that is a mark in his favor. This membership also gives you the chance to call the association and ask for information on his reputation and experience.

If you are satisfied that the contractor is capable after you have made your investigation and he is the lowest bidder, then sign the contract. Otherwise select the best qualified and pay a little more for construction.

There can be problems in working with some contractors: they may not work according to the time schedule you thought had been agreed on; they may do poor work; they may substitute materials or equipment. In other words the contractors do not perform according to the contracts they signed. To prevent this kind of thing from happening, you might investigate various kinds of inspection and control services which, for a very modest fee, will see that the contractor performs according to contract. Your local mortgage lender can probably tell you if such a service is available in your community.

You may also investigate the use of various kinds of bonds— performance, payment, license—which may reimburse you for any losses you suffer because a contractor fails to perform. They may also impose financial charges or even hire another contractor to complete the work. Bonds do carry some problems of enforcement so that you may not have immediate remedies when you use them. However, these are again items you should investigate locally through local mortgage lenders, lawyers, or even the professional contractors' association.

A very important fact to remember is that if a contractor is not paid for the materials and labor he provides, he can obtain a mechanic's lien—he can actually have your property seized and sold to satisfy the amounts owed him. The mechanic's lien law contains many provisions, which vary from state to state. Again a local mortgage lender can probably help you find out about the mechanic's lien law. On such matters, of course, a lawyer will help you.

Factors That Affect Costs

When you are building investment properties, you want to keep the costs as low as possible. Here is a checklist that may help you do this:

1. Keep shapes regular; do not ask for unusual designs or features.
2. Increasing size and shape increases costs. The more corners and indentations you add, the greater the costs are.
3. The number of rooms, their sizes, and the number of partitions within each apartment unit all will increase costs.
4. Doors, windows, and openings add to costs.
5. Quality workmanship and materials will increase costs, but in the long run they may reduce the costs of maintenance and operation.
6. Height increases costs as does area, so that tradeoffs should be considered, since there are conditions under which more height, rather than more area, can be used to reduce costs.
7. Other factors include ceiling heights, roof shapes, and pitch.
8. Finally, your design may result in problems relating to leveling the land, and the site itself may create problems relating to filled or low land. Always consider using a different site.

With care you will find that building an investment property can be an exciting and profitable adventure. Certainly it will keep you deeply involved in your investment for several months.

Are You Winning?
Some Ways to Check

6

After you have completed all your calculations, worried for the hundredth time about possible problems you may have overlooked, and finally decided to go ahead with the investment, you may be subjected to a bad case of "investor's fever." The symptoms include sleepless nights, cold sweats when you think of all the money you will owe, headaches as you wonder whether you should even consider such foolishness. Even if you have only the mildest case of "investor's fever," you will find the prescriptions in this chapter most useful for confirming your decisions. The prescriptions are simply the basic rules that all experienced investors follow as last checks before they finally commit to a new investment. Through careful checking you increase your winning potentials.

DEALING WITH DIFFERENT ANSWERS

A first step in reducing investor's fever is to determine what you know and what you want to do. One means of summarizing before you leap is provided in Exhibit 6-1. Completing this form permits you to see, in summary form, what you do and do not know and how much variation there may be among the answers you have developed on the most appropriate price of your property investment. Your last step is to reduce the different answers to a single investment amount that fits your investment goals.

Exhibit 6-1 Summary Statement and Major Conclusions

1. Property:
   Present use _____
   Year built _____
   Type of construction _____
   Architectural style _____
   Summary of physical condition _____
2. Date on which report was made: _____
3. Assessed value:
   Date of assessment _____
   Land _____ $ _____
   Building _____ $ _____
   Total $ _____
   Tax rate per $100 assessed value $ _____
   Total tax bill $ _____
4. Use constraints
   Most feasible use(s) _____
   Zoning restrictions _____
   Building code restrictions _____
   Deed restrictions _____
   _____
   _____

Other constraints: _____
_____

5. Value statement
   5.1 Estimates:
       Using market comparisons $ _____
       Using cost minus depreciation $ _____
       Using income capitalization $ _____
       Most probable value $ _____
   5.2 Schedules
       5.21 Depreciation
            Cost new $ _____
            Minus:
               Physical depreciation $ _____
               Functional depreciation $ _____
               Economic depreciation $ _____
            Plus:
               Land value $ _____
            Total estimate, cost minus
               depreciation $ _____

Exhibit 6-1 (cont.)

5.22 Income capitalization
Gross income $ _____
Total expenses (__% of gross) $ _____
Net income $ _____
Estimates:
Gross income × multiplier ( ) $ _____
Capitalization:
Capitalization rate _____%____
Capitalization period _____years____
Capitalization method _____
Estimate $ _____
5.23 Market comparison
Estimate value range _____to_____
Estimate $ _____
Terms: down payment $ _____
First mortgage: rate _____%
Total amount $ _____
Annual total payment $ _____
6. Feasibility summary
Feasible use(s) recommended: _____
_____
_____

Feasible use(s) considered: _____
_____
_____

Potential demand for property services: _____
_____
_____

Facilities/services to be offered: _____
_____
_____

Major benefits: _____
_____
_____

Major costs: _____
_____
_____

Reasons for Differences

Your answers about price should come out within a reasonably close range. An obvious, but frequently overlooked, reason for wide differences may be that you have made arithmetical errors. Review each of your approaches to determine whether you have added, subtracted, divided, and multiplied correctly. You should have a reasonably good idea of what the answers should be, so look for any wide deviations, and check the arithmetic.

Double check any information furnished to you—for example, sales and price data. Throw out any unusual or suspect answers. Remember that your final answer is only an estimate based on a number of limitations, most of which you have imposed, to arrive at an answer. At best, the price you have estimated is your idea of what you should pay. Variations from your idea could represent what others think they should pay. At some point both you and the seller must agree or there will be no sale.

Your first and most logical step, therefore, is to review all your information in order to reduce or eliminate any possible errors. Look at the information and eliminate any of it that does not help you make your decision. You may have included a host of descriptive material that cannot be used to calculate price. Information about family income of the area, the number of local parks, prices paid for commercial or large apartment properties have little value to you at this point—so eliminate them. Once you have narrowed your choice to the information that helps you make a decision, check it: Is it from a reliable source? Is it complete? Are all calculations correct?

Having checked the information you will use in your final decision-making, determine which of it is reliable and in sufficient quantity, and base most of your decisions on that information. Your data on property expenses, for example, may be based on only one or two properties and may have been derived from secondary sources rather than from the owner. On the other hand, your gross income multipliers may have resulted from your investigating many properties, and from talking to many property investors. Use the latter; forget the former. Finally, be sure that all data relate to the property in which you are interested. If you have a great deal of information on income and expenses from larger properties, or from apartments located in different areas, perhaps you should disregard it.

A Zone of Reasonableness

Hopefully you have managed to develop estimates of the value of your property by using income capitalization, market comparisons, and cost approaches. To reduce them to a single estimate you must first ask: "What were my investment goals—capital gains, income, or tax shelter? Does this property help me meet those goals?"

Next you might ask, "What would other investors like me, with my objectives, pay?" In other words, what would a typical informed investor, with sufficient time to undertake careful analysis, pay for this property? "How does my thinking fit with that of this typical investor?"

On these bases you can select an appropriate price if you recognize that:

1. the income capitalization approach reflects basically your particular goals, assumptions, and needs;
2. the market comparison approach reflects the average of what investors like you have paid for the kinds of properties in which you are interested; and
3. cost should set an upper limit on what you will pay if you can afford the special costs and delays of construction; or costs set a limit reflecting some of your special requirements in a new building.

The final price you select is still only an estimate, subject to further bargaining and change, but it should reflect the purposes you have in investing, the adequacy and accuracy of the data, and what you know about local real estate market trends.

On a rule-of-thumb basis, your price should reflect the market in these ways:

1. it relates to market gross multipliers;
2. the per rental unit, per square foot prices should support the multipliers;
3. the price does not do violence to your income capitalization and cost estimates of price; and
4. you can explain why you selected the price.

At this point you may still be concerned about the correctness of the price you have estimated, or you may still be faced with worrisome differences among your estimates. Fortunately, there are still other methods of checking out your answers, although they require some additional mathematical calculations. These methods can be used if you have reliable information only on land prices, or only on construction or building costs, or only on total net income estimates. More importantly, you may still buy the property even if you do not have sufficient cash for the down payments you believe the market requires.

At the end of the chapter you will have a chance to test what you know by giving investment advice to Fred and Lola Samson, who were the "amateur" investors you met in earlier chapters.

DIRECT METHODS AND INCOMPLETE DATA

The direct method of capitalization (income divided by a rate) always produces the lowest and most conservative investment value estimate. However, its use is limited to three applications:

1. *Building residual*—the land value is known and you must estimate building value;
2. *Land residual*—the building value is known but the land value is not known; and
3. *Property residual*—the total value of the property can be estimated and the property has no value at the end of the investment period.

The three methods are illustrated in the following examples. Each requires that you first develop a net income estimate and select an earning rate and an investment period. (Remember all calculations are based on annual amounts.)

Example 1—Building Residual. Land value is known, $300,000; building value is not known and must be estimated by using a cost method.

Net Income		$ 112,480
Income earned by land (300,000 × .08)		24,000
Income earned by building		88,480
Capitalization rate:		
Interest rate	.08	
Recovery rate (25 years)	.04	
	.12	
Building value ($88,480/.12)		$ 737,333
(based on cost to construct new minus depreciation if building is old)		
Land value (derived from market comparisons)		300,000
Investment value of property		$1,037,333

This is the most reliable method of estimating price, and the one we have illustrated most frequently. As you have discovered, land values can be estimated more accurately than the construction costs of the building.

Example 2—Land Residual. The building value is known; land value is not known. The building value is derived by using a cost estimate or using the actual cost to construct. Obviously this method will be most successful if you know costs on newly completed buildings. You can see that if you make an error on building costs and are too high, you will understate the land value, and if your costs are too low, your land value will be high.

Net Income	$ 112,480
Income earned by building ($500,000 × .12)	60,000
Income earned by land	$ 52,480
Land value ($52,480/.08)	$ 656,000
Building value	500,000
Investment value of property	$1,156,000

Example 3—Property Residual. This method is useful when you have estimated the net income but have no effective way of allocating it to land and building. This is considered by many to be the only way to estimate property investment value because they consider dividing income between building and land is very artificial—they firmly believe that building and land must work together; they cannot work separately. On the other hand, the method first understates the investment value because the assumption is made that at the end of the investment period the property would have no value (very frequently used by cautious investors). This would be valid perhaps only when the area is deteriorating or at the end of the investment period, and some new kind of use would be more appropriate on the site; under these conditions, the costs of converting to that new use probably would equal the costs of buying a vacant parcel of land.

Net Income	$ 112,480
$112,480/.12	937,333
Investment value of property	$ 937,000

What if you felt that the property might have some net value at the end of the investment period? You might have found that twenty-five-year-old properties like yours do have a value. Or, you might have discovered that properties like this suffer an annual percentage loss of value which would leave some value in the property at the end of the investment period. Here is how you would estimate the impact of these assumptions on your property residual estimate.

Example 4. The value of a twenty-five-year-old property at present is $450,000. Let's assume your building would have this value at the end of your investment twenty-five years from now. The present value of the building of $450,000 at 12 percent is (using a present value of one table) $450,000 × .0588, or $26,460. That figure can be rounded to $26,500. The value of the property, using a residual method, would therefore be:

Value of the income stream	$937,000
Present value of future residual value of property	26,500
Present total investment value	$963,500

Example 5. The present investment value of the income stream is $937,000. Market trends indicate this capacity will decline by 40 percent in twenty-five years; therefore the value at the end of the investment period would be $562,000 ($937,000 × .60).

Present investment value of income stream	$ 937,000
Present value of $562,000 residual	
($562,000 × .0588 = $33,057.36)	$ 33,000
Present total investment value	$ 970,000

Internal Rate of Return
(Earning on Your Equity)

Suppose you wanted to consider the impact of mortgage financing, and you were interested only in the rate you would earn on your down payment. You might estimate the property value as follows:

Net income stream annually		$ 112,480
Total investment	1,000,000	
Mortgage (25 years, 8%)	800,000	
Down payment	200,000	
Mortgage payments, annual amount,		
monthly payments ($800,000 × .00718 × 12)		74,745
Net income earned on the equity		$ 38,094
Total net earnings in 25 years ($38,094 × 25)		$ 952,350
Internal rate of return:		
$952,350/200,000 = 4.661750		

Using a direct method:

Total return on investment 466.17%
Annual average return 466.17/25 = 18.65%

Using an annuity method (referring to the present value of an annuity, one per period, table, using a twenty-five-year investment period):

5.466906 factor for 25 years annuity at 18%
−4.947587 factor for 25 years annuity at 20%
 .519399

4.661750/4.947587 = investment factor/.519399

or 4.947587 investment factor = (4.661750 × .519399) 2.421308

Investment factor = 2.421308/4.947587 = .4894 or 48.94%

20% minus 18% = 2% = .02

.02 × .4894 = .009788

18% + .98% (.18 + .0098) = 18.98% (internal rate of return using the annuity method)

Each of these methods suggests that you earned slightly more than 18 percent annually on your initial down payment of $200,000.

RECOGNIZING THE IMPACT OF FINANCING

In the previous example, the equity you built up through mortgage payments has not been recognized, even though you would receive this additional amount when you finally sold the property. Also, suppose you wanted to know whether financing might change your estimate of what you could pay for the property. Consider the following:

Net income produced by the property after financing	$ 38,094
Present value of the income stream, using an annuity table ($38,094 × 7.843139 25 years, 12%) =	298,776
Add: Equity buildup in mortgage (principal payments)	800,000
Value of property recognizing financing	$1,098,776

---

or, using a direct method:

Net income produced by the property after financing	$ 38,094
Present value of that income stream ($38,094/.12)	317,450
Add: Equity buildup in mortgage principal payments	800,000
Value of property recognizing financing	$1,117,450

THE IMPACT OF SECOND MORTGAGE FINANCING

Suppose you decided to pay $1,000,000 for the property but had only $100,000 for a down payment and could secure a mortgage for only $800,000. You might consider using another mortgage—a "second" or "junior" mortgage. Suppose you asked the seller of the property to accept the second mortgage as part of the purchase. The seller's problem is as follows:

1. Cash proceeds using a first mortgage $1,000,000
   (Down payment of $200,000 plus a $800,000 mortgage)
2. Cash proceeds using a second mortgage 900,000
   ($100,000 down plus proceeds of first mortgage $800,000)

If he still wanted the $1,000,000 in cash proceeds, he might determine for what amount of cash he could sell your second mortgage of $100,000. Typically, buyers of such mortgages will not pay $100,000 for the mortgage because they consider owning a mortgage much riskier than owning a property. Suppose the seller of the property found he could obtain only $80,000 by selling the $100,000 mortgage you offer. He might do this:

Accept your down payment	$ 100,000
Accept first mortgage proceeds	800,000
Accept a second mortgage from you for	120,000
Price he would charge you for the property	$1,020,000

He would sell your second mortgage for a 20-percent discount or about $100,000 and still have his $1,000,000 in cash proceeds. You would now own the property for only $100,000 down payment instead of $200,000. If your second mortgage was for only fifteen years and at a rate of 10 percent:

Annual total payments ($100,000 × .10746 × 12)	$12,895
First mortgage payments	74,745
Total mortgage payments	$97,640
Net return on equity	
Net income before financing	$112,480
Financing charges	97,640
Net after financing	$15,840

Total return on equity for 15 years	
$15,840 × 15	$237,600
Total return on equity remaining 10 years	
$38,094 × 10	380,940
Total return on down payment of $100,000	$618,540

$618,540/25 years = 24.74% average return annually (24,741/100,000)

In other words, by assuming additional debt you have increased your rate of return on your down payment (internal rate of return) from approximately 18 percent to over 24 percent.

FINANCING NEW CONSTRUCTION
WITH LIMITED CASH

Perhaps you have decided you will build the apartment house that interests you because you have found a lot in an area showing every sign of growing in the near future. At present, lenders may be reluctant to provide mortgage financing because the area is new and untried.

Your previous calculations indicate that you should pay not more than $500,000 to $600,000 for the lot, and plan to construct a building that would cost not more than the same amount. However, since this is a new and untested market area, you decide that your maximum land price will be $500,000. Your survey of the market indicates that values are rising for apartment houses at about 10 to 15 percent per year and that construction of a new apartment would take twelve months from the time you have title to the property. Your financial status and market conditions are:

Your cash for a down payment	$100,000
Land price	500,000
Cost to construct the building	500,000
Transfer, architect, and other building costs	50,000
Net income estimate for the property	112,480
Gross income estimate	200,000
Anticipated market gross multiplier	6/7
First mortgage, 25 years, 9.0%	800,000

You might finance this investment, assuming that you want a return on your equity and are not seeking a long-term investment:

Agreement to purchase the land but using an option to purchase subject to your receiving a loan. (The owner of the land agrees to subordinate his interest to a first mortgage in return for a share of the profits equal to 25% of his investment of $400,000.)

Agreement... of his investment of $400,000.)		$100,000
Proceeds from the mortgage		800,000
Transfer, sales and other costs		50,000
Total costs of the investment		$950,000

Sales price of the property			
$200,000 × 6 = $1,200,000 (Gross multiplier)		$1,200,000	
$200,000 × 7 = $1,400,000 (Gross multiplier)			$1,400,000
Costs of construction	$500,000		
Other costs	50,000		
Down payment (option)	100,000		
Land owner interest	400,000		
Land owner profit share	100,000	1,150,000	1,150,000
Net proceeds to investor		50,000	250,000
Total investor cash invested		100,000	100,000
Return on investment (1 year)		50%	250%

This is the kind of potential that attracts investors to the purchase of raw land for construction purposes. The basic requirements for success in this type of transaction are: (1) reliable information on market trends; (2) no delays in construction which increase the costs; (3) location of another investor who will purchase the entire package; (4) careful checking on the accuracy of your calculations.

In this type of transaction you may never have to undertake construction of the property. You can create a legal package that includes all agreements—option, purchase agreements, financing, permits for construction—and sell the package. You might, for example, create an agreement in which you agree to purchase the land from the original land owner within 120–180 days or forfeit your down payment. You can then proceed to create the paper work and try to sell the package to another investor within the option period. In this case you would have completed the entire investment process in six months. Perhaps the single most important key to this form of investing is knowing your areas and local market trends.

WRAP-AROUND MORTGAGE FINANCING

"Wrap-around financing" is used when an investor has a mortgage on a property but must use the property as security to obtain additional funds. A new mortgage is placed on the property without the original mortgage being repaid.

The investor makes a total payment on that mortgage which provides for repayment of the mortgage plus sufficient amounts for the lender to also pay on the original mortgage. The new mortgage is a wrap-around mortgage.

Not all lenders will agree to this type of financing. Not many investment advisors or real estate brokers understand how this type of financing works. There are also many variations other than the one illustrated, any of which can be used to secure lower overall financing costs.

Remember these ideas when thinking about using wrap-arounds:

1. You own property on which you are paying loan interest lower than current rates.
2. You have a substantial equity in the property and wish to keep it.
3. Any financing you may get for your new investment will probably require you to secure more financing than can be obtained from the first mortgage (trust deed).
4. The lender gains from
   a. the difference between the 9.25 percent you pay and the 8.5 percent paid for you on the $50,000 unpaid mortgage on the first property, and
   b. a loan with more security even though only 9.25 instead of 9.5 percent is being received.
5. You have earnings from two properties without increasing your overall financial liability as much as if you had tried to finance the second property with current loan market terms.

CHECKING OUT WHAT YOU KNOW

You may recall Fred and Lola Samson from earlier chapters. They have embarked on the process of investing in income-producing real estate and have located an apartment project they would like to have evaluated. Read the information they have provided and then prepare an analysis to answer their questions. There are many possible answers you can give but to help you, one set of answers follows the problem presented.

The Property

The property is a one-year-old 100-unit apartment house located in an area of new apartment houses. The area appears to be properly suited for apartment construction, with shopping centers, schools, and other public service facilities within walking distance. Employment for most residents is only a short bus or car ride away. The population in the area has been increasing steadily, but the current rate is 5 percent annually.

At present the property is fully occupied by tenants on two-year leases, with a 10-percent reduction to those tenants who signed the two-year leases.

At the time the land was purchased for $300,000, and the apartment house was constructed for $500,000.

Property Income and Expenses

The current property owner has furnished the following information about his one-year operation of the property:

Gross income 100 units × $100 × 12 months		$120,000
Expenses:		
Resident manager/janitor	Free apartment rent	
Trash/garbage collection	$900	
Utilities for public areas	1,800	
(Tenants are metered and pay own utilities)		
Maintenance, cleaning	1,200	
License fees, annually	200	
Furniture costs ($100 per apartment)	10,000	
Mechanical equipment ($150 per apartment)	15,000	
Interior painting and repairs	5,000	
Property taxes	20,000	
Property insurance, 3-year premium	3,000	
Total expenses		57,100
Net income		$ 62,900

Mortgage financing is available for 80 percent of the market value, 25-year term, 9.0 percent interest rate.

Market Comparisons

	Property A	*Property B*	*Property C*
Number of units	110	100	95
Gross income	$165,000	$144,000	$144,780
Sales price	$1,160,000	$1,100,000	$998,000
Expenses	$82,500	$79,200	$79,200
Age of the apartments	1 year	1 year	2 years
Condition	Excellent	Good	Excellent

The Samsons ask you to indicate various investment alternatives they might consider and to make recommendation on what they should pay for the property, including the terms of purchase. They want to hold the apartment for a number of years. They do not want you to consider the impact of income taxes.

Possible Solution
to the Samsons' Investment Problem

1. Analyze the market information on the comparable apartments

	Property A	*Property B*	*Property C*
Rents per unit	$125	$120	$127
Gross multiplier	7.03	7.64	6.89
Expenses as % of income	50%	55%	55%

2. Reconstruct the owner's statement to conform more closely to the above market information

Gross rents ($125 × 12 × 100)	$150,000	
(Leases should be eliminated since the market is good and there is no reason to provide lease discounts)		
Minus: Expected losses due to tenants moving, rental collection problems (5% provided)	−7,500	
Expense schedule		$142,500
Operating expenses		
Manager, resident ($125 × 12)	$ 1,500	
(Even though the apartment is provided free, it is an expense to be considered)		
Manager, professional (5% of expected collected rents)	7,125	
Maintenance	1,200	
(This amount can be verified by asking the professional manager. You will want to maintain rent levels)		
Trash, garbage collection	900	
Utilities	1,800	
Total operating expenses		$12,525

Fixed expenses

License fees	$ 200	
Property taxes	20,200	
Property insurance ($3,000/3)	1,000	
Total fixed expenses		$21,400

Reserves for maintenance, repairs, improvements

Furniture ($10,000/5-year life)	$ 2,000	
Mechanical equipment ($15,000/10-year life)	1,500	
Interior repairs, painting, renovation ($5,000/3-year life)	1,667	
Exterior repairs, painting, renovation	1,700	
(With no other information available, make it equal to the interior expenditures)		
Total reserve expenses		$ 6,867
Total of all expenses		$ 40,792
Net earned income		$101,708

Now, try calculating the market value of the property several different ways.

Market Value Based on Multipliers

$150,000 × 7.3 = $1,054,500
 150,000 × 7.64 = 1,146,000
 150,000 × 6.89 = 1,033,500
Possible sale price: $3,234,000/3 = $1,078,000

Market Value Based on the Net Income:
Direct Capitalization

Expenses as % of gross income ($62,900/$120,000) = 52%
Market averages on expenses (50 + 55 + 55 = 160/3) = 53%
The expenses seem about right, so they will be used.

From the market place:	
Investors buying these apartments want to 10%, 62,900/.10	$629,000
Typically an investor stays invested for 10 years. Total costs to build, $800,000, assume 2% depreciation for 10 years equals value in 10 years based on cost of $720,000. Present value of $720,000 for 10 years at 10% = $720,000 × .385543 =	$277,590
Estimated value on an overall rate approach	$906,590

Net income	$ 62,900
Earnings attributed to land ($300,000 × 10%)	30,000
	$ 32,900
Value of the building ($32,900/10% earning, + 2% depreciation)	$274,166
Recovery value of property at end of 10 years with 2% a year depreciation or 20% at end of period: $800,000 × .80 = $640,000; present value of $640,000 at 10% ($640,000 × .092296)	$246,700
Estimated investment value, direct capitalization, building residual:	
Land	$300,000
Building	274,166
Residual	246,700
	$820,866

Market Value Based on Net Income Capitalization Using Annuity Tables

Net income	$ 62,900
Earning attributed to land ($300,000 × .10)	30,000
Net income to building	$ 32,900
Using present value of one per year, 10%, 10 years, building income ($32,900 × 6.1445)	$202,154
Residual value, 10 years, 10%, based on costs and assumed 2% per year depreciation ($800,000 × .20 = $640,000 × .3855)	246,720
Land value	300,000
Present value of total property	$748,874

Summary

Market price: using gross multipliers	$1,078,000
(10% earning and 2% recovery = 12%, $150,000/.12)	1,250,000
Overall rate, net income	906,590
Market comparisons ($1,160,000 + 1,100,000 + 998,000/3)	1,086,000
Net income, direct capitalization	820,866
Net income, annuity capitalization	748,874

Recognizing the Impact of Mortgage Financing

Net income before mortgage financing $ 62,900

Assume an $800,000 mortgage, 25 years, 9%
   Monthly payments, $800,000 × .008392
   = $6,713.60 × 12 months;   80,563
   See tables for the mortgage factor.
Obviously this is too large a mortgage.

   $600,000 × .008392 = $5,035.20 × 12 = $60,422.40, leaving $2,477 for investor.
   $500,000 × .008392 = $4,196 × 12 = $50,352, leaving $12,548 for investor.

Estimated Value Taking into Account the Impact of Financing

Possible purchase price: $1,000,000

Down payment: $12,548 = $12,548/$500,000 down payment = 3% annual return.

Conclusions

The gross multipliers indicate that the price would have to be about
$1,000,000. Given the levels of rents, expenses, and financing, the investor would not earn a satisfactory return. The Samsons would be able to buy
this kind of investment and let it pay for itself, hoping that growth in the
area would raise both prices and rental levels. On the other hand, the
Samsons might try to bargain to obtain a price closer to $800,000, which
reflects a conservative investment analysis based on net income. In any
case, you would review your findings with the Samsons to determine what
they hope to accomplish by investing in this property.

Clearly compromises can be made:

1. the Samsons could accept a lower rate of return;
2. the Samsons could stay invested longer and plan their income/expense ratios
   and capitalization accordingly;
3. the rents could be raised and the expense schedule reviewed to reduce
   items; for example, the Samsons might become resident managers; and
4. the Samsons could speculate on inflation and growth continuing.

At this point you may wonder if real estate is a good investment, if
this problem is representative of what actually happens. Because local

markets vary, this example may not correspond to what is happening in your area, so check locally before you decide what to do. On the other hand, this example represents what many investors are finding out about real estate investing.

Despite an occasional disappointment, investors continue to invest because of an additional factor—Federal income tax laws that make it possible to have good investments while apparently losing money. This legal feature will be discussed next, as you are introduced to some new, important strategies that will help you raise your investment score.

Winning By Losing—
The Magic
Of Federal Income
Tax Law

7

Real estate investments can have several distinct advantages for you as an investor because of the operations of the Federal income tax law:

1. interest on money borrowed to pay for the real estate may be deducted fully from earned income,
2. buildings and furnishings may be depreciated annually and that amount deducted from reportable income even though the amount may not represent actual cash losses,
3. any increases in value may be treated as capital gains and taxed at rates lower than those paid on equivalent earned income,
4. taxes due may be postponed and paid at a time more favorable to the tax payer/investor, and
5. through exchanges, the investor can acquire increasingly valuable property and new income tax advantages without paying a tax on each exchange.

If the real estate investment loses money, as defined under Internal Revenue Service codes, the losses may be deducted from other earned income. In other words, it is possible to use Federal income tax laws in ways that permit you to make money by losing it.

HOW FEDERAL INCOME TAX LAW
CAN HELP YOU

An illustration of some of the ways in which Federal income tax laws can be used to advantage by you as a real estate investor are indicated in Exhibit 7-1. We will refer to it from time to time to illustrate some of the rules of the income tax game.

Before becoming too enthusiastic about the tax advantages of real estate, remember that such advantages cannot overcome poor location, bad building design, and other factors basic to the "economic aspects" of real estate investments. Also remember that the laws relating to income taxes are being changed continually and new interpretations are being applied to

Exhibit 7-1 Financial Advantages of Federal Income Tax Law as Applied to Real Estate Investments

Assumptions:

1. The investor has income of $10,000 on which he must pay a 50-percent tax.
2. The property owned has a gross scheduled income of $14,300, a gross multiplier of 7 which produces a current market value of $100,000.
3. The property is mortgaged with an $80,000 loan, with a 9-percent interest rate and a 25-year term.
4. Income tax laws allow the investor to take a percentage of the value of the building ($80,000), of stoves and refrigerators ($8,000), and of apartment furnishings ($4,000), none of which necessarily has a relationship to the actual replacement life of these items.
5. After one year of ownership the investor can sell the property for $120,000.

Assume that the property is sold at the end of the first year of ownership for $120,000. The tax consequences would be:

Sales price	$120,000	
Minus: Original purchase price	100,000	
Capital gain	$ 20,000	
Plus: Building depreciation taken	1,600	
New capital gain calculation	$21,600	
Minus: Capital improvements	10,000	
Capital gain for tax purposes	$ 11,600	
Potential capital gains tax ($11,600 × .25)		$2,900
Potential income tax if gain were earned income (.50)		5,500
Net income gain to investor because of capital gains		$2,600

Income and Expense Analyses

Income:

Purchase price	$100,000

Exhibit 7-1 (cont.)

(Gross income = 14,300, gross multiplier = 7)

Gross scheduled income		14,300
Vacancy and collection losses allowance (5%)		715
Gross operating income		$13,585

Expenses:

Operating:

Maintenance, including janitor	$1,000	
Trash, landscaping	900	
Utilities	800	
Management	3,500	
Miscellaneous	500	$6,700

Fixed:

Property taxes	$2,500	
Insurance	1,000	3,500

Reserves:

Stoves, refrigerators	$ 800	
(Original cost = $8,000, 10-year life)		
Apartment furnishings	400	
(Original cost = $4,000, 10-year life)		
Exterior painting, decorating, repairs	300	
(5-year investment life)		1,500
Total expenses		11,700
Net income, earned, to be capitalized for value estimate		$ 1,885

The Additional Impact of Federal Income Tax Laws:

Other deductions:

Mortgage interest ($80,000 loan at 9%, first year only)	$7,200	
Building depreciation ($80,000 value, 2% annual depreciation)	1,600	
Shorter life permitted for refrigerators, stoves	800	
(5-year life instead of 10-year life, double depreciation)		
Apartment furnishings (same as refrigerator, etc.)	800	
Added deductions because of income tax laws	$10,400	

New Financial Status:

Net income earned from the property	$ 1,885
Minus: additional deductions permitted under income tax law	− 10,400
Net income loss for tax purposes	−8,515

Overall Impact on Tax Liabilities:

Other income earned by the taxpayer	$10,000
Tax due on this income, 50% bracket	5,000
Impact of the tax loss on real estate:	
Other income earned	$10,000
Income loss from real estate	8,515
New income level to report for tax purposes	1,485
New tax liability to replace former liability of $5,000	742.50
Tax shielded income from real estate investment ($5,000–742.50)	$ 4,257.50
Actual net income from building and land investment	1,885.00
Tax shielded income for first year	$ 6,142.50
Return on equity for first year 6,142.50/20,000	31%

laws that have been in existence for some time. However, let us look at the bright side of the tax laws first so that you can understand the basic rules of this tax law game. Once you understand the basics, then you can use tax consultants to keep you advised on the newest interpretations and laws. (And deduct their charges from the income earned by your investments!)

In order to appreciate the impact of Federal income taxes on real estate investments, assume that you have $10,000 in income on which you must pay 50 percent for taxes (Exhibit 7-1). Obviously, you must have earned much more income than this, but for the purposes of this illustration the last $10,000 of your earned income is in the 50-percent bracket. On a straight income basis, you would have to write out a check to the IRS for $5,000.

But suppose on the other hand that you have purchased a property with a gross income of $14,300 on a gross multiplier of 7, or $100,000. You are financing the property with an $80,000 loan (9-percent interest, twenty-five-year term) and a $20,000 down payment (equity) from your own resources. You have consulted with a tax accountant, and he recommends the rate at which you can depreciate the building and how to use money spent to improve the property on your tax return. After one year, you sell the property for $20,000 more than you paid. After allowances for capital improvements and depreciation, the net gain is taxed as capital gains, *not* as straight income. On a net capital gain of $11,600, you pay only $2,900 in taxes. (Check the figures shown in Exhibit 7-1.)

SPECIAL ASPECTS OF FEDERAL INCOME TAX LAW

Federal income tax law is so complex and it changes so frequently that the ordinary real estate investor cannot act as his own tax accountant. An experienced, well-trained tax advisor should always be used in connection with negotiating for any substantial real estate investment. However, some initial questions to the advisors will help them appreciate your investment situation and generate more suggestions regarding the applications of the most recent rules and interpretations of regulations to your situation. To help you in this aspect of your investment, a number of questions are offered and some of the possible answers discussed to give you some "feeling" for the advantages, pitfalls, and complexities of using Federal income tax law to further your investment opportunities. The most important classes of questions are:

1. How much depreciation can be taken? And how will it impact on the cash flow and investment situation?
2. How much interest from the use of mortgage loans can be charged? In what amounts? Over what periods of time?
3. If others are involved and a partnership or syndicate is formed, how are the expenses of the organization treated for income tax purposes? Can they all be deducted immediately or over time, or must they be capitalized and added to the tax basis?
4. What items of expense have to be added to the purchase price and treated as capital investment?
5. How can the investment amount be divided between land and building?
6. What opportunities exist now for deferring tax liability for any investment now being disposed of as a part of this investment situation?
7. Is some form of tax-free property exchanges possible and warranted?

Depreciation

Buildings and the furnishings in them, when used to produce earned income, may have a portion of their original purchase price deducted from earned income each year as a depreciation charge (Exhibit 7-1). The amount of depreciation charged each year is determined either by applicable Federal income tax schedules or through negotiation with the Internal Revenue Service (IRS). Schedules published by the IRS indicate the usual period over which various types of real estate buildings and furnishings may be depreciated.

The rate at which depreciation can be taken on buildings or furnishings is dependent upon IRS regulations and any negotiations you may make with them. The basic (straight-line) method of depreciation allocates equal amounts of the depreciable item over its anticipated economic life. However, there are other depreciation methods which the IRS has allowed, although their regulations have changed over time, so be sure to use the most current regulations on depreciations. Some examples of the kinds of depreciation presently allowed, or allowed in the past are presented in Exhibit 7-2.

In negotiating or planning for depreciation, it is advantageous to use the shortest possible depreciable life, which may or may not have some relationships to the economic life of the property. Actually, there are some standards for depreciation which the IRS has used: Apartment buildings—forty years, homes—forty-five years, factories—forty-five years, office

Exhibit 7-2 Examples of Depreciation Methods Recognized by the Internal Revenue Service (US-IRS) Assuming a Ten-Year Depreciation Period

End of year	Straight Line**	RL*	("Normal")†	RL	Declining Balance*** 150%††	RL	Declining Balance*** 200%†††	RL	Sum of years digits§		RL
1	1.00–.10	.90	1.00–.10	.90	1.00–.15	.85	1.00–.20	.80	10/55§§	.1818	.8182
2	.90–.10	.80	.90–.090	.81	.85–.1275	.7225	.80–.16	.64	9/55	.1636	.6546
3	.80–.10	.70	.81–.081	.729	.7225–.1084	.6141	.64–.128	.5120	8/55	.1454	.5092
4	.70–.10	.60	.729–.0729	.6561	.6141–.0921	.5220	.5120–.1024	.4096	7/55	.1272	.3820
5	.60–.10	.50	.6561–.0656	.5905	.5220–.0783	.4437	.4096–.0819	.3277	6/55	.1090	.2730
6	.50–.10	.40	.5905–.0590	.5314	.4437–.0666	.3771	.3277–.0655	.2622	5/55	.0909	.1821
7	.40–.10	.30	.5314–.0531	.4783	.3771–.0566	.3206	.2622–.0524	.2098	4/55	.0727	.1094
8	.30–.10	.20	.4783–.0478	.4305	.3206–.0481	.2725	.2098–.0419	.1679	3/55	.0545	.0549
9	.20–.10	.10	.4305–.0435	.3874	.2725–.0409	.2316	.1679–.0335	.1344	2/55	.0363	.0186
10	.10–.10	0	.3874–.0387	.3487	.2316–.0347	.1969	.1344–.0268	.1076	1/55	.0181	.0005

*RL = Remaining Life
**Minus salvage value
***Must not depreciate below a reasonable salvage value
†Depreciation is 10% annually but is applied to remaining balance
††Depreciation rate is 15%, i.e. 150% of "normal"
†††Depreciation rate is 20%, i.e. 200% of "normal"
§Sum of digits 1 through 10 years is 55
§§The depreciation amount or percent is subtracted from the original unrecovered amount but is expressed as a percent of the original, not the remaining, balance.

buildings—forty-five years, stores—forty-five years. Information on "usual standards" is provided in the IRS publication *Guidelines for Depreciation*, which can be obtained from the IRS.

Recent regulations require that under given conditions any depreciation recovered in excess of the straight-line method must be treated as earned income and taxed at that rate. For example, *The 1976 Tax Reform Act* provides that for commercial and residential real estate, any gain realized at the time of sale is to be treated as ordinary income to the extent that depreciation has been taken in excess of straight-line depreciation. A comparison of the amounts recovered under depreciation charges using "accelerated" (that is, other than straight-line) methods of depreciation is shown in Exhibit 7-2.

Sometimes a financial advantage can be achieved by using a component method of depreciating. In this method the property is divided into its major components—walls, floors, roof, wiring, plumbing, mechanical equipment—with each component given a useful life and a rate of depreciation. Such a method may be used on both new and used real estate, but all computations must be supported by a well-documented appraisal.

Interest Payments

Any interest paid on a loan to purchase real estate is fully deductible, but the amount that can be deducted in a given year is subject to regulation. In earlier years investors would pay more than one year of interest at the time of purchase, and the entire amount could be deducted as an expense. The use of prepaid interest as an expense is now severely limited. For example, if an income property is purchased late in a given year, such as in September, the only deductible interest charges are those that are due in the months of September to December. Formerly, the entire year's interest could have been deducted no matter on what date the purchase was made. Now any prepaid interest or points included should not "materially distort" income.

If a new property is being constructed and financing is used, interest sometimes may not be treated as an expense. Under certain conditions some of the interest (and even property taxes) may have to be added to the purchase price base and treated as a capital cost.

One method of taking advantage of interest deductions has been the use of a "wrap-around" mortgage. This mortgage is used when a property already has one mortgage on it, which the buyer wants to keep, but more financing is needed to buy the property. Suppose you want to purchase an income property for $150,000 on which there is an existing mortgage for

30 years at 7.5 percent. Current mortgage terms are 25 years at 8.5 percent. First, you can agree to assume the first mortgage. Then you write another mortgage for an amount equal to the difference between the sale price plus the down payment and the amount yet to be repaid on the original mortgage. The entire property is pledged as security, and the interest is at the current rate. In this example you might assume the first mortgage with an unpaid principal of $90,000, make a cash down payment of $20,000, and write a wrap-around mortgage for the remaining $40,000, with the mortgage due in 25 years at 8.5 percent.

The IRS looks with suspicion upon wrap-around mortgages. Some of the conditions under which its use might be accepted are:

1. the need for paying a heavy prepayment penalty if the original mortgage were paid off,
2. the desire to keep the lower interest rate and payments of the original mortgage,
3. the inability to acquire title because of clauses in the original mortgage,
4. the seller's desire to simplify his financing by having only one mortgage to consider, and
5. the seller's tax requirements.

Investment Expenses

Frequently the purchase of real estate involves certain fees and expenses such as loan fees, escrow costs, and the like. Again, the rules are complex about whether such items can be deducted as expenses or treated as investment amounts to be capitalized.

If several persons form a partnership for real estate investment purposes, some of the costs of the partnership can be treated as expenses. The determination of how much an individual investor-partner can allow for expenses relates to such things as his profit and loss interests, cash flow, and distribution rights when the project is completed and sold. Most of the costs of creating the partnership, such as fees paid to general partners, have to be treated as capital costs and added to the invested amounts. On the other hand, costs related to organizing the partnership can be amortized over at least sixty months.

Land and Building

For IRS purposes only buildings and improvements may be depreciated. Obviously, if the building value can be established as a major portion of the total investment, then the amount of depreciation that can be charged is also increased. In order to establish the division of the purchase price between land, building, and improvements, a certified appraisal prepared by an appraiser with a professional designation is usually required. The IRS expects the appraisal to include a number of items that the appraiser should know how to prepare.

Deferring Tax Liabilities

Installment Buying and Selling. One method of spreading the tax liability over several years, so as to reduce its immediate financial impact, is to buy or sell on an installment basis. To qualify, any payments made in the year in which the sale occurs must not exceed 30 percent of the total sales price. If you as a buyer give the seller notes payable at later dates, these are not treated as cash payments. The total sales price includes cash, mortgage indebtedness assumed, and any property, such as notes, received as part of the price. Other complex and interrelated conditions must be met, requiring a review by an experienced tax advisor in this type of transaction so that no additional tax liability is incurred inadvertently.

Exchanging Properties. Another method of deferring tax liabilities is to exchange a property you own for the one you desire. In exchanges the goal is to avoid the use of cash, since any cash paid creates a tax liability. Mortgages can be used effectively to avoid cash problems. In the process of exchanging, you carry with you the tax basis on which your tax liabilities are estimated, but you can develop a new depreciation schedule on the acquired property.

Only like kinds of properties can be exchanged, but the definition of "like" is rather broad. The IRS defines "like," but normally if you are using a property for income production. No matter what the actual use may be, you may exchange for another income/producing property without regard for the actual uses of the property.

Assume that you own an apartment house you can sell for $200,000, for which you have a tax basis of $100,000. There is a mortgage of $90,000 on the property. You wish to buy a property with a market price of $225,000 and a mortgage loan of $120,000. The situation is as follows:

	Your property	*Property to be purchased*
Market value	$200,000	$225,000
Mortgage	90,000	130,000
Equity	$130,000	$120,000
Basis	$100,000	

Property exchanges involve exchanges of equities with the new buyers assuming any mortgages. In this case you might be asked to pay in cash the difference between your equity and that on the other property. If you did, the cash could be subject to tax payments. Instead you could pay off $10,000 on the mortgage on the second property, thus making the equities equal.

Your gain on this transaction would be:

Value of property acquired	$225,000
Mortgage liabilities subject to which you exchanged your property	90,000
Total consideration received	$315,000
Minus: Tax basis for property transferred	$100,000
Mortgage liability on the new property	120,000
Credits in exchange	$220,000
Total consideration received	$315,000
Minus credits	−220,000
Non-taxable gain on the exchange	$115,000

WORKING YOUR WAY AGAINST THE TAX OPPONENTS

You can organize your investment game plan so that you are always ready to obtain maximum financial advantage of current tax laws and interpretations. If you follow these principles, you will not have to be a tax "expert," even though you can obtain all the advantages of one.

Basic Philosophy of Federal Income Taxing

All income is taxed in varying degrees depending upon how the income was earned.

Income is earned as payment for the use of services or materials

Income is earned by the increase in the value of an asset held and the realization of the income by sale.

Higher taxes are paid on income from services and materials, but the expenses of earning this income are deductible.

Expense deduction for tax depreciation need not equal actual.

Lower taxes are paid on income from asset value increase, but there are fewer deductions that can be charged against the earning of this income.

Property held more than six months may be classified as an asset, and the increase in value is a *capital gain*. For tax purposes, only a portion of the gain is counted for tax purposes, and the amount of taxes to be paid is a fixed percentage regardless of the taxpayer's bracket.

Income from the sale of a property held less than six months is not capital gain and is fully taxable as earned income.

Short-term losses may be offset against long-term gains.

General rules when dealing with taxes are:

When a gain is anticipated, capital assets should be considered.

When a loss is anticipated, ordinary business income should be considered.

Capital Asset
Versus a Noncapital Asset

What is a capital asset?

It is defined in negative terms.

All property except that held for resale or for use in the taxpayer's business.

Typically, it would be a residence or property held for appreciation in value.

Some examples and problems:

Property used in a trade or business, held for more than six months and for the income it produces. Property is actually an adjunct to the business—net result of such property sales could be a capital gain.

Property held for resale—that is, a dealer's assets, such as property held by a real estate broker—depending on how it is handled, could be a capital gain or fully reportable income.

Noncapital asset

Property held as stock in trade

Depreciable property—scheduling depreciation

Real property used in a trade or business

Principles in Working with Federal Income Taxes

Only a qualified expert should be used to settle these matters.

These rules and regulations are subject to change and re-interpretation yearly in the light of laws passed by Congress and interpretations of the Internal Revenue Bureau and the courts.

Federal income tax considerations may not be the only things to consider when handling a property—state laws, license fees, franchise taxes, sales taxes, effects of irrevocable trusts—must all be remembered.

In any one situation there may be several regulations that must be considered since they may all affect a particular parcel of property.

An expert should be qualified in several ways: education, experience, library, legal, and accounting background, clients he has served, breadth of view, field of specialization.

Purpose is to give taxpayer some choice as to when he pays taxes.

Avoiding taxes is perfectly proper, and taxpayers should seek to take full advantage of the law and get taxes to as low a level as possible. Evasion is illegal and can result in fines and imprisonment.

Chronological, Accurate, Fully Documented Records

When a property is purchased—cost price, legal fees, title insurance, surveys, commissions.

When property is held for investment—cost of maintenance, management expenses, expenses of preservation and operations, expenses of looking after the property.

Capital expenses add to tax basis—they are expenses that lengthen life of property, relate to more than one year of property operation.

Expenses of operating add to expense deductions—do not add to life, merely maintain it.

Each property to have a separate bank account and records—check stubs and deposit books are cheap and accurate.

Tax Savings in Exchanges

No gain or loss recognized when property is exchanged for *like kind*.

Cash or other than real property, when included as part of price, must be counted for taxes.

Exchanges are useful when it is desired to postpone tax payments.

Example of advantages of an exchange:

Able owns an industrial property purchased for $30,000. It has depreciated so that tax base is now $25,000. The market value is $40,000.

If Able sells the property and purchases a store, sale would result in $15,000 gain.

If an industrial building were exchanged for a store, there would be no tax at this time; but the basis for the building is $25,000.

Methods of Influencing the Taxes Due or Payable

Control type of property being sold by selection prior to purchase.

Change the identity of the seller—private person, corporation, partnership, trust, etc.

Control the time of the sale by postponing closing date of sale and postponing date of payment.

Use installment buying.

CHECKING YOUR TAX SAVINGS POTENTIALS

By now you may wonder whether you can ever understand how to take maximum investment advantage of Federal income tax law—a familiar feeling even for those investors who think they understand the *ins* and *outs* of income tax regulations. Do not be overly concerned about your inability to deal with income tax laws initially, or even eventually. Experienced tax advisors can help you achieve substantial savings in your income tax liabilities, as long as they know what you intend to accomplish. To that end the following questions are provided to help you deal with the advisors on an "expert" basis:

What is the distribution between capital gains and earned income?

Can the ownership form be arranged to maximize investment objectives?

Have all requirements been considered to be able to maximize all income and capital gain goals?

Is an acceptable appraisal available to substantiate decisions about capital gains and income earned and to identify depreciable and nondepreciable real estate?

If there are tenants in the income-producing properties, can any improvements made by them be treated to maximize capital improvement record crediting potentials?

Have all opportunities to recognize and document income and expenses been maximized?

Can all losses be documented?

Can maximum allowable depreciation charges be arranged for?

Are all interest payments recognized and deductions arranged?

Are all *ad valorem* property taxes recognized and included for estimation purposes?

Are tenants on lease arrangements that convert their rents to business expenses for them; or, if you are a tenant, have you considered that all rental expenses are deductible compared to some restrictions on property you own and use? Are tenant financial liabilities fully described?

Are all potential repairs, improvements, property changes fully described, documented and all amounts expended fully accounted for, so that capital improvements and expenses can be differentiated?

Are all expenses related to the investment identified, documented, and fully accounted for in figuring investment potentials?

Have all opportunities been considered for postponing or deferring tax liabilities to fit investment objective?

Any potentials for tax-free exchanges?

Any potentials for installment sales?

Have sales-leaseback potentials been discussed with tenants and potential buyers and sellers of all properties considered?

In this situation the investor buys the property from the current owner (or in agreement with a possible tenant) with the understanding that the old owners (or future tenant) will sign a lease to continue to use the property. The lease can be used by the investor as security for the mortgage money and as a means to assure continued income to pay off the investment. The seller (or future tenant) will therefore receive the cash he may need in his business and rental payments, which can be a total deductible expense.

Can property be mortgaged and proceeds be used for investment potentials?

These questions soon lead to more complex questions and better answers on how Federal income tax law can be used to help you attain your real estate investment objectives.

SAMPLES OF HOW TO WIN BY LOSING

Because income tax laws change annually and there are many rulings to be considered when determining the impact of taxes on your real estate investment, you have to keep current on these laws. You can do it in a number of ways:

1. Professional journals such as *The Appraisal Journal, The Real Estate Review, The Property Management Journal, The National Association of*

Realtors Journal all usually contain articles on the latest laws and rulings and how they will affect real estate.

2. You can secure from the Internal Revenue Service free booklets on the current laws and rules for your personal income tax reports and for any business. Simply call the nearest Internal Revenue Service office for information on this.

3. Libraries carry Federal income tax services. For example, there is the Prentice-Hall income tax service with special sections on real estate.

4. Approximately one or two months after the new tax laws are passed, any major accounting, management consulting, and securities dealer firms hold invitational seminars at which they discuss the latest changes. Usually you can call and get an invitation.

Some illustrations relating to current (1976) tax laws indicate how you may use tax laws to improve your investment potentials:

1. When you are building a new property, there are some expenses connected with construction before completion that can be capitalized and added to your investment total, but only for a short period of time (ten years).

2. If you buy a second home for investment, you can actually use it for personal, or pleasure, purposes for more than the fourteen days or 10 percent of the number of days the home is rented, as specified by the income tax laws. Deductions may still be made, but they cannot exceed the gross income. If the property is rented for less than fifteen days in a year, then the rental income need not be reported, and property expenses may not be deducted on your income tax return.

3. Prepaid interest has to be prorated over the life of the loan, no matter when the interest is paid or how much is paid.

4. If you buy and rehabilitate low-income housing, you can deduct the write-off for depreciation in sixty months.

5. If residential real estate is held for less than one hundred months, depreciation can be charged only on a straight-line (equal annual depreciation rate) basis. If the property is sold in a shorter time, any depreciation above the allowed depreciation must be treated as earned income.

6. Condominium management and home owner associations can choose to be treated as tax-exempt organizations under certain conditions.

Of course, other provisions and details can alter your situation. Perhaps these examples will encourage you to get good income tax advice before you undertake a real estate investment. Almost any good tax consultant will save you in income taxes the amount you pay for the services, or at least keep you from losing money by your not taking full advantage of all possible tax provisions.

Remember, the game is to avoid taxes, using maximum opportunities to decide when to pay and how much—but do not try to evade taxes. You must expect to pay your legal "fair share."

Using
Other People's
Money

8

Suppose you cannot find a "friendly" neighborhood bank or savings institution to furnish you a loan—what then? All is not lost. There are many other sources of loans.

PARTNERSHIPS

You may be able to find others who are as convinced as you that you have found a good investment. They are ready to invest some of their money, so you form a partnership. A *partnership* is a legal agreement based on how much each partner invests, the sharing of expenses and other liabilities connected with the investment, and the distribution of profits (or losses). The agreement should be prepared by a lawyer and can consist of one of two major types of partnerships: (a) general and (b) limited.

To understand the differences between the two forms of partnerships, you should determine the following:

1. On what basis will each partner be responsible for the debts occurring from the investment—maintenance, repairs, improvements, labor and so on? Under what conditions can you be assessed for additional amounts?

2. On what basis will each partner share in any income or increases in capital value or in the distribution of assets if the partnership is dissolved?
3. Who will be responsible for "managing" the investment, and how, and how much will the manager be paid?
4. What happens if for any reason one of the partners wants to dissolve the partnership?
5. What are the tax advantages and disadvantages?

If there is a sharing of all these responsibilities and benefits, you have a general partnership. If one or a few of the partners assume major responsibilities, leaving the remaining partners with only a "limited" relationship (as legally defined), the partnership is limited.

Why would you want to use a partnership? Because:

1. More money is available for the investment.
2. All partners receive the full benefit of income tax laws as they would if they were investing individually.
3. Risk can be less than what it would be if you were an individual.
4. The costs of organizing are low and the agreement can be prepared easily.
5. Management of the investment can be shared.
6. The purpose for which the partnership is organized can be limited.

The secret of a successful partnership is finding persons who can work well with each other and who agree fully on all the terms and conditions necessary to make the investment a success. Before you finally agree to a partnership, be sure to have the partnership agreement reviewed by an experienced lawyer/tax advisor so that you understand fully all your obligations and opportunities.

SYNDICATES (OR JOINT VENTURES)

A *syndicate* is a group that joins together for a specific reason and dissolves the group when that reason no longer exists. For example, a group of persons can join together to buy a single piece of property. When the property is sold the syndicate is dissolved. A syndicate can be any form of business organization—partnership, corporation, or any of the other more particular forms. As with a partnership, the members of the syndicate should be in agreement as to the purpose, as well as to the responsibilities related to the investment.

If you are thinking of using a syndicate form, mortgage lenders and real estate brokers can help you locate experienced real estate persons and lawyers to help you with the technicalities of forming the organization and to provide expert assistance in managing the assets of the organization.

The primary advantage of a syndicate is that many persons with small amounts to invest can join together to purchase a large, expensive real property. Since this type of activity represents the sales of "shares," syndicates are often subject to public review and regulation by a state or Federal agency. If the syndicate is small in terms of the number of investors and amount invested, it may escape regulation. On the other hand, if the syndicate is large and many investors will be invited to participate, its offerings may be subject to review by the Securities and Exchange Commission (SEC). Government inspection and approval will help you avoid many of the common errors made by inexperienced investors.

Syndicates may be formed either for the purchase of an identified property or for particular investment purposes with the types of properties to be purchased not specified. The latter type of investment poses some problems for you since you may not know how much you will have to invest, and the property finally purchased may not be suitable to your investment objectives. Since all syndicates publish information about how they will be formed and operated, be sure to acquire this publication and read it carefully. If you find difficulty in interpreting it, pay for the review and advice of an experienced real estate investment advisor/lawyer, real estate broker, CPA, or tax accountant.

CORPORATIONS

A corporation is an attractive way to raise money for investments through the sale of shares of interest in the corporation in reasonably small amounts—perhaps as low as five or ten dollars. A corporation, as a "legal" identity, can create agreements, borrow money, sell assets, or do anything else provided for in its articles of incorporation. If you plan to form a corporation you will need expert legal advice, since there are many Federal and state laws to comply with before the corporation can begin operations.

Like anything else in life, corporations have some advantages you may like:

1. Liability is limited to the assets of the corporation, so that none of the stockholders has personal liability in case of financial disasters.

2. Shares in the corporation can be divided into smaller price units.
3. Stockholders elect the management, but management can be professional, chosen on the basis of merit rather than the amounts invested.
4. The life of the corporation can extend indefinitely.

And some disadvantages:

1. Organizing a corporation is costly, complicated, and sometimes time-consuming.
2. The corporation must pay taxes before it distributes profits or dividends.
3. The corporate charter limits the activities of the corporation. If stock is sold publicly, various regulatory agencies affect the operations of the corporation.

REAL ESTATE INVESTMENT TRUSTS (REITs)

Real estate investment trusts (REITs) were created through special legislation that permits them to have some of the characteristics of partnerships and corporations. A group of trustees form the REIT and sell ownership shares to the general public. The REIT can invest in real estate, in mortgages, or in both. The liabilities of the stockholders are limited as they are in any corporation. However, some of the tax advantages of the partnership are offered to the REIT stockholders.

REIT can sometimes be the source of funds for developing or buying existing properties.

Because the special qualities of REITs are difficult to explain in a short space, contact a local mortgage lender or a stock broker and ask for a fuller explanation of REITs.

BEFORE YOU LEAP ...

If you are planning to invest with others in a partnership, syndication, or another form of organization, you should ask some basic questions. If you cannot answer "yes" to any of the following questions, get additional information until you are satisfied that you can give an affirmative answer.

1. Can the organizer (syndicator) provide evidence of successful development or management of the project in which you will invest?

2. Have all payments to the syndicator been fully disclosed?

3. Have all costs of organization and other front-end costs been fully disclosed?

4. Are you provided with an accurate and full statement as to when you will begin receiving "profits" or "dividends" from the investment?

5. Are all financial statements certified by competent legal and accounting persons? (A CPA certification is best.)

6. Are the investment prospects for the project detailed by income and expenses for all years during which you will be invested and on a detailed annual basis?

7. Have you had your own tax advisor evaluate the promised "income tax advantages" of the investment as they relate to your particular situation?

8. Have you visited the property and the area in which it is located?

9. Apart from the obvious income tax advantages, does the project make economic sense according to the principles outlined in this book?

10. Will the project be managed by an experienced property manager?

11. Will you receive periodic, certified reports on the financial status of the project?

12. Has the project been reviewed and approved by appropriate state authorities and the Securities and Exchange Commission? Or, is it a smaller project not requiring governmental approval or review? Has it been reviewed and certified by a professional appraiser and property manager?

13. Are those organizing and managing the project providing you with the following reports? Are they satisfactory to you?
    a. Form or organization?
    b. Credit standing?
    c. Ability to keep the project feasible as an investment?
    d. Reputation for integrity and interest in protecting all investors in the project?
    e. Interest in any other projects that might conflict with interests in this project?
    f. Reports of all visits and evaluations made by the organizers of the project?

14. Are all possible assessments outlined and your financial responsibilities carefully delineated?

15. Can you "drop out" of the project without serious legal or financial problems?

16. Will you receive regular reports on all compensation paid to the organizers, brokers, or others who are used as experts in the organization, management, and sale of the project?

17. Is the plan for distributing profits, proceeds, or other financial returns specific as to your situation?

18. Will the project organizer and managers be compensated in direct proportion to the earnings to the investors?

THE FORM OF INVESTMENT ORGANIZATION AND INCOME TAX LAW

An important element in selecting any form of investment organization is to determine how it will affect your Federal income tax liabilities. Though you should use professional assistance in making this determination, here are some basic ideas to remember:

1. As a partner, you have a tax liability equal to that of an individual. However, the partnership agreement can be arranged so that expenses may give you some tax shelters.
2. Joint venture is the same as a partnership.
3. Syndication creates liabilities related to the syndicate agreement, but in most cases the liability is the same as in a partnership.
4. Incorporating creates a tax liability for the corporation after which the stockholders receive any profits or capital distributions on which, in turn, they must also pay income taxes.

MISCELLANEOUS AND OFTEN OVERLOOKED . . .

Many kinds of organizations collect money that they must invest: trusts, endowments, pension funds, commercial credit companies, to name a few. If, for instance, your prospective investment has some "unusual" features that are discouraging the "usual" lenders, or if it exceeds their financial interests or legal limitations, you might look into these other sources of financing.

Unfortunately, these sources are often overlooked because they are off the beaten path, so to speak. An experienced financial advisor, your local banker, or your local real estate agent can probably help you locate and identify such potential lenders. Since each of the sources invests under different conditions and/or requirements, each has to be contacted individually.

1. Lines of credit. If you are planning to build something new and have a good credit reputation, materials suppliers, even building contractors, may give you ninety to a hundred and twenty days in which to pay what is owed.

During that time you may find financing from regular sources and save interest while you are building and searching.

2. *Trust*. Trusts are legal forms of holding property in which the trustee is expected to look for appropriate forms of investment for his trust funds. Frequently the trust officer has certain restrictions to which you may have to agree, but you may also get the amount you need to borrow at attractive, even if higher, interest rates.

3. *Endowments*. Colleges, universities, and nonprofit organizations frequently hold assets on which they must earn but which they cannot sell. Perhaps you can find an endowment with cash to invest at rates higher than the rates they receive on their current investments. You would need to talk to the endowment fund director or board to tailor your proposal to meet their limitations.

4. *Pension Funds*. Pension funds have many legal limitations placed on their investment programs, but more and more are able to consider either real estate investments or real estate securities. Again, each pension fund has special requirements so that if you are thinking of inviting one to become an investment partner or to provide loan funds, you must expect to spend considerable time talking with their legal and investment advisors.

5. *Commercial Credit Companies*. Many commercial credit companies that make consumer loans (for cars, furniture, appliances) are becoming increasingly interested in the higher earnings associated with real estate investments. They would expect you to submit a very professional proposal but also can be very flexible in providing financing.

6. *Private persons*. Professional persons—lawyers, doctors, corporate managers—have large incomes for which they seek some form of tax shelter or investment that provides continued income in later years. Usually they have investment counsellors who will work with you in preparing your investment. These persons frequently are willing to take large risks for high profits—tax-sheltered income or long-term capital gains.

Becoming
A Professional
Player

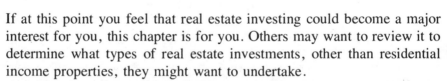

9

If at this point you feel that real estate investing could become a major interest for you, this chapter is for you. Others may want to review it to determine what types of real estate investments, other than residential income properties, they might want to undertake.

First we will review the principles of leverage and pyramiding in an investment example involving constant exchanging for larger, better properties. This is followed by checklists summarizing the kinds of information you need for evaluating the investment potentials of apartment houses, undeveloped land, subdividing and developing, and recreational land. (These are the most common types of property uses found in investors' portfolios.)

USING PYRAMIDING TO BUILD EQUITY

Exhibit 9-1 is a more realistic picture of pyramiding than the previous illustration, which was largely hypothetical.

Pyramiding is successful only when property values are increasing.

Exhibit 9-1 Using Pyramiding to Build Equity

	Property A (Home)	Property B (Duplex)	Property C (4 Apts)	Property D (10 Apts)
Purchase Information:				
Purchase price	$25,000	$48,000	$140,000	$285,000
Down payment	$ 2,500	**$12,000**	**$ 28,000**	**$ 57,000**
First mortgage	$22,500	$36,000	$112,000	$228,000
Terms in years	25	25	25	25
Interest rate	8%	8.5%	9%	9.5%
Monthly payments	$174.26	$259.32	$ 939.90	$1,992.03
Investment Period (Years):	5	5	5	5
Value at end of period	$32,000	$45,946	$163,000	$371,000
Unpaid mortgage amount	$22,578	$29,882	$104,500	$213,707
Total interest paid	$ 9,126*	$13,000*	$ 48,019	$103,424
Property taxes paid	$ 2,500	$ 4,800	$ 19,500	$ 35,600
Tax deductible expenses	$11,626	$17,800	$67,519	$139,024
Equity at End of Period:				
Down payment	$2,500	$12,000	$26,000	$57,000
Equity buildup (mortgage payments)	$2,422	$ 6,118	$ 8,000	$14,300
Value increase	$ 7,000	$ 9,946*	$23,000	$ 86,000
Total equity	$11,922	$28,064	**$57,000**	**$157,300**
	(or **$12,000**)	(or **$28,000**)		
Costs of exchanging for next property (cash outlays):		$3,400		
Potential gross income	$ 3,600	$ 7,200	$ 20,000	$ 41,000
annual (5 years)	$18,000	$36,000	$100,000	$205,000
Available for all other property expenses (5 years)	$ 6,374	$18,200	$ 32,481	$ 65,976

*Rounded

The limited down payment allows you to use borrowed money to buy the property, during which time the value of the property increases—thus giving you an increased equity.

In the illustration the investor starts by renting out a home and then exchanging it for a duplex apartment. Holding each investment for five years, the increased equity is exchanged at the end of each period for a larger income-producing apartment.

Pyramiding and leverage are effective means of adding to your rate of profit return. In Exhibit 9-1 a down payment of only $2,500 is pyramided, with the use of borrowed funds, into a $285,000 apartment investment, with an equity of $157,300. The time to accomplish this might vary from as few as five or ten years to as many as twenty. Given the inflationary spiral and an apparently undiminished need for rental units, the process could occur in a period of months. However, remember that each market differs in its timing and in its growth curve, and these factors determine whether your investment succeeds.

Exhibit 9-1 exemplifies the goals of all real estate investors— earned income and capital gains. Principles you should keep in mind if you decide to pursue this route include:

1. Maintain a cash reserve that can be used to meet expenses when market turns down or rising expenses reduce the cash flow.
2. Diversify your investments by property type, by area, and by entering the market at different periods of time.
3. Select properties that are convertible at minimum expense to a variety of uses.
4. Structure the financing so that refinancing is possible without extensive time delays or additional money costs.
5. Be ready to pay for all the required expert advice, particularly for the management of the property and its exchange for other properties.
6. Keep track of the growth curves of the market in which you are investing and always try to get out of that market while the curve is still ascending sharply.
7. Do not wed yourself to a particular type of property. Let your choice relate to your investment objectives and market opportunities.
8. Buy development rights as a bundle, but break down the bundle into individual rights and place a price on each.
9. Emphasize location in your investment selection and then maximize its potential through appropriate development or changes in the existing developments.
10. Through careful analysis and skillful negotiation secure the property on the terms and price that meet your goals.
11. Associate with others only when you are certain their investment goals are the same as yours and they are willing to invest on terms and conditions that you feel are necessary.

APARTMENTS

After paying for mortgage payments (principal and interest) and property taxes, there is a relatively small percentage of the gross income available for paying all the rest of the expenses. Probably this type of investment would require paying some of the expenses from other income, perhaps not. If you are able to do much of the janitorial and maintenance work, you can keep the expenses down.

Some factors you might want to think about before selecting an apartment include:

1. *How much of your time and effort will you apply?*
   Apartments require considerable attention and you may not be able to afford full-time experienced property managers and maintenance personnel.
2. *An older or a new building?*
   Older units command smaller rents and may have higher operational and maintenance costs, but you can get a good record of past income and expenses. Newer units are easier to maintain, must produce higher rents, but present better chances for higher depreciation write-off for tax purposes. An older building may have been neglected so that with minimum investment of time and money you can rehabilitate it so that it brings in higher rents without a proportionate increase in costs.
3. *Furnished or unfurnished?*
   Furnished units command higher rents and the furnishings provide an opportunity for high depreciation for tax purposes. However, tenants in such units tend to move more often and sometimes abuse the furnishings and the apartment so that maintenance and repair costs may be high.
4. *Should the apartment build equity, current income, or both?*
   In the illustration the chief advantage of the apartments is that they build the equity of the investor—but there is no earned income. Shopping for an apartment that meets both equity buildup and income production goals can be very time-consuming. You may have to make a choice between equity and income.

RAW (UNDEVELOPED) LAND INVESTMENTS

Raw land is sometimes seen as an attractive investment because the down payment is small and the potential returns appear to be high. But many problems are associated with buying land for investment purposes because it is really a form of speculation, not investment. Land can be an investment only when you have sound guarantees that it will be used shortly in a development project; otherwise, do not invest in land unless you are willing to lose all you invest.

Unfortunately, raw land investment always sounds so attractive that very often the heart overcomes the mind in buying it. You have probably been attracted to: ". . . price covers land near a lake where your family can enjoy boating and fishing. Enough land to put in a small garden plot or to keep horses. Room enough to put a cabin without being near your neighbors. Blue sky and quiet, away from the smog and congestion of your city living.'' Admittedly the advertising is almost irresistible.

You may have also seen an advertisement in your local newspaper, or perhaps you have received an announcement in the mail, for land auctions. Is this an opportunity for investment—or loss?

PUBLIC LAND AUCTION—LOTS AND ACREAGE

Lots and acreage have become available in the metropolitan area only short driving times from the very center of the city. The owners of these lands have asked us to liquidate their holdings. Some of these lands have been in family holdings for years, others are being sold because the owners need cash now.

This is your opportunity to obtain half- to five-acre parcels at exceptional prices. Your choice of desert, lake mountain, or foothills properties—a few near major bodies of water.

Minimum bid: $10 and up. Write or call:

Professional Land Liquidators
5322 Oliver Boulevard, Box 32, Albustate,————
Call toll free: 800-500-0000

The important rule in approaching such a purchase is: *there are no bargains in real estate*. You receive in value just about what you pay. Too frequently this method of selling encourages spirited competition among prospective buyers. Lotteries are used increasingly in cases where inflation or land fever has reached a high pitch. All potential buyers receive numbers. When the numbers are drawn, those who win must make a down payment and complete the transaction within a given period or give up their rights to purchase. Some winners actually make their profits by selling their rights to buy. Sometimes the sellers put limits on prices, but the new buyers all too frequently try to sell quickly and take their profits.

As a sad result of all this fierce buying, the final prices are far too high for the kinds of land purchased. Often these lands are not even accessible over anything but very primitive roads. *So do not be rushed into buying!* Recheck everything we have said about land purchases and be careful. *Again, do not allow the "fever" to cause you to buy unwisely*—you will make money by using the principles presented in this book. Rarely do any bargains occur in auctions and lotteries, particularly for the second buyers.

Fortunately, sound investigative techniques are very effective "prescriptions'' for this kind of fever. Exhibit 9-2 gives you some idea of how to organize your thinking on an investment idea.

Your first task is, of course, to make a careful financial analysis of the potentials:

1. How much down payment? _____

2. Costs of acquiring land? _____

3. Financing costs and monthly payments? _____

4. Special assessments for roads, water, trash and garbage disposal, parks, etc.? _____

5. Payments for recreational or club house privileges, if offered? _____

6. Typical costs of bringing electricity, water, sewage disposal to site? _____

Another way of calculating the potential costs would be:

		Your *Investment:*
1. Percentage of purchase price down × earnings on money down		_____
Example: 10% down and you could earn 5.75% on this money if it were in a savings deposit; .10 × .0575 =	.00575	_____
2. Interest payments on the loan *Example:* 90% loan at 9%, .90 × .09	.081	_____
3. Costs of holding the property—taxes, insurance, special assessment *Example:* taxes = 2%. Insurance ¼%. Assessment 1% of total value.	.0325	_____
4. Profit you wish to make on the total investment	.1500	_____
5. Cost of selling at end of five years (averaged on an annual basis)	.0200	_____
Average percentage by which land must increase in value to meet your investment goals.	.28925 or 28.9%	

If you are still interested in the land, here are some other questions. If you cannot answer in the affirmative, you should consider not investing or doing more market research.

Exhibit 9-2 Underdeveloped Land as an Investment

Assumptions:

Price per acre	$1,000
Down payment	$ 100
Loan (15 years @ 9%)	$9,900
Monthly payment	$ 100.41
Annual payment	$1,204.95
Brokerage Commissions 15% sales price	$1,500
Maintenance, additional cost 1% of original value annually	$ 100

Holding Costs	*% of Original Price*
Mortgage payments (price and interest)	12.17
Property taxes	2.75
Return on equity 10%	1.00
Maintenance, other holding cost	1.00
Annual holding costs as % of original price	16.92%

Assume 20% annual price increase
Assume a 5-year holding period and sale

	Total	*Annual Average*
Price increase	$14,883.20	$2,976.64
Brokerage Commission 10%	2,488.32	497.66
Net after commission	$12,394.88	$2,478.98
Total tax (3% annual increase)	1,460.02	292.00
	$10,934.86	$2,186.98
Mortgage interest paid	3,977.12	795.42
	$ 6,957.74	$1,391.56
10% on original equity	61.05	12.21
	$6,896.69	$1,379.35
Maintenance and holding costs	61.05	12.21
1% on original price 10% earnings		
	$6,835.64	$1,367.14
Original equity	100.00	
Price increase	14,883.20	
Equity build up, mortgage	2,073.46	
	$17,956.66	

Assume 10% annual price increase, 5 years holding period.

Price increase	$6,105.10	$1,221.02
Brokerage Commission 10%	1,610.05	302.01
	$4,495.05	$ 919.01
Mortgage interest paid	3,977.12	795.42
	$ 517.93	$ 123.59
10% on original equity	61.05	12.21
	$ 556.88	$ 111.38

Exhibit 9-2 (cont.)

		Total	*Annual Average*
Maintenance holding cost		61.05	61.05
		$ 495.83	$ 50.33
Original equity	$ 100.00		
Price increase	6,105.10		
Equity buildup, mortgage	1,973.46		
Equity increase	$8,178.56		

1. Is there a report from a Federal or state agency that informs you of the problems and costs of buying this land?
2. Have you visited the area and seen the land you will purchase?
3. Have you been furnished with a list of building restrictions or other rules that will affect your use of the land and possible construction of improvements on the site?
4. Is there a neighborhood organization or a set of land use covenants to control building on the land and its use?
5. Are utilities (water, electricity, gas, sewage disposal) available to the lot line so that you can hook into them inexpensively when you are ready to build?
6. Is there a scarcity of land like this, or does there seem to be an ample supply nearby? What are the prices of the adjacent lands?
7. If you must resell, who will do it and how much would the resale cost?
8. Do you obtain underground mineral, oil, and other development rights?
9. Is the land subject to flooding or other periodic natural hazards?
10. How much land is available for sale in this project and how many buyers are there so far?
11. Do you get a fee title, or only use rights?
12. Who is offering the land for sale and can you verify the reputation for honest dealing of the seller?
13. Can you obtain financing and on what terms if you decide to build?
14. Will you have continued, free access to your land?
15. Has the seller pledged any portion of the land for his debts?
16. Has the seller any financial obligations which are unpaid and which might prevent him from giving you a clear title?
17. Do you have in writing an agreement that includes everything the sales personnel promised?

Interstate land sales are controlled by Federal regulations administered by the Department of Housing and Urban Development (HUD),

Washington, D.C. 20411. If you are thinking of investing in raw land, you should write to them and ask for any information they can supply on buying raw land. You can obtain free the pamphlet *Consumer Protection, Interstate Land Sales* from the Office of Interstate Land Sales Registration. HUD, Washington, D.C. 20411.

SUBDIVIDING AND DEVELOPING

As you become more experienced in real estate investing, you will be given opportunities to participate in the buying and developing of land. Typically a builder or contractor will approach you with this kind of offering:

Anticipated costs:	
Land purchase, cost per acre	$ 3,000
Development of land to a buildable basis	2,000
Construction of homes, 5 per acre @ $25,000	125,000
Sales, holding, and financing costs	10,000
Total Costs	$140,000
Costs per home ($140,000/5)	$28,000
Anticipated income:	
Sales price per home $32,000 × 5	$160,000
Anticipated profits	20,000
Distribution of proceeds:	
To land owner for furnishing land	1,500
Investors'	9,250
Builder's profits	9,250
	$ 20,000
Investors' initial investment	$ 28,000
(to pay for land and provide down payments needed to secure construction loan)	
Investors' return $9,250/$28,000	33%

On the basis of this financial analysis the investment opportunities appear very bright. However, if these opportunities are so great why doesn't the builder invest more of his own funds and retain more of the profits? Why is the land owner paid such a high profit for his land? Why wouldn't the lender provide a 100 percent construction loan and perhaps ask for participation in the potential profits? The answer, briefly, is that full development requires twelve to eighteen months minimum from the time that the land is purchased until the last home is sold. In the meantime markets change, financing may become difficult to obtain, costs may rise more rapidly than anticipated. A number of problems can develop that cannot be anticipated but that can reduce profits, perhaps even create losses.

Builders and investors do make high profits, but there are a number of precautions investors should keep in mind before participating. The following checklist should help you decide what to do. Before you rely too heavily on your findings, however, you should check out the answers with an experienced mortgage lender, builder, and appraiser. You can expect to spend perhaps two or three weeks collecting the information; do not allow the builder-developer or the syndicates to pressure you into making a decision before you are satisfied that you have the answers you need to these questions:

1. Has the builder had experience in developing such projects?
2. Do other investors with whom he has worked report that they were satisfied with the builder's performance?
3. Do the builder's creditors give a good recommendation about the builder's payment record?
4. Is the development plan supported by an informative feasibility analysis that establishes a market need for the development?
5. Is the financial plan supported by a professional and detailed appraisal report that supports the proposed sales prices and sales volume?
6. Will an inspection service be used to make sure that the builder uses his financial proceeds on the development as scheduled and will these reports be furnished to investors on a monthly basis?
7. Has a lawyer and a tax consultant reviewed the partnership (syndication) agreement and approved of it in light of your investment goals and potentials?
8. If the project fails, are you free of any additional liability except for your initial investment?
9. Does the builder have an effective marketing organization or plan to help promote sales?
10. Will the builder construct model units immediately and use them to gauge the rate at which he should plan to build and sell?
11. Will you be able to visit the project regularly and check personally on what progress is being made?
12. Will the builder provide you with regular certified reports on income and expenditures made on the project?

13. Does the planned development appear to be competitive with other nearby developments and is it responsive to local market demands?

You may not be able to obtain clear, affirmative answers to all these questions, but, whenever you cannot, your investment risks increase and your potentials for that high rate of return are reduced.

The pitfalls in such developments are many so high rates of return should be expected. To give you some idea of how complex the process of subdividing and developing can be, look at Exhibit 9-3 listing the steps and procedures in analyzing the potential. Clearly this is not a field of investment for amateurs. Just below the diagram is a typical financial breakdown for such developments. Notice that the builder will probably limit his cash investment to paying for the option. On the other hand the private investor usually furnishes cash for the purchase of the land. The returns for the private investor are usually between 80 and 100 percent of the cash that is furnished. The return for the builder on his cash investment is 650 percent in the illustration. However, the builder must use this return to compensate for all the time he invests and the experience he brings to the project.

RECREATIONAL DEVELOPMENTS

An increasingly attractive extra investment for many families is the remote recreational development. Typically this type of property is advertised as being available for family recreation while the family is young and for retirement when the children leave. Advertisements show pictures of wooded lots, lakes or rivers, club houses, horses, hiking and bike trails, golf courses, and many other amenities. The lots for sale are described as being ready for building with utilities, water and sewage disposal facilities, and roads available to the site. Sometimes swimming, golf, and other recreational facilities are promised coincident or shortly after lot sales begin.

Recreational developments can be good investments, but they can also be absolute financial disasters. A basic rule in purchasing such property is to visit the development and have the site you wish to buy identified for you. Some of the major questions to have affirmative answers to before investing are:

1. Have you read—and did you understand—the statement which the developer is required to furnish either by your state or by the Federal government?

Exhibit 9-3   Appraisal Processes for Subdividing and Developing

Analysis	Procedure
1. Vacant land market	1. Prices—costs of developing Terms of availability Sizes of parcels and locations
2. Location analysis	2. Adjacent uses Direction of city growth Use limitations Available services
3. Government regulations	3. Planning, zoning, codes Taxes State and local controls and procedures
4. Title problems	4. Private agreements—easements, covenants Liens—financial, taxes Above and sub-surface rights Title clearance
5. Market considerations	5. Size of market Property sizes Prices, terms, state of market
6. Engineering, developing costs	6. Grading Streets, sewers, utilities, drainage, sidewalks Construction staking Maps
7. Financial arrangements	7. Equity needs Mortgage amounts and costs Marketing costs Holding costs
8. Marketing	8. Sales plans—advertising Sales staff

Used by permission: Frederick E. Case, *Real Estate* (Boston: Allyn and Bacon, Inc., 1962).

This statement should tell you precisely what facilities and developments will be provided and when they will be available. It will also inform you of any potential problems that could arise from using the land.

2. Are you given a reasonable period, at least 48 hours, in which to withdraw from your agreement even though you have signed a purchase agreement?

3. Has the developer furnished you with a certified statement relating to his financial condition and ability to complete the project as promised?

4. Have you been furnished with a time table of when all improvements will be provided and how the developer plans to guarantee the financing of such improvements?

5. Have you visited and inspected the site you wish to buy?

6. Has the developer provided you with full information on all financial outlays

expected of you during the periods of development and when you want to use the facilities?

7. Have you talked to persons who have already purchased?

8. Has the developer created other similar types of developments and can you get information on the experience of buyers in these developments?

9. What use restrictions are placed on you with respect to the site:
   a. Can you put tents or recreational vehicles on the site before you erect a permanent building?
   b. Can you keep animals on the site?
   c. Can you install tennis courts, swimming pools, or other kinds of recreational facilities on the site?

10. Are there size and architectural restrictions that will guarantee appropriate development of the entire project?

11. Will there be a property owners organization to determine use restrictions, payments for community facilities?

12. Do the property owners, rather than the developer, receive title to all common facilities and can they determine what the ''dues'' will be?

13. Have you discussed with the developer all the kinds of uses you intend for the site and received assurances that these uses will be possible?

14. Has the developer assured you as to when utilities, sewage disposal, and roads will be provided to your site, and the costs you may incur in bringing these facilities onto your site for your development?

15. Do you have full information on all local zoning and building code requirements?

16. Have you compared the prices and terms of sale for these sites with other comparable properties in the vicinity?

17. Do your property rights include mineral rights?

After you have received positive answers to these questions, you should still check out what you have discovered with an experienced real estate counsellor, perhaps a professional appraiser, developer or tax counsellor—or all of them.

Now that you are ready and capable of entering the investment game, you will have to develop your game schedule—the subject of the next chapter.

Major Types
Of Investment
Games

10

As you develop your ability to analyse potential real estate investments you are ultimately attracted to some of the better known investment games, particularly those relating to planned unit developments, office complexes, shopping centers, industrial parks, and special use properties. Do not undertake these ventures on your own, without all the expert advice you can obtain. The financial investments required are so large you will definitely need partners. In this chapter you will be provided with checklists to help you decide, in a preliminary way, whether you might want to analyze a particular investment in some depth.

The best means of getting precise information on the investment qualities of any of these properties is to ask for a feasibility study, prepared by a professional appraiser who can prove to you that he has the experience and knowledge to undertake such a study. A feasibility study is not an appraisal to set a market value. Instead, it is an analysis of the investment qualities of the project in comparison with your own investment standards, goals, or policies. For this reason you should have clearly in mind at least:

1. the amount of financial risk you wish to take,

2. your objectives—tax shelter, earned income, capital gains, cash flow, a particular rate of return,
3. the period you wish to stay invested, and
4. the extent to which you are willing to engage in the supervision and management of the investment and the property or to use experts for these purposes.

One element of the report is an estimate of the value of the property and the probable price you will have to pay to acquire it. You can use the feasibility study to guide you in negotiating for the price and the terms of purchase for the property. You need not follow the analysts' recommendations closely, but you will know the risks and the limits you should accept to make the investment feasible from your viewpoint.

PLANNED UNIT DEVELOPMENTS (PUD)

As the demand for home ownership continues, land prices rise, and home sites become scarcer, developers are providing a form of residential development in which the units are grouped more closely together but open spaces are preserved for parks, swimming pools, and common recreational facilities. In a typical single-family, detached dwelling development, the homes may average five to eight per acre; but in a planned unit development (PUD), the densities may be two to four—or more—times greater.

Sometimes developers purchase existing apartment buildings and try to change them sufficiently to qualify as PUDs; such conversions do not have the appeal of the true PUD. However, by offering common ownership (condominium or cooperative), the developer offers home ownership with amenities at prices sufficiently below the costs of detached homes; the purchase of an apartment with such a development becomes, therefore, extremely attractive.

If you are approached to invest in converting an apartment rental project to a PUD, with common ownership, seek answers to these questions prior to asking for a feasibility study:

1. Has the developer had experience in converting to PUDs?
2. Has the developer provided you with certified statements about the financial results of other conversions he has made?
3. Will local building codes and zoning regulations permit the conversion?

4. Does the developer have certified accurate estimates of costs that will be incurred in meeting public requirements relating to zoning and building codes?

   Note: These costs can include providing more parking spaces, better insulation, different kinds of access from public streets, installation of sidewalks, curbs, fire plugs.

5. Does the developer have at least three certified bids or estimates of the costs connected with improving the property so that sales can be made?

6. Have you been provided with a professional appraisal report that confirms the market potential at the prices and terms for which the units will be sold?

7. Have you been provided with a plan for development indicating what will be done, when, and at what costs?

8. Have you visited the project and does it look like a reasonable undertaking to you?

9. Have you walked or driven around the neighborhood to determine what kinds of competitive projects exist and what their prices are?

10. Are you convinced that the proposed development will fit into the local area?

COMMON OWNERSHIPS

Three kinds of common ownership residential units may be created:

1. Condominium. If the development is to be sold as a common ownership project it will probably be in the form of a condominium. In a condominium the buyer acquires full use rights to a given living unit and parking space, as well as shared use rights to all public areas—particularly the swimming pool, tennis courts, community rooms, and open spaces. The unit owner must also pay all costs incident to his ownership including mortgage payments, property taxes, maintenance, utilities in his own unit plus costs of creating, maintaining, and using common facilities and areas. The responsibilities of the unit buyers are spelled out in a condominium agreement which each must sign. The contents of such agreements are fully defined under some state laws and are always a necessary part of condominium sales.

2. Cooperative. The buyer receives stock in the cooperative which then gives him rights and responsibilities equivalent to those in a condominium form of ownership. The owner must pay all corporation charges. The management is usually reserved to the board of directors who may or may not be owners of units. When the owner sells, he sells the stock back to the corporation and may or may not be paid for any capital value increases, but usually receives the full original purchase price.

3. Own-your-own Condominium or Cooperative Forms of Ownership. Common ownership properties may take many forms. They can be low- or high-rise multiple units or townhouses in which all units have their lower floor on land. The style of construction has nothing to do with the forms of ownership.

If you are invited to invest in the creation of any of these forms of residential developments first be sure to get "yes" answers to these questions:

1. Has the builder had experience in building this type of unit?
2. Can you visit other projects of this type constructed by this builder, talk with people in the area, and see what quality of construction he provides?
3. Can you talk to other investors who have had experience with this builder?
4. Are you provided with a detailed market study showing that the kinds of units planned will be salable in the proposed market?
5. Has the builder contacted all necessary public officials and received all necessary approvals, or can he show you his plans for securing such approvals?
6. Can the builder show you his "build-out" schedule?
7. Have all cost estimates been certified and checked by an experienced real estate broker, property manager, or other real estate expert familiar with this type of project?
8. Has your investment advisor approved the proposed financial plan?
9. Have you been provided with full information on all financial responsibilities with respect to the project? For example, if some of the units are not sold, will you have to provide some funds to help buy them from the developer?
10. Has a responsible lender indicated a willingness, perhaps a guarantee, to provide funds for construction and for mortgage financing for future buyers?
11. Will the proposed units contain the quality of sound insulation, heating and lighting, and power use efficiencies appropriate to ownership units in this quality and price of development?
12. Will the developer turn over to the unit owners all rights to uses of common facilities?
13. Will the developer be providing supportive parking, office, or retail shop facilities in which you can also invest for the owners of project units?

14. Have other projects been converted to condominiums or have condominiums been built in this market area? Have they been financial successes?

15. Will the builder assist the buyers in securing the services of a professional, competent property manager or management service during the period prior to releasing the project to the buyers?

16. Have you been informed of all of your financial responsibilities if the project does not succeed?

17. Have you been provided with full information on what the living units will be like in appearance, size, and price? What common use facilities will be provided? At what costs?

18. Do you believe, after answering all of the above questions, that this unit will be competitive with other residential units for sale in the local market?

19. Will the costs of owning a unit compare favorably with the costs of renting locally similar kinds of units?

If you are satisfied with the answers from this preliminary investigation, you are now ready to consult the experts to finalize your investment.

OTHER KINDS OF INVESTMENT GAMES

You must always keep in mind that when you become a serious investor and plan to enter the larger, more important investment games, you need the advice of experts. Even if you are offered an investment opportunity from one of these experts, use the others to check out the offer. Detailed checklists should be available for so many types of real estate investment opportunities—but they are not. Nonetheless, you can do some evaluative work of your own by keeping in mind:

1. the market for the property uses,
2. the location potentials for that property,
3. the capacity of the site to permit maximum access to the local market and maximum attraction for potential property tenants and users, and
4. the ability of the building to provide the income potentials necessary to warrant the investment.

A standard form of analysis is illustrated with applications to rental apartment properties, shopping centers, office buildings, industrial properties, and special use properties. After studying these carefully you should know how to go about preparing an appropriate investment checklist for any other property in which you are interested.

The checklists can be used by you to make a quick initial analysis of any property offered to you for investment purposes and then to help you discuss with your experts the kinds of information you need before you can decide on investing. Remember, however, that these checklists relate only to the properties and not to your personal investment plan.

Rental Apartment Houses

The Market.   Will the market absorb this type of apartment project?

Can inexpensive investments be made in modernizing, repairing, and rehabilitating the project so that it will be unique and more competitive in this market? Will the proposed rental schedules be competitive? Are vacancy rates in competitive apartments at 5 percent or lower? And have they been at these levels, or are they dropping to these levels during the last year?

Are the kinds of tenant services this project offers competitive? Are the sizes and characteristics of the rental units such that they can command market or higher rentals?

Locally, is renting more of a bargain, more attractive for potential tenants than home ownership?

Can the properties attract the quality of tenants necessary to make the project financially feasible?

Are the operational costs for the project staying level or dropping? Will they do either in the future? And are they similar to those for competing projects?

Do local housing market trends indicate a market demand for this type of rental unit?

Location.   Is this an attractive, improving rental market area?

Does the location offer tenants supporting services such as shopping, public transportation, access to work centers, parks, theatres, churches?

Is the quality of tenants renting in this location being sustained so that rental unit management problems are minimal?

Is the area readily accessible by both automobiles and public transportation?

Is the area on a growth curve that promises sustained economic life for the location?

Are nuisances from noise, air pollution, sight pollution minimal or nonexistent?

Are the levels of property taxes and special assessments reasonable with current assessed values stable?

Is the general physical environment conducive to "quality" apartment living?

Are the current or contemplated uses in conformity with local zoning, building codes, deed restrictions?

Are there any plans for redeveloping or rezoning the area?

Is the overall appearance of the area appealing to the types of tenants the property will attract?

Site. Does the site provide ample parking for tenants and guests?

Does the site appear large enough to accommodate the project and also provide some room for open space or future expansion?

Does the property give evidence of deterioration because of poor soil or subsoil conditions?

Does the site provide drainage from rains and water runoff?

Is there easy access from the site to the local street systems?

Are the assessed land values for this and other sites reasonable?

Have you been provided with evidence that there are no outstanding violation charges against the property because of zoning or building code or environmental regulations?

Improvement. Is the property's condition equal to or better than what might be expected, given its age?

Can the improvements be adapted without too much expense to other uses than those now in existence?

Can the improvements be modernized, rehabilitated, or improved to competitive market levels in a financially feasible manner?

Is the interior of the building such as to permit easy functional uses of the spaces?

Have you been provided with, or can you obtain, a certified five-year statement of rent collections and all expenses of operating the building?

Have you reviewed the lease terms now in existence?

Have you investigated the availability of financing if you decide to buy and will this financing make the project financially feasible for you?

Shopping Centers
(Or Any Kind of Retail Store Center)

Market. Do you have full information on the types and locations of potential competing shopping centers?

Have you been provided with a certified statement on the volume of sales activity, product and service sales, price ranges for the tenants in the center and their nearest competitors?

Does the adjacent market have enough buying power to support the centers in the market areas?

Are the levels of vacancies in competing centers and in this center at or below 5 percent?

Is the trading area a stable or improving economic area?

Does the market indicate a need for tenants of the kinds who would locate in this center?

What are the typical leasing terms in this market?

What are the overall renting potentials and lease terms in this area?

Location. Do the families who would be attracted to this center have incomes and shopping habits that would make this center financially viable?

Do the spending patterns of the potential clients represent a potential that can be capitalized on by this center?

Have you been provided with a certified estimate of the numbers and kinds of people who would have access to this center in terms of travel times and public transportation?

Has the competitive impact of adjacent centers been analyzed?

Have you determined if this site is likely to be affected by existing and future freeways, major traffic arteries, public transportation?

Is there an employment base in the area that will give stability to local populations and their incomes?

Is the location in the path of future city growth patterns?

Is the population representing the potential clientele increasing?

Site. Does the size and shape accommodate any present or contemplated future buildings?

Does or will the soil and subsoil accommodate all future building developments?

Is the site well drained from rains, flooding, and ground water flows?

Is the site amply provided with all necessary utilities, sewage, and garbage and trash disposal?

Can the site be reached easily from public streets and transportation?

Have you been provided with full information on all public (building codes, zoning, environmental controls) and private (deed) use restrictions?

Can the site be accessed readily by service and delivery vehicles without proving hazardous to clients using the center?

Is there room for expanding the facilities if business increases?

Improvements.   Is there ample parking for present and future users of the center?

Are the parking spaces easily accessed and of sufficient size to prevent undue crowding of cars?

Are all parking spaces within 300 feet or less of the stores?

If stacked or underground parking is provided, are the areas well lighted and marked for convenient, safe use by shoppers?

Are the stores positioned for easy access by shoppers?

Are the controls over the use of signs and ways of doing business for all of the tenants?

Can the space be rearranged at minimum cost to accommodate changing store uses and tenant needs?

Are lighting, air conditioning and other services adequate and designed to attract quality tenants and shoppers?

Are the lease terms designed to control the selection, location, and activities of the kinds of tenants appropriate to this center?

Are the costs of renting, operating, and maintaining the center available for the last five years?

Have you examined all tenant leases and income payments?

Office Buildings

Market.   Do you have a survey of what kinds of office buildings local business activity currently supports?

Have you a market survey of office space needs and what is now being developed?

Do you have a report covering at least the last five years of vacancies and rates of absorption of office space?

Has a survey been made of the kinds of business that will be needing office space and the kinds of space they will need?

What kinds of services must be offered to office building tenants?

What kinds of office buildings exist and are still needed to meet tenant demands?

Is the local business climate stable or improving and supportive of an office building market?

Have you an accurate inventory of competitive office buildings?

Location. Have you found the most favorable locations for office building in this area?

Do you have an analysis of the characteristics of areas that seem to be attracting office buildings?

Is the proposed office development accessible to future tenants and their clients by public streets and transportation?

Are the levels of taxes and other assessments reasonable for office buildings?

Have you been provided with a good analysis of office building location trends for this area?

Will local ordinances and other public regulations permit the kind of office building you plan or wish to buy?

Site. Is the parking ample for current and future tenants and their clients?

Does the size and shape of the site provide room for the building and other improvements?

Can the soil, subsoil, and drainage support the proposed or current uses?

Is the site readily accessible to public streets and transportation?

Are there adequate utilities, sewage, garbage and trash disposal facilities?

Have you a record of current assessed valuations and any trends in these?

Are you fully informed on all public and private land use restrictions?

Will the property comply with all restriction, or can it be changed to meet them?

Improvements. Is the condition of the improvements appropriate to the age of the improvements?

Have you a five-year record of income and the costs of operation and maintenance?

Have you used a property manager to determine the rental capacities, use alternatives, interior use arrangements for the improvements?

Have you a report on all tenants, lease terms, and vacancies—past and present?

Are the mechanical facilities appropriate, economical, and well maintained—lighting, heating, air conditioning, plumbing, elevators?

Does the property have an overall attractive appearance or appeal for the potential tenants and their clients?

Industrial Properties

Market.   Is there a level of industrial activity to support the project?

Do the levels of industrial activity appear to be strong and improving?

Is there sufficient industrial land in the area to support the kinds of industrial development appropriate to local markets?

Is the overall level of economic activities in the area either stable or increasing?

Has a survey been provided on competing projects?

Have you a survey of competitive leasing terms?

Have you a report on the tenant and rental potentials for such properties in this market?

Location.   Are there available the necessary raw materials, labor, markets, finished parts to support the kinds of industrial activity planned for this project?

Are industrial activities improving and growing or at least stable?

Is there space available and zoned for industrial uses?

Will the economic activity of the area support the proposed project?

Are you aware of the prevailing rents and lease terms of industrial properties?

What are the tenant potentials for your project?

Can your tenants secure the materials, labor, and equipment they need?

Is there an acceptance locally of industrial activities?

Are local public and private land use restriction favorable to your project?

Is housing available for the potential workers in the industrial projects?

Is there available to your future tenants sufficient amounts of the kinds of labor skills needed at wage rates future tenants can afford?

Is local union activity favorable to the development of your project?

Are you aware of competing and supplementary industrial activities?

Are utilities and other services available at reasonable rates and in sufficient volume to support your project?

Site. Is the site sufficient to support the present and any future expansion of industrial uses on the site?

Is the size, shape, and topography of the site conducive to most efficient layouts and construction of modern industrial facilities?

Will the soil and subsoil support the proposed industrial developments?

Are there available to the site in sufficient quantities and at reasonable rates utilities, water, sewage, garbage and trash disposal?

Is there adequate fire and police protection?

Is there freedom from hazards and nuisances from adjacent sites?

Is the site accessible to tenants, their employees, their clients and their suppliers?

Improvements. Is the building laid out for efficient industrial activities?

Can the building be adapted to varying use requirements without great expense?

Are the buildings well lighted, ventilated, heated, and cooled?

Are docking facilities sufficient?

Is there room for expansion?

Are there spaces for the operating activities as well as for warehousing and storage needs?

Special Use Properties

These are, typically, a single use for a limited market—doctors, pharmacies, nursing homes, tennis courts, bowling alleys, and the like.

Market. Has an analysis been made of the characteristics of the type of market that has to exist to make the project feasible?

Is there a market mix that will provide both users for the property and their clients appropriate facilities?

Have you a survey of the kinds of competitive facilities available?

Have the competing facilities left portions of the market unsatisfied?

Will local economic activity support the proposed project now and in the future?

Have you been provided with a professional market survey on the potentials for the kinds of uses intended for the project?

Can the local markets provide sufficient clientele to your future tenants to permit them to pay economic rents?

Location. Is the location in the line of market growth potentials?

Is the location readily accessible to future clients of the tenant?

Will the levels of property taxes and other assessments permit economic operations?

Have you reports on the lease and franchise or other terms which investors in this type of property must sign and have you read it carefully?

Will local planning, building codes, and environmental restrictions permit the intended uses?

Does the location meet the special locational needs of your contemplated uses?

Site. Will the site accommodate the planned developments?

Is there appropriate access from public streets and transportation?

Will there be ample parking or other room for clients?

Is the size, shape, and topography of the site appropriate to the proposed uses?

Will the soil and subsoil support the intended developments?

Are the utilities, water, sewage and trash disposal facilities available to the site in sufficient quantities and at appropriate prices?

Is there police and fire protection?

Is the site located with respect to any supporting or supplementary adjacent uses?

Is the site free from dangerous hazards, pollution, and similar kinds of annoyances?

Improvements. Are the improvements appropriate to the intended use or can they be adapted at reasonable costs?

Can appropriate new facilities be constructed at financially feasible costs?

Can the facilities be readily adapted to other uses if the contemplated uses cannot be achieved or fail?

Does the building have an expansion potential?

Is the building supplied with appropriate heating, lighting, and ventilating facilities?

INFORMATION SOURCES

By following these suggestions you will soon uncover many more local sources of information.

Location and Site Analysis.

Local building and planning departments
State departments of highways, economic development
Automobile clubs
Title insurance companies
Tax assessor records
Federal government reports from the Departments of Housing and Urban Development, Commerce, Census
Real estate boards, chambers of commerce, map service companies
Local utility companies—power, water, phones, sewers
Contractor and builder professional organizations

Market Analysis.

Business trade publications—*Sales Management, Business Week, Fortune*
Chambers of commerce
Research departments of banks, newspapers, utility companies
Research organizations
Periodic reports issued by all kinds of local business organizations
Planning reports and environmental impact reports submitted to public agencies.

Improving
Your Professional
Investing Standing

11

Before summarizing the more important rules in the real estate investing game, a short discussion is offered on the general goals of all investors and the use of these goals to define your real estate investment goals. The purpose of this discussion is to remind you that real estate investments should have a well-defined role in connection with other kinds of investment games you should be playing. Finally, a few of the major rules of the real estate investment game are presented by way of review and summary.

REAL ESTATE VERSUS OTHER FORMS OF INVESTMENT

An important element in real estate investing is risk, of which there are four kinds:

1. loss of investment,
2. earning potentials,
3. liquidity potentials, and
4. capital gains potential (see Exhibit 11-1).

Exhibit 11-1   Risk Levels in Real Estate and Other Forms of Investment

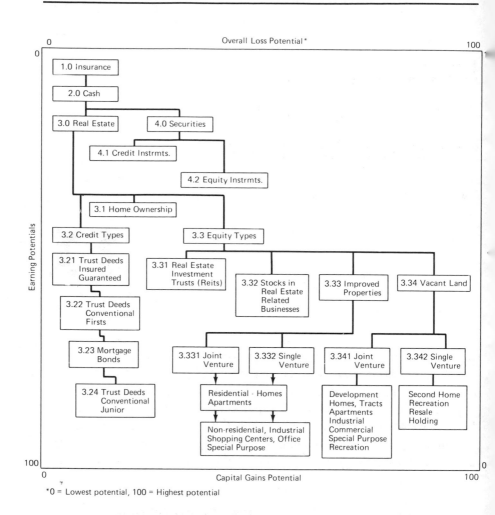

*0 = Lowest potential, 100 = Highest potential

You should decide which of these associated risks you want to assume in your investment. Remember that the greater the risk, the greater the return may be for profit potential; but the greater the profit potential, the greater the loss potential. You have to decide for yourself what kind of a risk taker you are, how much you can afford to win, and how much you can afford to lose. Finally, there will be cash and financial considerations peculiar to your situation. For example, decide what other kinds of investments you have and where they fit into your investment plan, how much cash you need, where it will come from, how long you want to stay invested, and what your income tax position will be (see Exhibit 11-1).

Typically, investors have four primary goals:

1. Risk Reduction.   Risk reflects the possibility that the investment will not be completed as planned, that all monies invested may be lost, or that not only all monies invested will be lost but also that additional amounts may be owed.

2. Earnings.   Most investors want an investment to yield income periodically. Such returns do not represent returns of any portion of the amount invested originally. Earnings are typically expressed as a percentage, either of equity or of the value of the investment.

3. Capital Gains.   Some investors seek investments that increase in dollar value greater than amounts invested originally. Capital gains are not realized until the investment has been sold. Hopefully, the capital gains will have been sufficient to maintain or exceed the purchasing power of the original amounts invested.

4. Liquidity.   When investors wish to get rid of an investment, they hope to recover the full value of the investment.

A rough approximation of how real estate compares on these four bases is indicated in Exhibit 11-1. Perhaps the greatest advantage of real estate investments is that, with care, they can be made to meet any or all of the four criteria. However, not all four can be realized to their fullest potentials, so that an investor usually has to decide what compromises he will accept in his investment objectives.

To understand how to use Exhibit 11-1, begin your analysis in the upper left hand corner, item one. The order of recommended investments is based on the assumption that you begin investing in real estate by first making sure that you have taken care of the basics for your own financial protection. For example, you have an adequate life insurance program and some kind of a cash or liquidity reserve. Once you have these, then you might want to make some balance between your real estate investment objectives and investments in securities.

Securities can include credit instruments (such as bonds) or equity instruments (such as stocks).

When you venture into real estate investing, start with home owner-ship, an equity type of real estate investment.

However, if you decide that either you don't care for the equity route or for home ownership, you may look into certain types of credit real estate investments. For reasonably modest sums you can buy trust deeds or mortgages, which may be insured or guaranteed but which carry higher interest rates. You can frequently contact a local real estate broker or local bank who might be able to refer you to persons who, needing money, might want to borrow from you and give you a trust deed or mortgage as a guarantee of their debt. Typically the bank or the savings and loan associa-tion will collect the payments from this mortgage for you for only a nominal charge.

Other real-estate-related credit instruments include mortgage bonds which companies use to raise money by pledging real properties as security for the repayment of the bonds. The most risky type of credit instruments—but also ones paying the highest rates of interest—are the conventional junior trust deed or mortgage. "Junior" refers to the fact that there is another mortgage that has priority in any funds paid up by the borrower. If the borrower cannot pay on the first mortgage, you may not be able to collect either the payments or the loan amount due you. On the other hand, these junior mortgages typically carry higher interest rates and earn a greater return. At this point you should know how to use this potential for securing funds for your own forms of investments.

Equity Real Estate Types

If you wish to own an equity investment but have only a very modest amount to invest, you might investigate real estate investment trusts (REITs). Because they are organized as corporations, you can buy shares of stocks, sometimes for as little as ten or twenty dollars a share, and you can determine how many shares you want to buy. Because of special legislation, you also secure with your stock purchase the same income tax shelter advantages that go with any other form of real estate investment. If you want to find out more about trusts, you can always talk to a stock broker.

Your next (but more risky) type of investment is improved properties. We've indicated you can either get into this kind of investment by yourself or in conjunction with other people by starting with residential properties and then going on to nonresidential properties. The most risky thing you can do is to invest in vacant land; and, again, you can do it by yourself or in conjunction with other people. You can decide either to buy the vacant land and hold it as vacant land, and hope to sell it later for some gain in value, or to develop something on the land. All these real estate investment potentials are the subject of this book.

PRINCIPLES OF REAL ESTATE INVESTING

If you are investing in real estate, the following principles, or guiding rules of action, may help:

1. All the major types of real estate investment objectives can be achieved in real estate investing—income, capital gains, liquidity, and loss minimization—but neither in equal proportion nor simultaneously. Before you invest, decide on the priority and emphasis you wish to give each objective.

2. Analyse all real estate investments in an objective manner, using all possible information and expert opinion, in the light of your goals. Do not allow feelings, emotions, or "pride of ownership" to sway you from your investment plan.

3. In determining your investment price, remember that it can vary widely and that you can still reach your investment objectives, so be ready to bargain wisely for the price and terms.

4. Successful investing requires the use of borrowed funds. Borrowed funds reduce the amount of equity you have to invest and so increase the rate of earnings on your investment. For example:

a. You purchase a real property for $100,000 cash and it earns $12,000 net income. Your return is 12 percent.

b. Instead of paying all cash you borrow $80,000 at 7 percent interest. In the first year you pay $5,600 in interest ($80,000 × .07) from the $12,000 income, leaving you a net income of $6,400. You have earned $6,400 with an investment of $20,000 for a 32-percent interest.

5. Selection of the best investment and operating it at a maximum profit level require the use of many kinds of experts:

a. Tax counsellor—to advise on how to obtain maximum advantage of Federal and state tax laws.

b. Property manager—to help on rent levels, rent collection, property operation; to advise on and execute needed repairs, modernization, improvements.

c. Appraiser—to advise on proper price and terms of purchase.

d. Mortgage lender—to advise on where to secure proper financing.

e. Real estate broker—to prepare and maintain a list of potential investments suited to your needs and interests.

f. Lawyer—to prepare, review, advise on all contracts.

6. If you want large and quick returns you will have to take large risks so you must be prepared to take large losses.

7. Your net income must be enough to pay you an adequate interest rate on your investment and also permit you to recover the amount you have invested in the building.

a. A security, such as a stock or bond, earns interest when you no longer wish to own the security. You can normally sell it for an amount that is at least equal to the amount you paid originally.

b. When you buy real property, the building deteriorates and loses value because of its age and use. You must include an amount in your net earnings to permit you to recover each year some of your investment in the building.

8. You increase your chances of losing your investment as you reduce the amount of equity in the property.

a. As you borrow more money, you increase the amount of fixed debt that you must repay. The income stream of your property will tend to fluctuate and may, in some years, be below the amount you need to meet property expenses and mortgage payments.

b. A mortgage that is a high percentage of the purchase price tends to increase your risk of losing your property, as well as the opportunity of not receiving returns in some years. It also lowers the overall risk quality of your investment.

9. In order to maximize your long-run returns and resale value of your property, you must plan a continuous program of qualified operations, maintenance, repairs, and modernization.

10. Changes in the value of real property tend to coincide with changes in the purchasing power of the dollar.

a. The capital value of the investment is more likely to coincide with changes in the value of the dollar than is the net spendable income.

b. In periods of rapidly rising prices, property expenses may rise more rapidly than rents, so that spendable income may decline or even disappear even in prosperous markets with rising prices.

11. The purchase of a real estate investment may be accomplished through the use of a variety of financing instruments.

    a. Mortgages or deeds of trust—permit pledging the property as security for the repayment of borrowed funds but with rights of property use relatively unimpaired.

    b. Personal note—a pledge of personal assets for repayment of a debt.

    c. Stocks—a division of equity ownership into small financial shares that are sold to others.

    d. Bonds—assets or property are pledged as security for shares that are sold with guaranteed payments of interest and redemption under given conditions.

    e. Land contracts—periodic payments are made that eventually permit passing of titles. During the payment period, the title remains with the seller of the property. All rights of the buyer may be cancelled if the buyer fails to make even one payment.

    f. Hypothecation—assets other than the property may be pledged as security for the repayment of funds borrowed to buy the real property. Failure to repay the loan means that the hypothecated assets are sold to satisfy the debt.

    g. Option—payment of a smaller sum for the privilege of purchasing the property at a later date on terms decided upon at the time of the option. This permits the buyer to secure funds from others and test the market for his planned uses of the property before he pays the entire price.

12. Real estate may be owned in many ways besides single ownership so that an individual may participate in the benefits of a large parcel of real property without having to buy the entire parcel.

    a. Syndicate—several persons pool their resources to acquire and operate the property. Once the property is sold, the syndicate dissolves.

    b. Partnership—several persons agree to share on a defined basis in the purchase, operations, and profits of a real property. The partnership continues to invest in properties and is not dissolved with the sale of a single investment.

    c. Corporation—a corporation is organized that has as its only assets the real property.

    d. Trust—a special form of organization that owns and operates real properties for the benefit of the holders of trust certificates. Trusts tend to pass on to certificate holders greater returns than do corporations.

13. Funds for the purchase of real estate investments can be secured from many sources.

    a. Savings and loan associations—prefer to provide funds for building, buying, or repairing residential properties.

b. Commercial banks—prefer to provide funds for building or buying nonresidential properties or apartment houses, although they do make loans for these purposes to single-family home buyers.

c. Insurance companies—prefer to make loans in larger amounts, typically for industrial properties, office buildings, shopping centers, large apartment houses, but they do make loans on almost all types of real estate.

d. Mortgage companies—typically provide funds for unusual properties on unusual conditions of purchase, but their interest rates and loan charges are typically among the highest in the money markets.

e. Trusts, estates—banks and other trustees may provide funds for high quality investment purposes.

f. Labor unions, pension funds—may provide funds for high quality real estate investments with reasonably firm income expectations.

g. Professional persons, others in high tax brackets—may provide funds that provide some form of tax relief or tax-free earning opportunities.

14. Constantly and carefully check your financial progress and be prepared to use the variable elements in your investment plan so that your investment plan moves according to plan.

15. Each real estate investment is a unique project, and it may or may not perform according to market trends and expectations.

a. The value of the investment may be determined by comparison with similar properties.

b. Uniqueness relates primarily to location; the site and improvements should be designed to maximize the location potential.

16. When using income streams to estimate investment value, be sure you understand the implications of the various mathematical tables and techniques on your investment conclusions. Careful financial analysis is always the key to effective real estate investing.

17. There are no bargains in real estate price; terms reflect risks and potential earnings.

Finally, you have been introduced to the rules of the real estate investment game and the basic strategies that should help you win. You are ready for the varsity. With the help of the proper team members, you should be able to win—and, with some luck and some science, to win big.

Tables for
Investment
Analysis

　　　　　　　　　　ANNUAL COMPOUND INTEREST TABLES　　　　　　　　　
　　　　　　　　　　　　　　　EFFECTIVE RATE　7.00

	1 AMOUNT OF $1 AT COMPOUND INTEREST	2 ACCUMULATION OF $1 PER PERIOD	3 SINKING FUND FACTOR	4 PRESENT VALUE REVERSION OF $1	5 PRESENT VALUE ORD. ANNUITY $1 PER PERIOD	6 INSTALMENT TO AMORTIZE $1
YEARS						
1	1.070000	1.000000	1.000000	0.934579	0.934579	1.070000
2	1.144900	2.070000	0.483092	0.873439	1.808018	0.553092
3	1.225043	3.214900	0.311052	0.816298	2.624316	0.381052
4	1.310796	4.439943	0.225228	0.762895	3.387211	0.295228
5	1.402552	5.750739	0.173891	0.712986	4.100197	0.243891
6	1.500730	7.153291	0.139796	0.666342	4.766540	0.209796
7	1.605781	8.654021	0.115553	0.622750	5.389289	0.185553
8	1.718186	10.259803	0.097468	0.582009	5.971299	0.167468
9	1.838459	11.977989	0.083486	0.543934	6.515232	0.153486
10	1.967151	13.816448	0.072378	0.508349	7.023582	0.142378
11	2.104852	15.783599	0.063357	0.475093	7.498674	0.133357
12	2.252192	17.888451	0.055902	0.444012	7.942686	0.125902
13	2.409845	20.140643	0.049651	0.414964	8.357651	0.119651
14	2.578534	22.550488	0.044345	0.387817	8.745468	0.114345
15	2.759032	25.129022	0.039795	0.362446	9.107914	0.109795
16	2.952164	27.888054	0.035858	0.338735	9.446649	0.105858
17	3.158815	30.840217	0.032425	0.316574	9.763223	0.102425
18	3.379932	33.999033	0.029413	0.295864	10.059087	0.099413
19	3.616528	37.378965	0.026753	0.276508	10.335595	0.096753
20	3.869684	40.995492	0.024393	0.258419	10.594014	0.094393
21	4.140562	44.865177	0.022289	0.241513	10.835527	0.092289
22	4.430402	49.005739	0.020406	0.225713	11.061240	0.090406
23	4.740530	53.436141	0.018714	0.210947	11.272187	0.088714
24	5.072367	58.176671	0.017189	0.197147	11.469334	0.087189
25	5.427433	63.249038	0.015811	0.184249	11.653583	0.085811
26	5.807353	68.676470	0.014561	0.172195	11.825779	0.084561
27	6.213868	74.483823	0.013426	0.160930	11.986709	0.083426
28	6.648838	80.697691	0.012392	0.150402	12.137111	0.082392
29	7.114257	87.346529	0.011449	0.140563	12.277674	0.081449
30	7.612255	94.460786	0.010586	0.131367	12.409041	0.080586
31	8.145113	102.073041	0.009797	0.122773	12.531814	0.079797
32	8.715271	110.218154	0.009073	0.114741	12.646555	0.079073
33	9.325340	118.933425	0.008408	0.107235	12.753790	0.078408
34	9.978114	128.258765	0.007797	0.100219	12.854009	0.077797
35	10.676581	138.236878	0.007234	0.093663	12.947672	0.077234
36	11.423942	148.913460	0.006715	0.087535	13.035208	0.076715
37	12.223618	160.337402	0.006237	0.081809	13.117017	0.076237
38	13.079271	172.561020	0.005795	0.076457	13.193473	0.075795
39	13.994820	185.640292	0.005387	0.071455	13.264928	0.075387
40	14.974458	199.635112	0.005009	0.066780	13.331709	0.075009
41	16.022670	214.609570	0.004660	0.062412	13.394120	0.074660
42	17.144257	230.632240	0.004336	0.058329	13.452449	0.074336
43	18.344355	247.776496	0.004036	0.054513	13.506962	0.074036
44	19.628460	266.120851	0.003758	0.050946	13.557908	0.073758
45	21.002452	285.749311	0.003500	0.047613	13.605522	0.073500
46	22.472623	306.751763	0.003260	0.044499	13.650020	0.073260
47	24.045707	329.224386	0.003037	0.041587	13.691608	0.073037
48	25.728907	353.270093	0.002831	0.038867	13.730474	0.072831
49	27.529930	378.999000	0.002639	0.036324	13.766799	0.072639
50	29.457025	406.528929	0.002460	0.033948	13.800746	0.072460

13.00% MONTHLY COMPOUND INTEREST TABLES 13.00%
EFFECTIVE RATE 1.083

	1 AMOUNT OF $1 AT COMPOUND INTEREST	2 ACCUMULATION OF $1 PER PERIOD	3 SINKING FUND FACTOR	4 PRESENT VALUE REVERSION OF $1	5 PRESENT VALUE ORD. ANNUITY $1 PER PERIOD	6 INSTALMENT TO AMORTIZE $1	
ONTHS							
1	1.010833	1.000000	1.000000	0.989283	0.989283	1.010833	
2	1.021784	2.010833	0.497306	0.978680	1.967963	0.508140	
3	1.032853	3.032617	0.329748	0.968192	2.936155	0.340581	
4	1.044043	4.065471	0.245974	0.957815	3.893970	0.256807	
5	1.055353	5.109513	0.195713	0.947550	4.841520	0.206547	
6	1.066786	6.164866	0.162210	0.937395	5.778915	0.173043	
7	1.078343	7.231652	0.138281	0.927349	6.706264	0.149114	
8	1.090025	8.309995	0.120337	0.917410	7.623674	0.131170	
9	1.101834	9.400020	0.106383	0.907578	8.531253	0.117216	
10	1.113770	10.501854	0.095221	0.897851	9.429104	0.106055	
11	1.125836	11.615624	0.086091	0.888229	10.317333	0.096924	
12	1.138032	12.741460	0.078484	0.878710	11.196042	0.089317	
EARS							**MONTHS**
1	1.138032	12.741460	0.078484	0.878710	11.196042	0.089317	12
2	1.295118	27.241655	0.036708	0.772130	21.034112	0.047542	24
3	1.473886	43.743348	0.022861	0.678478	29.678917	0.033694	36
4	1.677330	62.522811	0.015994	0.596185	37.275190	0.026827	48
5	1.908857	83.894449	0.011920	0.523874	43.950107	0.022753	60
6	2.172341	108.216068	0.009241	0.460333	49.815421	0.020074	72
7	2.472194	135.894861	0.007359	0.404499	54.969328	0.018192	84
8	2.813437	167.394225	0.005974	0.355437	59.498115	0.016807	96
9	3.201783	203.241525	0.004920	0.312326	63.477604	0.015754	108
10	3.643733	244.036917	0.004098	0.274444	66.974419	0.014931	120
11	4.146687	290.463399	0.003443	0.241156	70.047103	0.014276	132
12	4.719064	343.298242	0.002913	0.211906	72.747100	0.013746	144
13	5.370448	403.426010	0.002479	0.186204	75.119613	0.013312	156
14	6.111745	471.853363	0.002119	0.163619	77.204363	0.012953	168
15	6.955364	549.725914	0.001819	0.143774	79.036253	0.012652	180
16	7.915430	638.347406	0.001567	0.126336	80.645952	0.012400	192
17	9.008017	739.201542	0.001353	0.111012	82.060410	0.012186	204
18	10.251416	853.976825	0.001171	0.097548	83.303307	0.012004	216
19	11.666444	984.594826	0.001016	0.085716	84.395453	0.011849	228
20	13.276792	1133.242353	0.000882	0.075319	85.355132	0.011716	240
21	15.109421	1302.408067	0.000768	0.066184	86.198412	0.011601	252
22	17.195012	1494.924144	0.000669	0.058156	86.939409	0.011502	264
23	19.568482	1714.013694	0.000583	0.051103	87.590531	0.011417	276
24	22.269568	1963.344717	0.000509	0.044904	88.162677	0.011343	288
25	25.343491	2247.091520	0.000445	0.039458	88.665428	0.011278	300
26	28.841716	2570.004599	0.000389	0.034672	89.107200	0.011222	312
27	32.822810	2937.490172	0.000340	0.030467	89.495389	0.011174	324
28	37.353424	3355.700690	0.000298	0.026771	89.836495	0.011131	336
29	42.509410	3831.637843	0.000261	0.023524	90.136227	0.011094	348
30	48.377089	4373.269783	0.000229	0.020671	90.399605	0.011062	360
31	55.054699	4989.664524	0.000200	0.018164	90.631038	0.011034	372
32	62.654036	5691.141761	0.000176	0.015961	90.834400	0.011009	384
33	71.302328	6489.445641	0.000154	0.014025	91.013097	0.010987	396
34	81.144365	7397.941387	0.000135	0.012324	91.170119	0.010969	408
35	92.344923	8431.839055	0.000119	0.010829	91.308095	0.010952	420
36	105.091522	9608.448184	0.000104	0.009516	91.429337	0.010937	432
37	119.597566	10947.467591	0.000091	0.008361	91.535873	0.010925	444
38	136.105914	12471.315170	0.000080	0.007347	91.629487	0.010914	456
39	154.892951	14205.503212	0.000070	0.006456	91.711747	0.010904	468
40	176.273210	16179.065533	0.000062	0.005673	91.784030	0.010895	480

7.25%   MONTHLY COMPOUND INTEREST TABLES   7.25%
                        EFFECTIVE RATE 0.604

	1 AMOUNT OF $1 AT COMPOUND INTEREST	2 ACCUMULATION OF $1 PER PERIOD	3 SINKING FUND FACTOR	4 PRESENT VALUE REVERSION OF $1	5 PRESENT VALUE ORD. ANNUITY $1 PER PERIOD	6 INSTALMENT TO AMORTIZE $1	
MONTHS							
1	1.006042	1.000000	1.000000	0.993995	0.993995	1.006042	
2	1.012120	2.006042	0.498494	0.988025	1.982020	0.504536	
3	1.018235	3.018162	0.331328	0.982092	2.964112	0.337369	
4	1.024387	4.036396	0.247746	0.976194	3.940306	0.253787	
5	1.030576	5.060783	0.197598	0.970332	4.910637	0.203640	
6	1.036802	6.091358	0.164167	0.964504	5.875142	0.170209	
7	1.043066	7.128160	0.140289	0.958712	6.833854	0.146330	
8	1.049368	8.171226	0.122381	0.952955	7.786808	0.128422	
9	1.055708	9.220594	0.108453	0.947232	8.734040	0.114495	
10	1.062086	10.276302	0.097311	0.941543	9.675584	0.103353	
11	1.068503	11.338388	0.088196	0.935889	10.611473	0.094238	
12	1.074958	12.406891	0.080600	0.930269	11.541741	0.086642	
YEARS							**MON**
1	1.074958	12.406891	0.080600	0.930269	11.541741	0.086642	1
2	1.155535	25.743781	0.038844	0.865400	22.278661	0.044886	2
3	1.242152	40.080381	0.024950	0.805054	32.266882	0.030992	3
4	1.335262	55.491629	0.018021	0.748917	41.558610	0.024062	4
5	1.435351	72.058078	0.013878	0.696694	50.202413	0.019919	6
6	1.542942	89.866319	0.011128	0.648112	58.243472	0.017169	7
7	1.658599	109.009436	0.009174	0.602919	65.723817	0.015215	8
8	1.782924	129.587488	0.007717	0.560876	72.682548	0.013758	9
9	1.916569	151.708036	0.006592	0.521766	79.156037	0.012633	10
10	2.060232	175.486703	0.005698	0.485382	85.178120	0.011740	12
11	2.214664	201.047778	0.004974	0.451536	90.780276	0.011016	13
12	2.380671	228.524868	0.004376	0.420050	95.991786	0.010418	14
13	2.559122	258.061593	0.003875	0.390759	100.839890	0.009917	15
14	2.750950	289.812342	0.003451	0.363511	105.349929	0.009492	16
15	2.957156	323.943072	0.003087	0.338163	109.545477	0.009129	18
16	3.178819	360.632184	0.002773	0.314582	113.448464	0.008815	19
17	3.417098	400.071449	0.002500	0.292646	117.079291	0.008541	20
18	3.673238	442.467014	0.002260	0.272239	120.456934	0.008302	21
19	3.948578	488.040479	0.002049	0.253256	123.599051	0.008091	22
20	4.244557	537.030053	0.001862	0.235596	126.522063	0.007904	24
21	4.562721	589.691802	0.001696	0.219167	129.241249	0.007737	25
22	4.904735	646.300986	0.001547	0.203885	131.770823	0.007589	264
23	5.272386	707.153498	0.001414	0.189667	134.124007	0.007456	276
24	5.667595	772.567411	0.001294	0.176442	136.313100	0.007336	288
25	6.092428	842.884639	0.001186	0.164138	138.349544	0.007228	300
26	6.549106	918.472727	0.001089	0.152693	140.243984	0.007130	312
27	7.040016	999.726770	0.001000	0.142045	142.006323	0.007042	324
28	7.567724	1087.071477	0.000920	0.132140	143.645771	0.006962	336
29	8.134987	1180.963395	0.000847	0.122926	145.170898	0.006888	348
30	8.744772	1281.893291	0.000780	0.114354	146.589676	0.006822	360
31	9.400265	1390.388720	0.000719	0.106380	147.909521	0.006761	372
32	10.104893	1507.016781	0.000664	0.098962	149.137331	0.006705	384
33	10.862339	1632.387084	0.000613	0.092061	150.279524	0.006654	396
34	11.676561	1767.154931	0.000566	0.085642	151.342071	0.006608	408
35	12.551816	1912.024747	0.000523	0.079670	152.330525	0.006565	420
36	13.492679	2067.753757	0.000484	0.074114	153.250052	0.006525	432
37	14.504067	2235.155949	0.000447	0.068946	154.105460	0.006489	444
38	15.591267	2415.106324	0.000414	0.064138	154.901219	0.006456	456
39	16.759962	2608.545473	0.000383	0.059666	155.641489	0.006425	468
40	18.016260	2816.484491	0.000355	0.055505	156.330138	0.006397	480

12.00%   ANNUAL COMPOUND INTEREST TABLES   12.00%
                              EFFECTIVE RATE 12.00

	1 AMOUNT OF $1 AT COMPOUND INTEREST	2 ACCUMULATION OF $1 PER PERIOD	3 SINKING FUND FACTOR	4 PRESENT VALUE REVERSION OF $1	5 PRESENT VALUE ORD. ANNUITY $1 PER PERIOD	6 INSTALMENT TO AMORTIZE $1
YEARS						
1	1.120000	1.000000	1.000000	0.892857	0.892857	1.120000
2	1.254400	2.120000	0.471698	0.797194	1.690051	0.591698
3	1.404928	3.374400	0.296349	0.711780	2.401831	0.416349
4	1.573519	4.779328	0.209234	0.635518	3.037349	0.329234
5	1.762342	6.352847	0.157410	0.567427	3.604776	0.277410
6	1.973823	8.115189	0.123226	0.506631	4.111407	0.243226
7	2.210681	10.089012	0.099118	0.452349	4.563757	0.219118
8	2.475963	12.299693	0.081303	0.403883	4.967640	0.201303
9	2.773079	14.775656	0.067679	0.360610	5.328250	0.187679
10	3.105848	17.548735	0.056984	0.321973	5.650223	0.176984
11	3.478550	20.654583	0.048415	0.287476	5.937699	0.168415
12	3.895976	24.133133	0.041437	0.256675	6.194374	0.161437
13	4.363493	28.029109	0.035677	0.229174	6.423548	0.155677
14	4.887112	32.392602	0.030871	0.204620	6.628168	0.150871
15	5.473566	37.279715	0.026824	0.182696	6.810864	0.146824
16	6.130394	42.753280	0.023390	0.163122	6.973986	0.143390
17	6.866041	48.883674	0.020457	0.145644	7.119630	0.140457
18	7.689966	55.749715	0.017937	0.130040	7.249670	0.137937
19	8.612762	63.439681	0.015763	0.116107	7.365777	0.135763
20	9.646293	72.052442	0.013879	0.103667	7.469444	0.133879
21	10.803848	81.698736	0.012240	0.092560	7.562003	0.132240
22	12.100310	92.502584	0.010811	0.082643	7.644646	0.130811
23	13.552347	104.602894	0.009560	0.073788	7.718434	0.129560
24	15.178629	118.155241	0.008463	0.065882	7.784316	0.128463
25	17.000064	133.333870	0.007500	0.058823	7.843139	0.127500
26	19.040072	150.333934	0.006652	0.052521	7.895660	0.126652
27	21.324881	169.374007	0.005904	0.046894	7.942554	0.125904
28	23.883866	190.698887	0.005244	0.041869	7.984423	0.125244
29	26.749930	214.582754	0.004660	0.037383	8.021806	0.124660
30	29.959922	241.332684	0.004144	0.033378	8.055184	0.124144
31	33.555113	271.292606	0.003686	0.029802	8.084986	0.123686
32	37.581726	304.847719	0.003280	0.026609	8.111594	0.123280
33	42.091533	342.429446	0.002920	0.023758	8.135352	0.122920
34	47.142517	384.520979	0.002601	0.021212	8.156564	0.122601
35	52.799620	431.663496	0.002317	0.018940	8.175504	0.122317
36	59.135574	484.463116	0.002064	0.016910	8.192414	0.122064
37	66.231843	543.598690	0.001840	0.015098	8.207513	0.121840
38	74.179664	609.830533	0.001640	0.013481	8.220993	0.121640
39	83.081224	684.010197	0.001462	0.012036	8.233030	0.121462
40	93.050970	767.091420	0.001304	0.010747	8.243777	0.121304
41	104.217087	860.142391	0.001163	0.009595	8.253372	0.121163
42	116.723137	964.359478	0.001037	0.008567	8.261939	0.121037
43	130.729914	1081.082615	0.000925	0.007649	8.269589	0.120925
44	146.417503	1211.812529	0.000825	0.006830	8.276418	0.120825
45	163.987604	1358.230032	0.000736	0.006098	8.282516	0.120736
46	183.666116	1522.217636	0.000657	0.005445	8.287961	0.120657
47	205.706050	1705.883752	0.000586	0.004861	8.292822	0.120586
48	230.390776	1911.589803	0.000523	0.004340	8.297163	0.120523
49	258.037669	2141.980579	0.000467	0.003875	8.301038	0.120467
50	289.002190	2400.018249	0.000417	0.003460	8.304498	0.120417

8.00%   MONTHLY COMPOUND INTEREST TABLES   8.00
                                        EFFECTIVE RATE 0.667

	1 AMOUNT OF $1 AT COMPOUND INTEREST	2 ACCUMULATION OF $1 PER PERIOD	3 SINKING FUND FACTOR	4 PRESENT VALUE REVERSION OF $1	5 PRESENT VALUE ORD. ANNUITY $1 PER PERIOD	6 INSTALMENT TO AMORTIZE $1	
MONTHS							
1	1.006667	1.000000	1.000000	0.993377	0.993377	1.006667	
2	1.013378	2.006667	0.498339	0.986799	1.980176	0.505006	
3	1.020134	3.020044	0.331121	0.980264	2.960440	0.337788	
4	1.026935	4.040178	0.247514	0.973772	3.934212	0.254181	
5	1.033781	5.067113	0.197351	0.967323	4.901535	0.204018	
6	1.040673	6.100893	0.163910	0.960917	5.862452	0.170577	
7	1.047610	7.141566	0.140025	0.954553	6.817005	0.146692	
8	1.054595	8.189176	0.122112	0.948232	7.765237	0.128779	
9	1.061625	9.243771	0.108181	0.941952	8.707189	0.114848	
10	1.068703	10.305396	0.097037	0.935714	9.642903	0.103703	
11	1.075827	11.374099	0.087919	0.929517	10.572420	0.094586	
12	1.083000	12.449926	0.080322	0.923361	11.495782	0.086988	
YEARS							**MC**
1	1.083000	12.449926	0.080322	0.923361	11.495782	0.086988	
2	1.172888	25.933190	0.038561	0.852596	22.110544	0.045227	
3	1.270237	40.535558	0.024670	0.787255	31.911806	0.031336	
4	1.375666	56.349915	0.017746	0.726921	40.961913	0.024413	
5	1.489846	73.476856	0.013610	0.671210	49.318433	0.020276	
6	1.613502	92.025325	0.010867	0.619770	57.034522	0.017533	
7	1.747422	112.113308	0.008920	0.572272	64.159261	0.015586	
8	1.892457	133.868583	0.007470	0.528414	70.737970	0.014137	
9	2.049530	157.429535	0.006352	0.487917	76.812497	0.013019	1
10	2.219640	182.946035	0.005466	0.450523	82.421481	0.012133	1
11	2.403869	210.580392	0.004749	0.415996	87.600600	0.011415	1
12	2.603389	240.508387	0.004158	0.384115	92.382800	0.010825	1
13	2.819469	272.920390	0.003664	0.354677	96.798498	0.010331	1
14	3.053484	308.022574	0.003247	0.327495	100.875784	0.009913	1
15	3.306921	346.038222	0.002890	0.302396	104.640592	0.009557	1
16	3.581394	387.209149	0.002583	0.279221	108.116871	0.009249	1
17	3.878648	431.797244	0.002316	0.257822	111.326733	0.008983	2
18	4.200574	480.086128	0.002083	0.238063	114.290596	0.008750	2
19	4.549220	532.382966	0.001878	0.219818	117.027313	0.008545	2
20	4.926803	589.020416	0.001698	0.202971	119.554292	0.008364	2
21	5.335725	650.358746	0.001538	0.187416	121.887606	0.008204	2
22	5.778588	716.788127	0.001395	0.173053	124.042099	0.008062	2
23	6.258207	788.731114	0.001268	0.159790	126.031475	0.007935	2
24	6.777636	866.645333	0.001154	0.147544	127.868388	0.007821	2
25	7.340176	951.026395	0.001051	0.136237	129.564523	0.007718	3
26	7.949407	1042.411042	0.000959	0.125796	131.130668	0.007626	3
27	8.609204	1141.380571	0.000876	0.116155	132.576786	0.007543	3
28	9.323763	1248.564521	0.000801	0.107253	133.912076	0.007468	3
29	10.097631	1364.644687	0.000733	0.099033	135.145031	0.007399	3
30	10.935730	1490.359449	0.000671	0.091443	136.283494	0.007338	3
31	11.843390	1626.508474	0.000615	0.084435	137.334707	0.007281	3
32	12.826385	1773.957801	0.000564	0.077964	138.305357	0.007230	3
33	13.890969	1933.645350	0.000517	0.071989	139.201617	0.007184	3
34	15.043913	2106.586886	0.000475	0.066472	140.029190	0.007141	4
35	16.292550	2293.882485	0.000436	0.061378	140.793338	0.007103	4
36	17.644824	2496.723526	0.000401	0.056674	141.498923	0.007067	43
37	19.109335	2716.400273	0.000368	0.052330	142.150433	0.007035	44
38	20.695401	2954.310082	0.000338	0.048320	142.752013	0.007005	45
39	22.413109	3211.966288	0.000311	0.044617	143.307488	0.006978	46
40	24.273386	3491.007831	0.000286	0.041197	143.820392	0.006953	48

7.50%   MONTHLY COMPOUND INTEREST TABLES   7.50%
                           EFFECTIVE RATE 0 ·25

	1 AMOUNT OF $1 AT COMPOUND INTEREST	2 ACCUMULATION OF $1 PER PERIOD	3 SINKING FUND FACTOR	4 PRESENT VALUE REVERSION OF $1	5 PRESENT VALUE ORD. ANNUITY $1 PER PERIOD	6 INSTALMENT TO AMORTIZE $1	
ITHS							
	1.006250	1.000000	1.000000	0.993789	0.993789	1.006250	
	1.012539	2.006250	0.498442	0.987616	1.981405	0.504692	
	1.018867	3.018789	0.331259	0.981482	2.962887	0.337509	
	1.025235	4.037656	0.247668	0.975386	3.938273	0.253918	
	1.031643	5.062892	0.197516	0.969327	4.907600	0.203766	
	1.038091	6.094535	0.164081	0.963307	5.870907	0.170331	
	1.044579	7.132626	0.140201	0.957324	6.828231	0.146451	
	1.051108	8.177205	0.122291	0.951377	7.779608	0.128541	
	1.057677	9.228312	0.108362	0.945468	8.725076	0.114612	
	1.064287	10.285989	0.097220	0.939596	9.664672	0.103470	
	1.070939	11.350277	0.088104	0.933760	10.598432	0.094354	
	1.077633	12.421216	0.080507	0.927960	11.526392	0.086757	
ARS							**MONTHS**
1	1.077633	12.421216	0.080507	0.927960	11.526392	0.086757	12
2	1.161292	25.806723	0.038750	0.861110	22.222423	0.045000	24
3	1.251446	40.231382	0.024856	0.799076	32.147913	0.031106	36
4	1.348599	55.775864	0.017929	0.741510	41.358371	0.024179	48
5	1.453294	72.527105	0.013788	0.688092	49.905308	0.020038	60
6	1.566117	90.578789	0.011040	0.638522	57.836524	0.017290	72
7	1.687699	110.031871	0.009088	0.592523	65.196376	0.015338	84
8	1.818720	130.995147	0.007634	0.549837	72.026024	0.013884	96
9	1.959912	153.585857	0.006511	0.510227	78.363665	0.012761	108
0	2.112065	177.930342	0.005620	0.473470	84.244743	0.011870	120
1	2.276030	204.164753	0.004898	0.439362	89.702148	0.011148	132
2	2.452724	232.435809	0.004302	0.407710	94.766401	0.010552	144
3	2.643135	262.901620	0.003804	0.378339	99.465827	0.010054	156
4	2.848329	295.732572	0.003381	0.351083	103.826705	0.009631	168
5	3.069452	331.112274	0.003020	0.325791	107.073127	0.009270	180
6	3.307741	369.238599	0.002708	0.302321	111.628623	0.008958	192
7	3.564530	410.324766	0.002437	0.280542	115.113294	0.008687	204
8	3.841254	454.600560	0.002200	0.260332	118.346930	0.008456	216
9	4.139460	502.313599	0.001991	0.241577	121.347615	0.008241	228
0	4.460817	553.730725	0.001806	0.224174	124.132131	0.008056	240
1	4.807122	609.139496	0.001642	0.208025	126.716051	0.007892	252
22	5.180311	668.849794	0.001495	0.193039	129.113825	0.007745	264
23	5.582472	733.195558	0.001364	0.179132	131.338863	0.007614	276
24	6.015854	802.536650	0.001246	0.166227	133.403610	0.007496	288
25	6.482880	877.260872	0.001140	0.154252	135.319613	0.007390	300
26	6.986163	957.786129	0.001044	0.143140	137.097587	0.007294	312
27	7.528517	1044.562771	0.000957	0.132828	138.747475	0.007207	324
28	8.112976	1138.076109	0.000879	0.123259	140.278506	0.007129	336
29	8.742807	1238.849131	0.000807	0.114380	141.699242	0.007057	348
30	9.421534	1347.445425	0.000742	0.106140	143.017627	0.006992	360
31	10.152952	1464.472331	0.000683	0.098494	144.241037	0.006933	372
32	10.941152	1590.584339	0.000629	0.091398	145.376312	0.006879	384
33	11.790542	1726.486751	0.000579	0.084814	146.429801	0.006829	396
34	12.705873	1872.939621	0.000534	0.078704	147.407398	0.006784	408
35	13.692263	2030.762007	0.000492	0.073034	148.314568	0.006742	420
36	14.755228	2200.836555	0.000454	0.067773	149.156386	0.006704	432
37	15.900715	2384.114432	0.000419	0.062890	149.937560	0.006669	444
38	17.135129	2581.620647	0.000387	0.058360	150.662457	0.006637	456
39	18.465374	2794.459783	0.000358	0.054155	151.335133	0.006608	468
40	19.898889	3023.822174	0.000331	0.050254	151.959350	0.006581	480

9.00%   MONTHLY COMPOUND INTEREST TABLES   9.00%
                              EFFECTIVE RATE 0.750

	1 AMOUNT OF $1 AT COMPOUND INTEREST	2 ACCUMULATION OF $1 PER PERIOD	3 SINKING FUND FACTOR	4 PRESENT VALUE REVERSION OF $1	5 PRESENT VALUE ORD. ANNUITY $1 PER PERIOD	6 INSTALMENT TO AMORTIZE $1	
MONTHS							
1	1.007500	1.000000	1.000000	0.992556	0.992556	1.007500	
2	1.015056	2.007500	0.498132	0.985167	1.977723	0.505632	
3	1.022669	3.022556	0.330846	0.977833	2.955556	0.338346	
4	1.030339	4.045225	0.247205	0.970554	3.926110	0.254705	
5	1.038067	5.075565	0.197022	0.963329	4.889440	0.204522	
6	1.045852	6.113631	0.163569	0.956158	5.845598	0.171069	
7	1.053696	7.159484	0.139675	0.949040	6.794638	0.147175	
8	1.061599	8.213180	0.121756	0.941975	7.736613	0.129256	
9	1.069561	9.274779	0.107819	0.934963	8.671576	0.115319	
10	1.077583	10.344339	0.096671	0.928003	9.599580	0.104171	
11	1.085664	11.421922	0.087551	0.921095	10.520675	0.095051	
12	1.093807	12.507586	0.079951	0.914238	11.434913	0.087451	
YEARS							MONT
1	1.093807	12.507586	0.079951	0.914238	11.434913	0.087451	12
2	1.196414	26.188471	0.038185	0.835831	21.889146	0.045685	24
3	1.308645	41.152716	0.024300	0.764149	31.446805	0.031800	36
4	1.431405	57.520711	0.017385	0.698614	40.184782	0.024885	48
5	1.565681	75.424137	0.013258	0.638700	48.173374	0.020758	60
6	1.712553	95.007028	0.010526	0.583924	55.476849	0.018026	72
7	1.873202	116.426928	0.008589	0.533845	62.153965	0.016089	84
8	2.048921	139.856164	0.007150	0.488062	68.258439	0.014650	96
9	2.241124	165.483223	0.006043	0.446205	73.839382	0.013543	108
10	2.451357	193.514277	0.005168	0.407937	78.941693	0.012668	120
11	2.681311	224.174837	0.004461	0.372952	83.606420	0.011961	132
12	2.932837	257.711570	0.003880	0.340967	87.871092	0.011380	144
13	3.207957	294.394279	0.003397	0.311725	91.770018	0.010897	156
14	3.508886	334.518079	0.002989	0.284991	95.334564	0.010489	168
15	3.838043	378.405769	0.002643	0.260549	98.593409	0.010143	180
16	4.198078	426.410427	0.002345	0.238204	101.572769	0.009845	192
17	4.591887	478.918252	0.002088	0.217775	104.296613	0.009588	204
18	5.022638	536.351674	0.001864	0.199099	106.786856	0.009364	216
19	5.493796	599.172747	0.001669	0.182024	109.063531	0.009169	228
20	6.009152	667.886870	0.001497	0.166413	111.144954	0.008997	240
21	6.572851	743.046852	0.001346	0.152141	113.047870	0.008846	252
22	7.189430	825.257358	0.001212	0.139093	114.787589	0.008712	264
23	7.863848	915.179777	0.001093	0.127164	116.378106	0.008593	276
24	8.601532	1013.537539	0.000987	0.116258	117.832218	0.008487	288
25	9.408415	1121.121937	0.000892	0.106288	119.161622	0.008392	300
26	10.290989	1238.798494	0.000807	0.097172	120.377014	0.008307	312
27	11.256354	1367.513924	0.000731	0.088839	121.488172	0.008231	324
28	12.312278	1508.303750	0.000663	0.081220	122.504035	0.008163	336
29	13.467255	1662.300631	0.000602	0.074254	123.432776	0.008102	348
30	14.730576	1830.743483	0.000546	0.067886	124.281866	0.008046	360
31	16.112406	2014.987436	0.000496	0.062064	125.058136	0.007996	372
32	17.623861	2216.514743	0.000451	0.056741	125.767832	0.007951	384
33	19.277100	2436.946701	0.000410	0.051875	126.416664	0.007910	396
34	21.085425	2678.056697	0.000373	0.047426	127.009850	0.007873	408
35	23.063384	2941.784473	0.000340	0.043359	127.552164	0.007840	420
36	25.226888	3230.251735	0.000310	0.039640	128.047967	0.007810	432
37	27.593344	3545.779215	0.000282	0.036241	128.501250	0.007782	444
38	30.181790	3890.905350	0.000257	0.033133	128.915659	0.007757	456
39	33.013050	4268.406696	0.000234	0.030291	129.294526	0.007734	468
40	36.109902	4681.320272	0.000214	0.027693	129.640902	0.007714	480

8.50% ... MONTHLY COMPOUND INTEREST TABLES ... 8.50%
EFFECTIVE RATE 0.708

	1	2	3	4	5	6	
	AMOUNT OF $1 AT COMPOUND INTEREST	ACCUMULATION OF $1 PER PERIOD	SINKING FUND FACTOR	PRESENT VALUE REVERSION OF $1	PRESENT VALUE ORD. ANNUITY $1 PER PERIOD	INSTALMENT TO AMORTIZE $1	

NTHS

1	1.007083	1.000000	1.000000	0.992966	0.992966	1.007083	
2	1.014217	2.007083	0.498235	0.985982	1.978949	0.505319	
3	1.021401	3.021300	0.330983	0.979048	2.957996	0.338067	
4	1.028636	4.042701	0.247359	0.972161	3.930158	0.254443	
5	1.035922	5.071337	0.197187	0.965324	4.895482	0.204270	
6	1.043260	6.107259	0.163740	0.958534	5.854016	0.170823	
7	1.050650	7.150519	0.139850	0.951792	6.805808	0.146933	
8	1.058092	8.201168	0.121934	0.945098	7.750906	0.129017	
9	1.065586	9.259260	0.108000	0.938450	8.689356	0.115083	
0	1.073134	10.324846	0.096854	0.931850	9.621206	0.103937	
1	1.080736	11.397980	0.087735	0.925296	10.546501	0.094818	
2	1.088391	12.478716	0.080136	0.918788	11.465289	0.087220	

ARS

							MONTHS
1	1.088391	12.478716	0.080136	0.918788	11.465289	0.087220	12
2	1.184595	26.060437	0.038372	0.844171	21.999453	0.045456	24
3	1.289302	40.842659	0.024484	0.775613	31.678112	0.031568	36
4	1.403265	56.931495	0.017565	0.712624	40.570744	0.024648	48
5	1.527301	74.442437	0.013433	0.654750	48.741183	0.020517	60
6	1.662300	93.501188	0.010695	0.601576	56.248080	0.017778	72
7	1.809232	114.244559	0.008753	0.552721	63.145324	0.015836	84
8	1.969152	136.821455	0.007309	0.507833	69.482425	0.014392	96
9	2.143207	161.393943	0.006196	0.466590	75.304875	0.013279	108
10	2.332647	188.138416	0.005315	0.428698	80.654470	0.012399	120
11	2.538832	217.246858	0.004603	0.393882	85.569611	0.011686	132
12	2.763242	248.928220	0.004017	0.361894	90.085581	0.011101	144
13	3.007487	283.409927	0.003528	0.332504	94.234798	0.010612	156
14	3.273321	320.939504	0.003116	0.305500	98.047046	0.010199	168
15	3.562653	361.786353	0.002764	0.280690	101.549693	0.009847	180
16	3.877559	406.243693	0.002462	0.257894	104.767881	0.009545	192
17	4.220300	454.630657	0.002200	0.236950	107.724713	0.009283	204
18	4.593337	507.294589	0.001971	0.217707	110.441412	0.009055	216
19	4.999346	564.613533	0.001771	0.200026	112.937482	0.008854	228
20	5.441243	626.998951	0.001595	0.183782	115.230840	0.008678	240
21	5.922199	694.898672	0.001439	0.168856	117.337948	0.008522	252
22	6.445667	768.800112	0.001301	0.155143	119.273933	0.008384	264
23	7.015406	849.233766	0.001178	0.142543	121.052692	0.008261	276
24	7.635504	936.777024	0.001067	0.130967	122.686994	0.008151	288
25	8.310413	1032.058310	0.000969	0.120331	124.188570	0.008052	300
26	9.044978	1135.761595	0.000880	0.110559	125.568199	0.007964	312
27	9.844472	1248.631307	0.000801	0.101580	126.835785	0.007884	324
28	10.714634	1371.477676	0.000729	0.093330	128.000428	0.007812	336
29	11.661710	1505.182546	0.000664	0.085751	129.070487	0.007748	348
30	12.692499	1650.705711	0.000606	0.078787	130.053643	0.007689	360
31	13.814400	1809.091800	0.000553	0.072388	130.956956	0.007636	372
32	15.035468	1981.477780	0.000505	0.066509	131.786908	0.007588	384
33	16.364466	2169.101112	0.000461	0.061108	132.549457	0.007544	396
34	17.810936	2373.308640	0.000421	0.056145	133.250078	0.007505	408
35	19.385261	2595.566257	0.000385	0.051586	133.893800	0.007469	420
36	21.098742	2837.469426	0.000352	0.047396	134.485244	0.007436	432
37	22.963679	3100.754635	0.000323	0.043547	135.028655	0.007406	444
38	24.993459	3387.311862	0.000295	0.040010	135.527934	0.007379	456
39	27.202654	3699.198142	0.000270	0.036761	135.986665	0.007354	468
40	29.607121	4038.652333	0.000248	0.033776	136.408142	0.007331	480

10.00%   MONTHLY COMPOUND INTEREST TABLES   10.00%
                                              EFFECTIVE RATE 0.833

	1 AMOUNT OF $1 AT COMPOUND INTEREST	2 ACCUMULATION OF $1 PER PERIOD	3 SINKING FUND FACTOR	4 PRESENT VALUE REVERSION OF $1	5 PRESENT VALUE ORD. ANNUITY $1 PER PERIOD	6 INSTALMENT TO AMORTIZE $1	
MONTHS							
1	1.008333	1.000000	1.000000	0.991736	0.991736	1.008333	
2	1.016736	2.008333	0.497925	0.983539	1.975275	0.506259	
3	1.025209	3.025069	0.330571	0.975411	2.950686	0.338904	
4	1.033752	4.050278	0.246897	0.967350	3.918036	0.255230	
5	1.042367	5.084031	0.196694	0.959355	4.877391	0.205028	
6	1.051053	6.126398	0.163228	0.951427	5.828817	0.171561	
7	1.059812	7.177451	0.139325	0.943563	6.772381	0.147659	
8	1.068644	8.237263	0.121400	0.935765	7.708146	0.129733	
9	1.077549	9.305907	0.107459	0.928032	8.636178	0.115792	
10	1.086529	10.383456	0.096307	0.920362	9.556540	0.104640	
11	1.095583	11.469985	0.087184	0.912756	10.469296	0.095517	
12	1.104713	12.565568	0.079583	0.905212	11.374508	0.087916	
YEARS							**MONT**
1	1.104713	12.565568	0.079583	0.905212	11.374508	0.087916	12
2	1.220391	26.446915	0.037812	0.819410	21.670855	0.046145	24
3	1.348182	41.781821	0.023934	0.741740	30.991236	0.032267	36
4	1.489354	58.722492	0.017029	0.671432	39.428160	0.025363	48
5	1.645309	77.437072	0.012914	0.607789	47.065369	0.021247	60
6	1.817594	98.111314	0.010193	0.550178	53.978665	0.018526	72
7	2.007920	120.950418	0.008268	0.498028	60.236667	0.016601	84
8	2.218176	146.181076	0.006841	0.450821	65.901488	0.015174	96
9	2.450448	174.053713	0.005745	0.408089	71.029355	0.014079	108
10	2.707041	204.844979	0.004882	0.369407	75.671163	0.013215	120
11	2.990504	238.860493	0.004187	0.334392	79.872986	0.012520	132
12	3.303649	276.437876	0.003617	0.302696	83.676528	0.011951	144
13	3.649584	317.950102	0.003145	0.274004	87.119542	0.011478	156
14	4.031743	363.809201	0.002749	0.248032	90.236201	0.011082	168
15	4.453920	414.470346	0.002413	0.224521	93.057439	0.010746	180
16	4.920303	470.436376	0.002126	0.203240	95.611259	0.010459	192
17	5.435523	532.262780	0.001879	0.183975	97.923008	0.010212	204
18	6.004693	600.563216	0.001665	0.166536	100.015633	0.009998	216
19	6.633463	676.015601	0.001479	0.150751	101.909902	0.009813	228
20	7.328074	759.368836	0.001317	0.136462	103.624619	0.009650	240
21	8.095419	851.450244	0.001174	0.123527	105.176801	0.009508	252
22	8.943115	953.173779	0.001049	0.111818	106.581856	0.009382	264
23	9.879576	1065.549097	0.000938	0.101219	107.853730	0.009272	276
24	10.914097	1189.691580	0.000841	0.091625	109.005045	0.009174	288
25	12.056945	1326.833403	0.000754	0.082940	110.047230	0.009087	300
26	13.319465	1478.335767	0.000676	0.075078	110.990629	0.009010	312
27	14.714187	1645.702407	0.000608	0.067962	111.844605	0.008941	324
28	16.254954	1830.594523	0.000546	0.061520	112.617635	0.008880	336
29	17.957060	2034.847259	0.000491	0.055688	113.317392	0.008825	348
30	19.837399	2260.487925	0.000442	0.050410	113.950820	0.008776	360
31	21.914634	2509.756117	0.000398	0.045632	114.524207	0.008732	372
32	24.209383	2785.125947	0.000359	0.041306	115.043244	0.008692	384
33	26.744422	3089.330596	0.000324	0.037391	115.513083	0.008657	396
34	29.544912	3425.389448	0.000292	0.033847	115.938387	0.008625	408
35	32.638650	3796.638052	0.000263	0.030639	116.323377	0.008597	420
36	36.056344	4206.761236	0.000238	0.027734	116.671876	0.008571	432
37	39.831914	4659.829677	0.000215	0.025105	116.987340	0.008548	444
38	44.002836	5160.340305	0.000194	0.022726	117.272903	0.008527	456
39	48.610508	5713.260935	0.000175	0.020572	117.531398	0.008508	468
40	53.700663	6324.079581	0.000158	0.018622	117.765391	0.008491	480

9.50% MONTHLY COMPOUND INTEREST TABLES 9.50%
EFFECTIVE RATE 0.792

	1 AMOUNT OF $1 AT COMPOUND INTEREST	2 ACCUMULATION OF $1 PER PERIOD	3 SINKING FUND FACTOR	4 PRESENT VALUE REVERSION OF $1	5 PRESENT VALUE ORD. ANNUITY $1 PER PERIOD	6 INSTALMENT TO AMORTIZE $1	
MONTHS							
1	1.007917	1.000000	1.000000	0.992146	0.992146	1.007917	
2	1.015896	2.007917	0.498029	0.984353	1.976498	0.505945	
3	1.023939	3.023813	0.330708	0.976621	2.953119	0.338625	
4	1.032045	4.047751	0.247051	0.968950	3.922070	0.254967	
5	1.040215	5.079796	0.196858	0.961340	4.883409	0.204775	
6	1.048450	6.120011	0.163398	0.953789	5.837198	0.171315	
7	1.056750	7.168461	0.139500	0.946297	6.783496	0.147417	
8	1.065116	8.225211	0.121577	0.938865	7.722360	0.129494	
9	1.073548	9.290328	0.107639	0.931490	8.653851	0.115555	
10	1.082047	10.363876	0.096489	0.924174	9.578024	0.104406	
11	1.090614	11.445923	0.087367	0.916915	10.494940	0.095284	
12	1.099248	12.536537	0.079767	0.909713	11.404653	0.087684	
YEARS							**MONTHS**
1	1.099248	12.536537	0.079767	0.909713	11.404653	0.087684	12
2	1.208345	26.317295	0.037998	0.827578	21.779615	0.045914	24
3	1.328271	41.465760	0.024116	0.752859	31.217856	0.032033	36
4	1.460098	58.117673	0.017206	0.684885	39.803947	0.025123	48
5	1.605009	76.422249	0.013085	0.623049	47.614827	0.021002	60
6	1.764303	96.543509	0.010358	0.566796	54.720488	0.018275	72
7	1.939406	118.661756	0.008427	0.515622	61.184601	0.016344	84
8	2.131887	142.975186	0.006994	0.469068	67.065090	0.014911	96
9	2.343472	169.701665	0.005893	0.426717	72.414648	0.013809	108
10	2.576055	199.080682	0.005023	0.388190	77.281211	0.012940	120
11	2.831723	231.375495	0.004322	0.353142	81.708388	0.012239	132
12	3.112764	266.875491	0.003747	0.321258	85.735849	0.011664	144
13	3.421699	305.898776	0.003269	0.292253	89.399684	0.011186	156
14	3.761294	348.795027	0.002867	0.265866	92.732722	0.010784	168
15	4.134593	395.948628	0.002526	0.241862	95.764831	0.010442	180
16	4.544942	447.782110	0.002233	0.220025	98.523180	0.010150	192
17	4.996016	504.759939	0.001981	0.200159	101.032487	0.009898	204
18	5.491859	567.392681	0.001762	0.182088	103.315236	0.009679	216
19	6.036912	636.241570	0.001572	0.165648	105.391883	0.009488	228
20	6.636061	711.923546	0.001405	0.150692	107.281037	0.009321	240
21	7.294674	795.116775	0.001258	0.137086	108.999624	0.009174	252
22	8.018653	886.566731	0.001128	0.124709	110.563046	0.009045	264
23	8.814485	987.092874	0.001013	0.113450	111.985311	0.008930	276
24	9.689302	1097.595994	0.000911	0.103207	113.279165	0.008828	288
25	10.650941	1219.066282	0.000820	0.093888	114.456200	0.008737	300
26	11.708022	1352.592202	0.000739	0.085412	115.526965	0.008656	312
27	12.870014	1499.370247	0.000667	0.077700	116.501054	0.008584	324
28	14.147332	1660.715658	0.000602	0.070685	117.387195	0.008519	336
29	15.551421	1838.074212	0.000544	0.064303	118.193330	0.008461	348
30	17.094862	2033.035174	0.000492	0.058497	118.926681	0.008409	360
31	18.791486	2247.345541	0.000445	0.053216	119.593820	0.008362	372
32	20.656495	2482.925693	0.000403	0.048411	120.200725	0.008319	384
33	22.706602	2741.886606	0.000365	0.044040	120.752835	0.008281	396
34	24.960178	3026.548765	0.000330	0.040064	121.255097	0.008247	408
35	27.437415	3339.462955	0.000299	0.036447	121.712011	0.008216	420
36	30.160512	3683.433122	0.000271	0.033156	122.127671	0.008188	432
37	33.153870	4061.541498	0.000246	0.030162	122.505803	0.008163	444
38	36.444312	4477.176216	0.000223	0.027439	122.849795	0.008140	456
39	40.061322	4934.061676	0.000203	0.024962	123.162729	0.008119	468
40	44.037311	5436.291914	0.000184	0.022708	123.447408	0.008101	480

12.00%   MONTHLY COMPOUND INTEREST TABLES   12.00%
                                      EFFECTIVE RATE 1.000

	1	2	3	4	5	6
	AMOUNT OF $1 AT COMPOUND INTEREST	ACCUMULATION OF $1 PER PERIOD	SINKING FUND FACTOR	PRESENT VALUE REVERSION OF $1	PRESENT VALUE ORD. ANNUITY $1 PER PERIOD	INSTALMENT TO AMORTIZE $1

MONTHS

1	1.010000	1.000000	1.000000	0.990099	0.990099	1.010000
2	1.020100	2.010000	0.497512	0.980296	1.970395	0.507512
3	1.030301	3.030100	0.330022	0.970590	2.940985	0.340022
4	1.040604	4.060401	0.246281	0.960980	3.901966	0.256281
5	1.051010	5.101005	0.196040	0.951466	4.853431	0.206040
6	1.061520	6.152015	0.162548	0.942045	5.795476	0.172548
7	1.072135	7.213535	0.138628	0.932718	6.728195	0.148628
8	1.082857	8.285671	0.120690	0.923483	7.651678	0.130690
9	1.093685	9.368527	0.106740	0.914340	8.566018	0.116740
10	1.104622	10.462213	0.095582	0.905287	9.471305	0.105582
11	1.115668	11.566835	0.086454	0.896324	10.367628	0.096454
12	1.126825	12.682503	0.078849	0.887449	11.255077	0.088849

YEARS   MONT

1	1.126825	12.682503	0.078849	0.887449	11.255077	0.088849	12
2	1.269735	26.973465	0.037073	0.787566	21.243387	0.047073	24
3	1.430769	43.076878	0.023214	0.698925	30.107505	0.033214	36
4	1.612226	61.222608	0.016334	0.620260	37.973959	0.026334	48
5	1.816697	81.669670	0.012244	0.550450	44.955038	0.022244	60
6	2.047099	104.709931	0.009550	0.488496	51.150391	0.019550	72
7	2.306723	130.672274	0.007653	0.433515	56.648453	0.017653	84
8	2.599273	159.927293	0.006253	0.384723	61.527703	0.016253	96
9	2.928926	192.892579	0.005184	0.341422	65.857790	0.015184	108
10	3.300387	230.038689	0.004347	0.302995	69.700522	0.014347	120
11	3.718959	271.895856	0.003678	0.268892	73.110752	0.013678	132
12	4.190616	319.061559	0.003134	0.238628	76.137157	0.013134	144
13	4.722091	372.209054	0.002687	0.211771	78.822939	0.012687	156
14	5.320970	432.096982	0.002314	0.187936	81.206434	0.012314	168
15	5.995802	499.580198	0.002002	0.166783	83.321664	0.012002	180
16	6.756220	575.621974	0.001737	0.148012	85.198824	0.011737	192
17	7.613078	661.307751	0.001512	0.131353	86.864707	0.011512	204
18	8.578606	757.860630	0.001320	0.116569	88.343095	0.011320	216
19	9.666588	866.658830	0.001154	0.103449	89.655089	0.011154	228
20	10.892554	989.255365	0.001011	0.091806	90.819416	0.011011	240
21	12.274002	1127.400210	0.000887	0.081473	91.852698	0.010887	252
22	13.830653	1283.065278	0.000779	0.072303	92.769683	0.010779	264
23	15.584726	1458.472574	0.000686	0.064165	93.583461	0.010686	276
24	17.561259	1656.125905	0.000604	0.056944	94.305647	0.010604	288
25	19.788466	1878.846626	0.000532	0.050534	94.946551	0.010532	300
26	22.298139	2129.813909	0.000470	0.044847	95.515321	0.010470	312
27	25.126101	2412.610125	0.000414	0.039799	96.020075	0.010414	324
28	28.312720	2731.271980	0.000366	0.035320	96.468019	0.010366	336
29	31.903481	3090.348134	0.000324	0.031345	96.865546	0.010324	348
30	35.949641	3494.964133	0.000286	0.027817	97.218331	0.010286	360
31	40.508956	3950.895567	0.000253	0.024686	97.531410	0.010253	372
32	45.646505	4464.650519	0.000224	0.021907	97.809252	0.010224	384
33	51.435625	5043.562459	0.000198	0.019442	98.055822	0.010198	396
34	57.958949	5695.894923	0.000176	0.017254	98.274641	0.010176	408
35	65.309595	6430.959471	0.000155	0.015312	98.468831	0.010155	420
36	73.592486	7259.248603	0.000138	0.013588	98.641166	0.010138	432
37	82.925855	8192.585529	0.000122	0.012059	98.794103	0.010122	444
38	93.442929	9244.292938	0.000108	0.010702	98.929828	0.010108	456
39	105.293832	10429.383172	0.000096	0.009497	99.050277	0.010096	468
40	118.647725	11764.772510	0.000085	0.008428	99.157169	0.010085	480

11.00%   MONTHLY COMPOUND INTEREST TABLES   11.00%
                                     EFFECTIVE RATE 0.917

	1 AMOUNT OF $1 AT COMPOUND INTEREST	2 ACCUMULATION OF $1 PER PERIOD	3 SINKING FUND FACTOR	4 PRESENT VALUE REVERSION OF $1	5 PRESENT VALUE ORD. ANNUITY $1 PER PERIOD	6 INSTALMENT TO AMORTIZE $1	
ONTHS							
1	1.009167	1.000000	1.000000	0.990917	0.990917	1.009167	
2	1.018417	2.009167	0.497719	0.981916	1.972832	0.506885	
3	1.027753	3.027584	0.330296	0.972997	2.945829	0.339463	
4	1.037174	4.055337	0.246589	0.964158	3.909987	0.255755	
5	1.046681	5.092511	0.196367	0.955401	4.865388	0.205533	
6	1.056276	6.139192	0.162888	0.946722	5.812110	0.172055	
7	1.065958	7.195468	0.138976	0.938123	6.750233	0.148143	
8	1.075730	8.261427	0.121044	0.929602	7.679835	0.130211	
9	1.085591	9.337156	0.107099	0.921158	8.600992	0.116266	
10	1.095542	10.422747	0.095944	0.912790	9.513783	0.105111	
11	1.105584	11.518289	0.086818	0.904499	10.418282	0.095985	
12	1.115719	12.623873	0.079215	0.896283	11.314565	0.088382	
EARS							**MONTHS**
1	1.115719	12.623873	0.079215	0.896283	11.314565	0.088382	12
2	1.244829	26.708566	0.037441	0.803323	21.455619	0.046608	24
3	1.388879	42.423123	0.023572	0.720005	30.544874	0.032739	36
4	1.549598	59.956151	0.016679	0.645329	38.691421	0.025846	48
5	1.728916	79.518080	0.012576	0.578397	45.993034	0.021742	60
6	1.928984	101.343692	0.009867	0.518408	52.537346	0.019034	72
7	2.152204	125.694940	0.007956	0.464640	58.402903	0.017122	84
8	2.401254	152.864085	0.006542	0.416449	63.660103	0.015708	96
9	2.679124	183.177212	0.005459	0.373256	68.372043	0.014626	108
10	2.989150	216.998139	0.004608	0.334543	72.595275	0.013775	120
11	3.335051	254.732784	0.003926	0.299846	76.380487	0.013092	132
12	3.720979	296.834038	0.003369	0.268747	79.773109	0.012536	144
13	4.151566	343.807200	0.002909	0.240873	82.813859	0.012075	156
14	4.631980	396.216042	0.002524	0.215890	85.539231	0.011691	168
15	5.167988	454.689575	0.002199	0.193499	87.981937	0.011366	180
16	5.766021	519.929596	0.001923	0.173430	90.171293	0.011090	192
17	6.433259	592.719117	0.001687	0.155442	92.133576	0.010854	204
18	7.177708	673.931757	0.001484	0.139320	93.892337	0.010650	216
19	8.008304	764.542228	0.001308	0.124870	95.468685	0.010475	228
20	8.935015	865.638038	0.001155	0.111919	96.881539	0.010322	240
21	9.968965	978.432537	0.001022	0.100311	98.147856	0.010189	252
22	11.122562	1104.279485	0.000906	0.089907	99.282835	0.010072	264
23	12.409652	1244.689295	0.000803	0.080582	100.300098	0.009970	276
24	13.845682	1401.347165	0.000714	0.072225	101.211853	0.009880	288
25	15.447889	1576.133301	0.000634	0.064734	102.029044	0.009801	300
26	17.235500	1771.145485	0.000565	0.058020	102.761478	0.009731	312
27	19.229972	1988.724252	0.000503	0.052002	103.417947	0.009670	324
28	21.455242	2231.480981	0.000448	0.046609	104.006328	0.009615	336
29	23.938018	2502.329236	0.000400	0.041775	104.533685	0.009566	348
30	26.708098	2804.519736	0.000357	0.037442	105.006346	0.009523	360
31	29.798728	3141.679369	0.000318	0.033558	105.429984	0.009485	372
32	33.247002	3517.854723	0.000284	0.030078	105.809684	0.009451	384
33	37.094306	3937.560650	0.000254	0.026958	106.150002	0.009421	396
34	41.386816	4405.834459	0.000227	0.024162	106.455024	0.009394	408
35	46.176050	4928.296368	0.000203	0.021656	106.728409	0.009370	420
36	51.519489	5511.216961	0.000181	0.019410	106.973440	0.009348	432
37	57.481264	6161.592447	0.000162	0.017397	107.193057	0.009329	444
38	64.132929	6887.228627	0.000145	0.015593	107.389897	0.009312	456
39	71.554317	7696.834582	0.000130	0.013975	107.566320	0.009297	468
40	79.834499	8600.127195	0.000116	0.012526	107.724446	0.009283	480

7.25%   ANNUAL COMPOUND INTEREST TABLES   7.25%
                                EFFECTIVE RATE 7.25

	1 AMOUNT OF $1 AT COMPOUND INTEREST	2 ACCUMULATION OF $1 PER PERIOD	3 SINKING FUND FACTOR	4 PRESENT VALUE REVERSION OF $1	5 PRESENT VALUE ORD. ANNUITY $1 PER PERIOD	6 INSTALMENT TO AMORTIZE $1
YEARS						
1	1.072500	1.000000	1.000000	0.932401	0.932401	1.072500
2	1.150256	2.072500	0.482509	0.869371	1.801772	0.555009
3	1.233650	3.222756	0.310293	0.810603	2.612375	0.382793
4	1.323089	4.456406	0.224396	0.755807	3.368182	0.296896
5	1.419013	5.779496	0.173025	0.704715	4.072897	0.245525
6	1.521892	7.198509	0.138918	0.657077	4.729974	0.211418
7	1.632229	8.720401	0.114674	0.612659	5.342633	0.187174
8	1.750566	10.352630	0.096594	0.571244	5.913877	0.169094
9	1.877482	12.103196	0.082623	0.532628	6.446505	0.155123
10	2.013599	13.980677	0.071527	0.496623	6.943128	0.144027
11	2.159585	15.994276	0.062522	0.463052	7.406180	0.135022
12	2.316155	18.153861	0.055085	0.431750	7.837930	0.127585
13	2.484076	20.470016	0.048852	0.402564	8.240495	0.121352
14	2.664172	22.954093	0.043565	0.375351	8.615846	0.116065
15	2.857324	25.618264	0.039035	0.349978	8.965824	0.111535
16	3.064480	28.475588	0.035118	0.326320	9.292143	0.107618
17	3.286655	31.540069	0.031706	0.304261	9.596404	0.104206
18	3.524937	34.826724	0.028714	0.283693	9.880097	0.101214
19	3.780495	38.351661	0.026074	0.264516	10.144612	0.098574
20	4.054581	42.132156	0.023735	0.246635	10.391247	0.096235
21	4.348538	46.186738	0.021651	0.229962	10.621209	0.094151
22	4.663808	50.535276	0.019788	0.214417	10.835626	0.092288
23	5.001934	55.199084	0.018116	0.199923	11.035549	0.090616
24	5.364574	60.201017	0.016611	0.186408	11.221957	0.089111
25	5.753505	65.565591	0.015252	0.173807	11.395764	0.087752
26	6.170634	71.319096	0.014021	0.162058	11.557822	0.086521
27	6.618005	77.489731	0.012905	0.151103	11.708925	0.085405
28	7.097811	84.107736	0.011890	0.140889	11.849814	0.084390
29	7.612402	91.205547	0.010964	0.131365	11.981178	0.083464
30	8.164301	98.817949	0.010120	0.122484	12.103663	0.082620
31	8.756213	106.982251	0.009347	0.114205	12.217867	0.081847
32	9.391039	115.738464	0.008640	0.106484	12.324352	0.081140
33	10.071889	125.129503	0.007992	0.099286	12.423638	0.080492
34	10.802101	135.201392	0.007396	0.092575	12.516213	0.079896
35	11.585253	146.003492	0.006849	0.086317	12.602529	0.079349
36	12.425184	157.588746	0.006346	0.080482	12.683011	0.078846
37	13.326010	170.013930	0.005882	0.075041	12.758052	0.078382
38	14.292146	183.339940	0.005454	0.069969	12.828021	0.077954
39	15.328326	197.632085	0.005060	0.065239	12.893259	0.077560
40	16.439630	212.960411	0.004696	0.060829	12.954088	0.077196
41	17.631503	229.400041	0.004359	0.056717	13.010805	0.076859
42	18.909787	247.031544	0.004048	0.052883	13.063687	0.076548
43	20.280747	265.941331	0.003760	0.049308	13.112995	0.076260
44	21.751101	286.222078	0.003494	0.045975	13.158970	0.075994
45	23.328055	307.973178	0.003247	0.042867	13.201837	0.075747
46	25.019339	331.301234	0.003018	0.039969	13.241806	0.075518
47	26.833242	356.320573	0.002806	0.037267	13.279073	0.075306
48	28.778652	383.153815	0.002610	0.034748	13.313821	0.075110
49	30.865104	411.932466	0.002428	0.032399	13.346220	0.074928
50	33.102824	442.797570	0.002258	0.030209	13.376429	0.074758

7.75%   ANNUAL COMPOUND INTEREST TABLES   7.75%
                                   EFFECTIVE RATE   7.75

	1	2	3	4	5	6
	AMOUNT OF $1 AT COMPOUND INTEREST	ACCUMULATION OF $1 PER PERIOD	SINKING FUND FACTOR	PRESENT VALUE REVERSION OF $1	PRESENT VALUE ORD. ANNUITY $1 PER PERIOD	INSTALMENT TO AMORTIZE $1
YEARS						
1	1.077500	1.000000	1.000000	0.928074	0.928074	1.077500
2	1.161006	2.077500	0.481348	0.861322	1.789396	0.558848
3	1.250984	3.238506	0.308784	0.799371	2.588767	0.386284
4	1.347936	4.489490	0.222742	0.741875	3.330642	0.300242
5	1.452401	5.837426	0.171308	0.688515	4.019157	0.248808
6	1.564962	7.289827	0.137177	0.638993	4.658151	0.214677
7	1.686246	8.854788	0.112933	0.593033	5.251184	0.190433
8	1.816930	10.541034	0.094867	0.550379	5.801563	0.172367
9	1.957742	12.357964	0.080919	0.510792	6.312355	0.158419
10	2.109467	14.315707	0.069853	0.474053	6.786409	0.147353
11	2.272951	16.425174	0.060882	0.439957	7.226365	0.138382
12	2.449105	18.698125	0.053481	0.408312	7.634678	0.130981
13	2.638910	21.147229	0.047288	0.378944	8.013622	0.124788
14	2.843426	23.786140	0.042041	0.351688	8.365310	0.119541
15	3.063791	26.629566	0.037552	0.326393	8.691703	0.115052
16	3.301235	29.693357	0.033678	0.302917	8.994620	0.111178
17	3.557081	32.994592	0.030308	0.281129	9.275750	0.107808
18	3.832755	36.551673	0.027359	0.260909	9.536659	0.104859
19	4.129793	40.384428	0.024762	0.242143	9.778802	0.102262
20	4.449852	44.514221	0.022465	0.224727	10.003528	0.099965
21	4.794716	48.964073	0.020423	0.208563	10.212091	0.097923
22	5.166306	53.758788	0.018602	0.193562	10.405653	0.096102
23	5.566695	58.925095	0.016971	0.179640	10.585293	0.094471
24	5.998114	64.491789	0.015506	0.166719	10.752012	0.093006
25	6.462967	70.489903	0.014186	0.154728	10.906740	0.091686
26	6.963847	76.952870	0.012995	0.143599	11.050338	0.090495
27	7.503546	83.916718	0.011917	0.133270	11.183609	0.089417
28	8.085070	91.420264	0.010938	0.123685	11.307293	0.088438
29	8.711663	99.505334	0.010050	0.114789	11.422082	0.087550
30	9.386817	108.216997	0.009241	0.106532	11.528614	0.086741
31	10.114296	117.603815	0.008503	0.098870	11.627484	0.086003
32	10.898154	127.718110	0.007830	0.091759	11.719243	0.085330
33	11.742760	138.616264	0.007214	0.085159	11.804402	0.084714
34	12.652824	150.359024	0.006651	0.079034	11.883436	0.084151
35	13.633418	163.011849	0.006135	0.073349	11.956785	0.083635
36	14.690008	176.645267	0.005661	0.068073	12.024858	0.083161
37	15.828484	191.335275	0.005226	0.063177	12.088036	0.082726
38	17.055191	207.163759	0.004827	0.058633	12.146669	0.082327
39	18.376969	224.218950	0.004460	0.054416	12.201085	0.081960
40	19.801184	242.595919	0.004122	0.050502	12.251587	0.081622
41	21.335775	262.397103	0.003811	0.046870	12.298456	0.081311
42	22.989298	283.732878	0.003524	0.043499	12.341955	0.081024
43	24.770969	306.722176	0.003260	0.040370	12.382325	0.080760
44	26.690719	331.493145	0.003017	0.037466	12.419791	0.080517
45	28.759249	358.183864	0.002792	0.034771	12.454562	0.080292
46	30.988091	386.943113	0.002584	0.032270	12.486833	0.080084
47	33.389668	417.931204	0.002393	0.029949	12.516782	0.079893
48	35.977368	451.320873	0.002216	0.027795	12.544577	0.079716
49	38.765614	487.298240	0.002052	0.025796	12.570373	0.079552
50	41.769949	526.063854	0.001901	0.023941	12.594314	0.079401

ANNUAL COMPOUND INTEREST TABLES
EFFECTIVE RATE   8.00

	1 AMOUNT OF $1 AT COMPOUND INTEREST	2 ACCUMULATION OF $1 PER PERIOD	3 SINKING FUND FACTOR	4 PRESENT VALUE REVERSION OF $1	5 PRESENT VALUE ORD. ANNUITY $1 PER PERIOD	6 INSTALMENT TO AMORTIZE $1
YEARS						
1	1.080000	1.000000	1.000000	0.925926	0.925926	1.080000
2	1.166400	2.080000	0.480769	0.857339	1.783265	0.560769
3	1.259712	3.246400	0.308034	0.793832	2.577097	0.388034
4	1.360489	4.506112	0.221921	0.735030	3.312127	0.301921
5	1.469328	5.866601	0.170456	0.680583	3.992710	0.250456
6	1.586874	7.335929	0.136315	0.630170	4.622880	0.216315
7	1.713824	8.922803	0.112072	0.583490	5.206370	0.192072
8	1.850930	10.636628	0.094015	0.540269	5.746639	0.174015
9	1.999005	12.487558	0.080080	0.500249	6.246888	0.160080
10	2.158925	14.486562	0.069029	0.463193	6.710081	0.149029
11	2.331639	16.645487	0.060076	0.428883	7.138964	0.140076
12	2.518170	18.977126	0.052695	0.397114	7.536078	0.132695
13	2.719624	21.495297	0.046522	0.367698	7.903776	0.126522
14	2.937194	24.214920	0.041297	0.340461	8.244237	0.121297
15	3.172169	27.152114	0.036830	0.315242	8.559479	0.116830
16	3.425943	30.324283	0.032977	0.291890	8.851369	0.112977
17	3.700018	33.750226	0.029629	0.270269	9.121638	0.109629
18	3.996019	37.450244	0.026702	0.250249	9.371887	0.106702
19	4.315701	41.446263	0.024128	0.231712	9.603599	0.104128
20	4.660957	45.761964	0.021852	0.214548	9.818147	0.101852
21	5.033834	50.422921	0.019832	0.198656	10.016803	0.099832
22	5.436540	55.456755	0.018032	0.183941	10.200744	0.098032
23	5.871464	60.893296	0.016422	0.170315	10.371059	0.096422
24	6.341181	66.764759	0.014978	0.157699	10.528758	0.094978
25	6.848475	73.105940	0.013679	0.146018	10.674776	0.093679
26	7.396353	79.954415	0.012507	0.135202	10.809978	0.092507
27	7.988061	87.350768	0.011448	0.125187	10.935165	0.091448
28	8.627106	95.338883	0.010489	0.115914	11.051078	0.090489
29	9.317275	103.965936	0.009619	0.107328	11.158406	0.089619
30	10.062657	113.283211	0.008827	0.099377	11.257783	0.088827
31	10.867669	123.345868	0.008107	0.092016	11.349799	0.088107
32	11.737083	134.213537	0.007451	0.085200	11.434999	0.087451
33	12.676050	145.950620	0.006852	0.078889	11.513888	0.086852
34	13.690134	158.626670	0.006304	0.073045	11.586934	0.086304
35	14.785344	172.316804	0.005803	0.067635	11.654568	0.085803
36	15.968172	187.102148	0.005345	0.062625	11.717193	0.085345
37	17.245626	203.070320	0.004924	0.057986	11.775179	0.084924
38	18.625276	220.315945	0.004539	0.053690	11.828869	0.084539
39	20.115298	238.941221	0.004185	0.049713	11.878582	0.084185
40	21.724521	259.056519	0.003860	0.046031	11.924613	0.083860
41	23.462483	280.781040	0.003561	0.042621	11.967235	0.083561
42	25.339482	304.243523	0.003287	0.039464	12.006699	0.083287
43	27.366640	329.583005	0.003034	0.036541	12.043240	0.083034
44	29.555972	356.949646	0.002802	0.033834	12.077074	0.082802
45	31.920449	386.505617	0.002587	0.031328	12.108402	0.082587
46	34.474085	418.426067	0.002390	0.029007	12.137409	0.082390
47	37.232012	452.900152	0.002208	0.026859	12.164267	0.082208
48	40.210573	490.132164	0.002040	0.024869	12.189136	0.082040
49	43.427419	530.342737	0.001886	0.023027	12.212163	0.081886
50	46.901613	573.770156	0.001743	0.021321	12.233485	0.081743

8.50%   ANNUAL COMPOUND INTEREST TABLES   8.50%
                              EFFECTIVE RATE 8.50

	1	2	3	4	5	6
	AMOUNT OF $1 AT COMPOUND INTEREST	ACCUMULATION OF $1 PER PERIOD	SINKING FUND FACTOR	PRESENT VALUE REVERSION OF $1	PRESENT VALUE ORD. ANNUITY $1 PER PERIOD	INSTALMENT TO AMORTIZE $1
YEARS						
1	1.085000	1.000000	1.000000	0.921659	0.921659	1.085000
2	1.177225	2.085000	0.479616	0.849455	1.771114	0.564616
3	1.277289	3.262225	0.306539	0.782908	2.554022	0.391539
4	1.385859	4.539514	0.220288	0.721574	3.275597	0.305288
5	1.503657	5.925373	0.168766	0.665045	3.940642	0.253766
6	1.631468	7.429030	0.134607	0.612945	4.553587	0.219607
7	1.770142	9.060497	0.110369	0.564926	5.118514	0.195369
8	1.920604	10.830639	0.092331	0.520669	5.639183	0.177331
9	2.083856	12.751244	0.078424	0.479880	6.119063	0.163424
10	2.260983	14.835099	0.067408	0.442285	6.561348	0.152408
11	2.453167	17.096083	0.058493	0.407636	6.968984	0.143493
12	2.661686	19.549250	0.051153	0.375702	7.344686	0.136153
13	2.887930	22.210936	0.045023	0.346269	7.690955	0.130023
14	3.133404	25.098866	0.039842	0.319142	8.010097	0.124842
15	3.399743	28.232269	0.035420	0.294140	8.304237	0.120420
16	3.688721	31.632012	0.031614	0.271097	8.575333	0.116614
17	4.002262	35.320733	0.028312	0.249859	8.825192	0.113312
18	4.342455	39.322995	0.025430	0.230285	9.055476	0.110430
19	4.711563	43.665450	0.022901	0.212244	9.261720	0.107901
20	5.112046	48.377013	0.020671	0.195616	9.463337	0.105671
21	5.546570	53.489059	0.018695	0.180292	9.643628	0.103695
22	6.018028	59.035629	0.016939	0.166167	9.809796	0.101939
23	6.529561	65.053658	0.015372	0.153150	9.962945	0.100372
24	7.084574	71.583219	0.013970	0.141152	10.104097	0.098970
25	7.686762	78.667792	0.012712	0.130094	10.234191	0.097712
26	8.340137	86.354555	0.011580	0.119902	10.354093	0.096580
27	9.049049	94.694692	0.010560	0.110509	10.464602	0.095560
28	9.818218	103.743741	0.009639	0.101851	10.566453	0.094639
29	10.652766	113.561959	0.008806	0.093872	10.660326	0.093806
30	11.558252	124.214725	0.008051	0.086518	10.746844	0.093051
31	12.540703	135.772977	0.007365	0.079740	10.826584	0.092365
32	13.606663	148.313680	0.006742	0.073493	10.900078	0.091742
33	14.763229	161.920343	0.006176	0.067736	10.967813	0.091176
34	16.018104	176.683572	0.005660	0.062429	11.030243	0.090660
35	17.379642	192.701675	0.005189	0.057539	11.087781	0.090189
36	18.856912	210.081318	0.004760	0.053031	11.140812	0.089760
37	20.459750	228.938230	0.004368	0.048876	11.189689	0.089368
38	22.198828	249.397979	0.004010	0.045047	11.234736	0.089010
39	24.085729	271.596808	0.003682	0.041518	11.276255	0.088682
40	26.133016	295.682536	0.003382	0.038266	11.314520	0.088382
41	28.354322	321.815552	0.003107	0.035268	11.349788	0.088107
42	30.764439	350.169874	0.002856	0.032505	11.382293	0.087856
43	33.379417	380.934313	0.002625	0.029959	11.412252	0.087625
44	36.216667	414.313730	0.002414	0.027612	11.439864	0.087414
45	39.295084	450.530397	0.002220	0.025448	11.465312	0.087220
46	42.635166	489.825480	0.002042	0.023455	11.488767	0.087042
47	46.259155	532.460646	0.001878	0.021617	11.510384	0.086878
48	50.191183	578.719801	0.001728	0.019924	11.530308	0.086728
49	54.457434	628.910984	0.001590	0.018363	11.548671	0.086590
50	59.086316	683.368418	0.001463	0.016924	11.565595	0.086463

9.50%   ANNUAL COMPOUND INTEREST TABLES   9.50%
                              EFFECTIVE RATE   9.50

	1 AMOUNT OF $1 AT COMPOUND INTEREST	2 ACCUMULATION OF $1 PER PERIOD	3 SINKING FUND FACTOR	4 PRESENT VALUE REVERSION OF $1	5 PRESENT VALUE ORD. ANNUITY $1 PER PERIOD	6 INSTALMENT TO AMORTIZE $1
YEARS						
1	1.095000	1.000000	1.000000	0.913242	0.913242	1.095000
2	1.199025	2.095000	0.477327	0.834011	1.747253	0.572327
3	1.312932	3.294025	0.303580	0.761654	2.508907	0.398580
4	1.437661	4.606957	0.217063	0.695574	3.204481	0.312063
5	1.574239	6.044618	0.165436	0.635228	3.839709	0.260436
6	1.723791	7.618857	0.131253	0.580117	4.419825	0.226253
7	1.887552	9.342648	0.107036	0.529787	4.949612	0.202036
8	2.066869	11.230200	0.089046	0.483824	5.433436	0.184046
9	2.263222	13.297069	0.075205	0.441848	5.875284	0.170205
10	2.478228	15.560291	0.064266	0.403514	6.278798	0.159266
11	2.713659	18.038518	0.055437	0.368506	6.647304	0.150437
12	2.971457	20.752178	0.048188	0.336535	6.983839	0.143188
13	3.253745	23.723634	0.042152	0.307338	7.291178	0.137152
14	3.562851	26.977380	0.037068	0.280674	7.571852	0.132068
15	3.901322	30.540231	0.032744	0.256323	7.828175	0.127744
16	4.271948	34.441553	0.029035	0.234085	8.062260	0.124035
17	4.677783	38.713500	0.025831	0.213777	8.276037	0.120831
18	5.122172	43.391283	0.023046	0.195230	8.471266	0.118046
19	5.608778	48.513454	0.020613	0.178292	8.649558	0.115613
20	6.141612	54.122233	0.018477	0.162824	8.812382	0.113477
21	6.725065	60.263845	0.016594	0.148697	8.961080	0.111594
22	7.363946	66.988910	0.014928	0.135797	9.096876	0.109928
23	8.063521	74.352856	0.013449	0.124015	9.220892	0.108449
24	8.829556	82.416378	0.012134	0.113256	9.334148	0.107134
25	9.668364	91.245934	0.010959	0.103430	9.437578	0.105959
26	10.586858	100.914297	0.009909	0.094457	9.532034	0.104909
27	11.592610	111.501156	0.008969	0.086262	9.618296	0.103969
28	12.693908	123.093766	0.008124	0.078778	9.697074	0.103124
29	13.899829	135.787673	0.007364	0.071943	9.769018	0.102364
30	15.220313	149.687502	0.006681	0.065702	9.834719	0.101681
31	16.666242	164.907815	0.006064	0.060002	9.894721	0.101064
32	18.249535	181.574057	0.005507	0.054796	9.949517	0.100507
33	19.983241	199.823593	0.005004	0.050042	9.999559	0.100004
34	21.881649	219.806834	0.004549	0.045700	10.045259	0.099549
35	23.960406	241.688483	0.004138	0.041736	10.086995	0.099138
36	26.236644	265.648889	0.003764	0.038115	10.125109	0.098764
37	28.729126	291.885534	0.003426	0.034808	10.159917	0.098426
38	31.458393	320.614659	0.003119	0.031788	10.191705	0.098119
39	34.446940	352.073052	0.002840	0.029030	10.220735	0.097840
40	37.719399	386.519992	0.002587	0.026512	10.247247	0.097587
41	41.302742	424.239391	0.002357	0.024211	10.271458	0.097357
42	45.226503	465.542133	0.002148	0.022111	10.293569	0.097148
43	49.523020	510.768636	0.001958	0.020193	10.313762	0.096958
44	54.227707	560.291656	0.001785	0.018441	10.332203	0.096785
45	59.379340	614.519364	0.001627	0.016841	10.349043	0.096627
46	65.020377	673.898703	0.001484	0.015380	10.364423	0.096484
47	71.197313	738.919080	0.001353	0.014045	10.378469	0.096353
48	77.961057	810.116393	0.001234	0.012827	10.391296	0.096234
49	85.367358	888.077450	0.001126	0.011714	10.403010	0.096126
50	93.477257	973.444808	0.001027	0.010698	10.413707	0.096027

9.00%   ANNUAL COMPOUND INTEREST TABLES   9.00%
                              EFFECTIVE RATE   9.00

	1 AMOUNT OF $1 AT COMPOUND INTEREST	2 ACCUMULATION OF $1 PER PERIOD	3 SINKING FUND FACTOR	4 PRESENT VALUE REVERSION OF $1	5 PRESENT VALUE ORD. ANNUITY $1 PER PERIOD	6 INSTALMENT TO AMORTIZE $1
YEARS						
1	1.090000	1.000000	1.000000	0.917431	0.917431	1.090000
2	1.188100	2.090000	0.478469	0.841680	1.759111	0.568469
3	1.295029	3.278100	0.305055	0.772183	2.531295	0.395055
4	1.411582	4.573129	0.218669	0.708425	3.239720	0.308669
5	1.538624	5.984711	0.167092	0.649931	3.889651	0.257092
6	1.677100	7.523335	0.132920	0.596267	4.485919	0.222920
7	1.828039	9.200435	0.108691	0.547034	5.032953	0.198691
8	1.992563	11.028474	0.090674	0.501866	5.534819	0.180674
9	2.171893	13.021036	0.076799	0.460428	5.995247	0.166799
10	2.367364	15.192930	0.065820	0.422411	6.417658	0.155820
11	2.580426	17.560293	0.056947	0.387533	6.805191	0.146947
12	2.812665	20.140720	0.049651	0.355535	7.160725	0.139651
13	3.065805	22.953385	0.043567	0.326179	7.486904	0.133567
14	3.341727	26.019189	0.038433	0.299246	7.786150	0.128433
15	3.642482	29.360916	0.034059	0.274538	8.060688	0.124059
16	3.970306	33.003399	0.030300	0.251870	8.312558	0.120300
17	4.327633	36.973705	0.027046	0.231073	8.543631	0.117046
18	4.717120	41.301338	0.024212	0.211994	8.755625	0.114212
19	5.141661	46.018458	0.021730	0.194490	8.950115	0.111730
20	5.604411	51.160120	0.019546	0.178431	9.128546	0.109546
21	6.108808	56.764530	0.017617	0.163698	9.292244	0.107617
22	6.658600	62.873338	0.015905	0.150182	9.442425	0.105905
23	7.257874	69.531939	0.014382	0.137781	9.580207	0.104382
24	7.911083	76.789813	0.013023	0.126405	9.706612	0.103023
25	8.623081	84.700896	0.011806	0.115968	9.822580	0.101806
26	9.399158	93.323977	0.010715	0.106393	9.928972	0.100715
27	10.245082	102.723135	0.009735	0.097608	10.026580	0.099735
28	11.167140	112.968217	0.008852	0.089548	10.116128	0.098852
29	12.172182	124.135356	0.008056	0.082155	10.198283	0.098056
30	13.267678	136.307539	0.007336	0.075371	10.273654	0.097336
31	14.461770	149.575217	0.006686	0.069148	10.342802	0.096686
32	15.763329	164.036987	0.006096	0.063438	10.406240	0.096096
33	17.182028	179.800315	0.005562	0.058200	10.464441	0.095562
34	18.728411	196.982344	0.005077	0.053395	10.517835	0.095077
35	20.413968	215.710755	0.004636	0.048986	10.566821	0.094636
36	22.251225	236.124723	0.004235	0.044941	10.611763	0.094235
37	24.253835	258.375948	0.003870	0.041231	10.652993	0.093870
38	26.436680	282.629783	0.003538	0.037826	10.690820	0.093538
39	28.815982	309.066463	0.003236	0.034703	10.725523	0.093236
40	31.409420	337.882445	0.002960	0.031838	10.757360	0.092960
41	34.236268	369.291865	0.002708	0.029209	10.786569	0.092708
42	37.317532	403.528133	0.002478	0.026797	10.813366	0.092478
43	40.676110	440.845665	0.002268	0.024584	10.837950	0.092268
44	44.336960	481.521775	0.002077	0.022555	10.860505	0.092077
45	48.327286	525.858734	0.001902	0.020692	10.881197	0.091902
46	52.676742	574.186021	0.001742	0.018984	10.900181	0.091742
47	57.417649	626.862762	0.001595	0.017416	10.917597	0.091595
48	62.585237	684.280411	0.001461	0.015978	10.933575	0.091461
49	68.217908	746.865648	0.001339	0.014659	10.948234	0.091339
50	74.357520	815.083556	0.001227	0.013449	10.961683	0.091227

10.00%   ANNUAL COMPOUND INTEREST TABLES   10.00%
                                         EFFECTIVE RATE 10.00

	1 AMOUNT OF $1 AT COMPOUND INTEREST	2 ACCUMULATION OF $1 PER PERIOD	3 SINKING FUND FACTOR	4 PRESENT VALUE REVERSION OF $1	5 PRESENT VALUE ORD. ANNUITY $1 PER PERIOD	6 INSTALMENT TO AMORTIZE $1
YEARS						
1	1.100000	1.000000	1.000000	0.909091	0.909091	1.100000
2	1.210000	2.100000	0.476190	0.826446	1.735537	0.576190
3	1.331000	3.310000	0.302115	0.751315	2.486852	0.402115
4	1.464100	4.641000	0.215471	0.683013	3.169865	0.315471
5	1.610510	6.105100	0.163797	0.620921	3.790787	0.263797
6	1.771561	7.715610	0.129607	0.564474	4.355261	0.229607
7	1.948717	9.487171	0.105405	0.513158	4.868419	0.205405
8	2.143589	11.435888	0.087444	0.466507	5.334926	0.187444
9	2.357948	13.579477	0.073641	0.424098	5.759024	0.173641
10	2.593742	15.937425	0.062745	0.385543	6.144567	0.162745
11	2.853117	18.531167	0.053963	0.350494	6.495061	0.153963
12	3.138428	21.384284	0.046763	0.318631	6.813692	0.146763
13	3.452271	24.522712	0.040779	0.289664	7.103356	0.140779
14	3.797498	27.974983	0.035746	0.263331	7.366687	0.135746
15	4.177248	31.772482	0.031474	0.239392	7.606080	0.131474
16	4.594973	35.949730	0.027817	0.217629	7.823709	0.127817
17	5.054470	40.544703	0.024664	0.197845	8.021553	0.124664
18	5.559917	45.599173	0.021930	0.179859	8.201412	0.121930
19	6.115909	51.159090	0.019547	0.163508	8.364920	0.119547
20	6.727500	57.274999	0.017460	0.148644	8.513564	0.117460
21	7.400250	64.002499	0.015624	0.135131	8.648694	0.115624
22	8.140275	71.402749	0.014005	0.122846	8.771540	0.114005
23	8.954302	79.543024	0.012572	0.111678	8.883218	0.112572
24	9.849733	88.497327	0.011300	0.101526	8.984744	0.111300
25	10.834706	98.347059	0.010168	0.092296	9.077040	0.110168
26	11.918177	109.181765	0.009159	0.083905	9.160945	0.109159
27	13.109994	121.099942	0.008258	0.076278	9.237223	0.108258
28	14.420994	134.209936	0.007451	0.069343	9.306567	0.107451
29	15.863093	148.630930	0.006728	0.063039	9.369606	0.106728
30	17.449402	164.494023	0.006079	0.057309	9.426914	0.106079
31	19.194342	181.943425	0.005496	0.052099	9.479013	0.105496
32	21.113777	201.137767	0.004972	0.047362	9.526376	0.104972
33	23.225154	222.251544	0.004499	0.043057	9.569432	0.104499
34	25.547670	245.476699	0.004074	0.039143	9.608575	0.104074
35	28.102437	271.024368	0.003690	0.035584	9.644159	0.103690
36	30.912681	299.126805	0.003343	0.032349	9.676508	0.103343
37	34.003949	330.039486	0.003030	0.029408	9.705917	0.103030
38	37.404343	364.043434	0.002747	0.026735	9.732651	0.102747
39	41.144778	401.447778	0.002491	0.024304	9.756956	0.102491
40	45.259256	442.592556	0.002259	0.022095	9.779051	0.102259
41	49.785181	487.851811	0.002050	0.020086	9.799137	0.102050
42	54.763699	537.636992	0.001860	0.018260	9.817397	0.101860
43	60.240069	592.400692	0.001688	0.016600	9.833998	0.101688
44	66.264076	652.640761	0.001532	0.015091	9.849089	0.101532
45	72.890484	718.904837	0.001391	0.013719	9.862808	0.101391
46	80.179532	791.795321	0.001263	0.012472	9.875280	0.101263
47	88.197485	871.974853	0.001147	0.011338	9.886618	0.101147
48	97.017234	960.172338	0.001041	0.010307	9.896926	0.101041
49	106.718957	1057.189572	0.000946	0.009370	9.906296	0.100946
50	117.390853	1163.908529	0.000859	0.008519	9.914814	0.100859

11.00%   ANNUAL COMPOUND INTEREST TABLES   11.00%
                              EFFECTIVE RATE 11.00

	1 AMOUNT OF $1 AT COMPOUND INTEREST	2 ACCUMULATION OF $1 PER PERIOD	3 SINKING FUND FACTOR	4 PRESENT VALUE REVERSION OF $1	5 PRESENT VALUE ORD. ANNUITY $1 PER PERIOD	6 INSTALMENT TO AMORTIZE $1
YEARS						
1	1.110000	1.000000	1.000000	0.900901	0.900901	1.110000
2	1.232100	2.110000	0.473934	0.811622	1.712523	0.583934
3	1.367631	3.342100	0.299213	0.731191	2.443715	0.409213
4	1.518070	4.709731	0.212326	0.658731	3.102446	0.322326
5	1.685058	6.227801	0.160570	0.593451	3.695897	0.270570
6	1.870415	7.912860	0.126377	0.534641	4.230538	0.236377
7	2.076160	9.783274	0.102215	0.481658	4.712196	0.212215
8	2.304538	11.859434	0.084321	0.433926	5.146123	0.194321
9	2.558037	14.163972	0.070602	0.390925	5.537048	0.180602
10	2.839421	16.722009	0.059801	0.352184	5.889232	0.169801
11	3.151757	19.561430	0.051121	0.317283	6.206515	0.161121
12	3.498451	22.713187	0.044027	0.285841	6.492356	0.154027
13	3.883280	26.211638	0.038151	0.257514	6.749870	0.148151
14	4.310441	30.094918	0.033228	0.231995	6.981865	0.143228
15	4.784589	34.405359	0.029065	0.209004	7.190870	0.139065
16	5.310894	39.189948	0.025517	0.188292	7.379162	0.135517
17	5.895093	44.500843	0.022471	0.169633	7.548794	0.132471
18	6.543553	50.395936	0.019843	0.152822	7.701617	0.129843
19	7.263344	56.939488	0.017563	0.137678	7.839294	0.127563
20	8.062312	64.202832	0.015576	0.124034	7.963328	0.125576
21	8.949166	72.265144	0.013838	0.111742	8.075070	0.123838
22	9.933574	81.214309	0.012313	0.100669	8.175739	0.122313
23	11.026267	91.147884	0.010971	0.090693	8.266432	0.120971
24	12.239157	102.174151	0.009787	0.081705	8.348137	0.119787
25	13.585464	114.413307	0.008740	0.073608	8.421745	0.118740
26	15.079865	127.998771	0.007813	0.066314	8.488058	0.117813
27	16.738650	143.078636	0.006989	0.059742	8.547800	0.116989
28	18.579901	159.817286	0.006257	0.053822	8.601622	0.116257
29	20.623691	178.397187	0.005605	0.048488	8.650110	0.115605
30	22.892297	199.020878	0.005025	0.043683	8.693793	0.115025
31	25.410449	221.913174	0.004506	0.039354	8.733146	0.114506
32	28.205599	247.323624	0.004043	0.035454	8.768600	0.114043
33	31.308214	275.529222	0.003629	0.031940	8.800541	0.113629
34	34.752118	306.837437	0.003259	0.028775	8.829316	0.113259
35	38.574851	341.589555	0.002927	0.025924	8.855240	0.112927
36	42.818085	380.164406	0.002630	0.023355	8.878594	0.112630
37	47.528074	422.982490	0.002364	0.021040	8.899635	0.112364
38	52.756162	470.510564	0.002125	0.018955	8.918590	0.112125
39	58.559340	523.266726	0.001911	0.017077	8.935666	0.111911
40	65.000867	581.826066	0.001719	0.015384	8.951051	0.111719
41	72.150963	646.826934	0.001546	0.013860	8.964911	0.111546
42	80.087569	718.977896	0.001391	0.012486	8.977397	0.111391
43	88.897201	799.065465	0.001251	0.011249	8.988646	0.111251
44	98.675893	887.962666	0.001126	0.010134	8.998780	0.111126
45	109.530242	986.638559	0.001014	0.009130	9.007910	0.111014
46	121.578568	1096.168801	0.000912	0.008225	9.016135	0.110912
47	134.952211	1217.747369	0.000821	0.007410	9.023545	0.110821
48	149.796954	1352.699580	0.000739	0.006676	9.030221	0.110739
49	166.274619	1502.496534	0.000666	0.006014	9.036235	0.110666
50	184.564827	1668.771152	0.000599	0.005418	9.041653	0.110599

Index

Maintenance *(Cont.)*
  Federal tax law, 30
  Internal Revenue Service, 30
  maximizing of, 29–30
Market comparison, 140
Market prices, 125–27
  actuality of sale, 125
  appraiser, 127
  and circumstances of sale, 125
  comparison chart, 125–27
  neighborhood prices, 125
  and principals to sale, 127
  and property similarity, 125
  real estate brokers, 127
  tax assessor, 127
  terms of sales, 125
Masonry, 135
Market value:
  based on annuity tables, 154
  based on multipliers, 153
  based on net income, 153–54
  summary, 154
Materials, 135
  prices of, 134
Money, borrowing of, 173–79 *(See also* specific
    aspects of)
Mortgages:
  constant, use of, 117–18
    and loans, 118
    payment of mortgage, 117
    procedure, 117
  impact of financing, 155
    conclusions about, 155–56
  loan officers, 134
  payments, estimating, 116–17
    example, 116
    factors in, 116
    mortgage constant, 116

Narrowing of choice, 127–29
  appraisal, 128
  "Bigger fool" theory, 129
  averaging of prices, 128
  gross multiplier method, 129
  price estimates, 128
  reliability weights, 128
The National Association of Realtors Journal,
  171
Neighborhood, 61
Net income, 70
New structures, estimating cost of, 129–33
  acquisition costs, 131
  age of building, 129, 131
  appraiser, 130
  building, 131
  chart, 131–33
  contractors, information from, 130

New structures, estimating cost of *(Cont.)*
  cost per square foot, 132
  engineering, 131
  estimates, 130
  finances, 131
  garage, 131
  land, 131
  landscaping, 131
  miscellaneous costs, 131
  repairs, 131
  replacement, 131
  replica vs. updated problem, 129
  updating, 131
  walks, 131

Office buildings, 201–03
  improvements, 202–03
  location, 202
  market, 201–02
  site, 202
Overall rate, 121
  sales vs. income, 121

Partnerships, 173–74
  general, 173–74
  limited, 174
Pension funds, 179
Planned unit developments, 194–95
  conversions to, 194
  density of, 194
  questions about, 194–95
Planning strategy:
  comparison with other properties, 89
  estimating value of home, 89
  financing, 90
  gross income, 90
  investment, 90
  net income, 90
  potential net earnings, 89
  taxes, 90
Plastering, 135
Plumbing, 135
Prentice-Hall publications, 171
Present value of one, 114
  factors in, 114
  example, 114
Present value of one per period, 114–15
  example, 115
  factors, 114
  income stream, 114
  prepurchase, 114
Price, "fair" market, 31
  and gross income multiplier, 31, 142
    income capitalization, 142
    market comparisons, 142
    price per square foot, 142